MEDICAL NEGLIGENCE LITIGATION: EMERGING ISSUES

Medical Negligence Litigation: Emerging Issues

Edited by

CIARÁN CRAVEN

and

WILLIAM BINCHY

First Law

Published in 2008 by
First Law Limited
Merchant's Court
Merchants Quay
Dublin 8
Ireland.
www.firstlaw.ie

This book was typeset by
Gough Typesetting Services, Dublin.

ISBN 978-1-904480-36-5

A catalogue record for this book
is available from the British Library.

Printed by Lirda, Ireland

Contributors

Ciarán Craven B.L. is a medical practitioner and practising barrister. He practised medicine for a number of years before being called to the Bar. He lectures in Medical Law in the Master of Laws Degree Programme at Trinity College Dublin and is a regular contributor of conference papers and articles on topics in medical law. He is co-author of textbooks on *Military Law* (Round Hall) and *Psychiatry and the Law* (Oak Tree Press). His previous publication with First Law was as co-editor of *The Civil Liability and Courts Act 2004*.

Ray Ryan is a practising barrister. He holds the degrees of Bachelor of Laws (LL.B.) and Master of Laws (LL.M.) from Trinity College, Dublin and has written several articles and conference papers in the area of tort law.

Des Ryan is a Lecturer in Law in Trinity College Dublin and is a qualified Barrister. His areas of research interest include Tort Law and Employment Law. He lectures in Comparative Law, Legal Systems and Methods and Constitutional Law II on the LL.B. programme, and in Employment Litigation on the LL.M. programme. Legal journals in which his work has been published include *The Cambridge Law Journal*, the *Civil Justice Quarterly*, the *Commercial Law Practitioner*, T*he Conveyancer and Property Lawyer*, the *Dublin University Law Journal*, the *Irish Employment Law Journal*, the *Irish Law Times* and the *Northern Ireland Legal Quarterly*.

William Binchy is Regius Professor of Laws at Trinity College, Dublin. He is the co-author of books on tort law and is co-editor of books on the Personal Injuries Assessment Board Act 2003 and the Civil Liability and Courts Act 2004, both published by First Law.

Neville Cox, LL.B., Ph.D. FTCD is a practising barrister and a Senior Lecturer in the Law School in Trinity College Dublin where he lectures in Sports Law, Tort Law and Medical Law. He is co-author of *Annual Review of Employment Law 2005 and 2006* (First Law) and *Sport and the Law* (2004) and the author of *Defamation Law* (2007)(First Law).

Liz Heffernan LL.B. (Dublin), LL.M. (Dalhousie), LL.M. & J.S.D. (Chicago), B.L. lectures at the Law School, Trinity College Dublin. A former law clerk at the United States Court of Appeals for the Seventh Circuit, Chicago and the United States District Court for the Northern District of Illinois, Chicago, she has taught at Washington and Lee University, Lexington and University College Dublin.

She is the author of Scientific *Evidence: Fingerprints and DNA* (First Law, 2006) and *Evidence: Cases and Materials* (Thomson Round Hall, 2005).

Michael Boylan, Solicitor, Partner & Head of the Medical Negligence Group in Augustus Cullen Law, Solicitors, Wicklow. Over time he has specialised in the area of medical negligence and has been involved in many of the leading Irish medical negligence actions and he is a member of the Litigation Committee of the Law Society.

Estelle Feldman is a Research Associate in the School of Law, Trinity College and Lecturer in Constitutional Law for the University of Wales LL.B in Portobello College, Dublin. Formerly MBA Programme Director of the Trinity School of Business Studies, she has extensive experience in general management and consultancy including 15 years as a senior manager in the voluntary health sector. In addition to children's rights in healthcare, Estelle has publications on whistleblower protection, freedom of information and public service accountability. She writes on Constitutional Law and on Information Law and the Ombudsman for the Annual Review of Irish Law, is editor of Freedom of Information Law and Practice (First Law, 2006) and co-author of Access to Information in Developing Countries, (Transparency International, Berlin, 1998).

John Smith II is an Equity Partner of the Chicago law firm of Pretzel & Stouffer and a Board Member of the International Academy of Dispute Resolution. He is a graduate in Arts and a Juris Doctor of the University of Notre Dame. He has particular expertise in litigation in litigation relating to medical malpractice and hospital liability and has written widely on these subjects.

John H. Scheid is Professor of Law at John Marshall Law School, Chicago. He formerly was a lawyer in Chicago, concentrating on trial and appellate practice. He is an expert in tort law. He has lectured on medical negligence law to Irish lawyers, doctors and other health service personnel at several conferences organised by the Law School of Trinity College, Dublin.

Introduction

Medical negligence litigation, formerly a rarity, has become a daily feature of life in the Irish courts. There is no single reason for this transformation. In the past, the relationship between doctors and patients was different – less anonymous than today but also based on norms of social deference and paternalism which have no counterpart in today's society. Patients have far greater access to information about medicine and health care and more awareness of how things can go wrong, whether through error, neglect or the inevitability of the risk of misadventure.

In this book, the contributors try to capture these developments. The emphasis is on the position in Ireland but attention is paid to the wider common law world, especially the United States of America.

In Chapter 1, "Medical Negligence: the *Dunne* Principles and their Application", Ciaran Craven discusses the meaning and implications for medical practice of the principles set out by the Supreme Court in *Dunne v. National Maternity Hospital*[1] as governing medical negligence litigation. He examines the caselaw in the particular areas of medical expertise in which the test has been applied.

In Chapter 2, "Recent Judicial Approaches to 'Loss of Chance' in Medical Negligence Cases", Ray Ryan and Des Ryan analyse the recent jurisprudence in which judges have debated the proper approach to adopt where the defendant's negligence has deprived the patient of the chance of a better medical outcome. The traditional "but for" causation test, coupled with the requirement of proof of the plaintiff's case on the balance of probabilities, can yield outcomes considered by some to be unfair.

In Chapter 3, "Issues of Proof in Medical Negligence Litigation: New Questions Posed in the Irish Courts', William Binchy considers the conceptual difficulties and uncertainty of practical application of the *res ipsa loquitur* doctrine, in the context of medical negligence litigation.

In Chapter 4, "Suing Hospitals and Health Boards", Neville Cox examines the different possible bases of liability of these institutions, ranging from statutory liability under the Safety, Health and Welfare at Work Act 2005 and Occupiers' Liability Act 1995, to vicarious liability and, possibly, direct primary liability based on a non-delegable duty of care.

In Chapter 5, "Expert Evidence in Medical Negligence Litigation", Liz Heffernan analyses the rules of evidence relating to the testimony of expert witnesses in claims for medical negligence. She goes on to consider the impact

---

[1] [1989] I.R. 91.

on this kind of evidence of the changes brought about by the Civil Liability and Courts Act 2004, section 20 of which enables a court to appoint its own expert witness.

In Chapter 6, "Medical Negligence Litigation Challenges for the Plaintiff's Lawyers", Michael Boylan outlines the several hurdles facing those who act on behalf of plaintiffs in this area. The array of statutory changes that have taken place recently has increased their burden. He goes on to consider the possible impact on this type of litigation of the enactment of the European Convention on Human Rights Act 2003.

In Chapter 7, "Informed Consent. Should there be a Reasonable Parent Test?", Estelle Feldman examines an area of the law, on which Irish courts have yet to give full guidance, relating to the extent to which children's autonomy rights in regard to health care may be curbed by the guardianship functions of their parents or other carers. The difficulty in making confident statements about the present legal position is increased by the dearth of judicial analysis of children's autonomy rights in contrast to the elaborate – some say overelaborate – judicial analysis of parental autonomy.

In Chapter 8, "Defence Strategies in Medical Negligence Litigation: New Approaches", John V. Smith II offers insights into defence strategies, from the standpoint of a practitioner in the United States of America.

In Chapter 9, "Some Statutory Responses to the American Medical Malpractice Crisis", John J. Scheid examines the various statutory initiatives, such as caps on damages, 'Good Samaritan' Acts and shortened limitation periods, which have been adopted in the United States of America over the past couple of decades. Consideration of these developments is timely in view of recent proposals to introduce similar changes in Ireland.

We are very grateful to the several contributors for their chapters. In editing this volume, we received very considerable guidance from Therese Carrick of First Law. We are most appreciative of her patient support as well as that of Bart Daly, Managing Director of First Law. We also want to thank Shane Gough for his excellent professional help, and Eoin Craven for his overall assistance with the text at a very busy time.

Ciáran Craven and
William Binchy,
April 11, 2008.

Table of Contents

Table of Cases

C

D

E

F

L

M

N

O

P

Q

R

Table of Legislation

UNITED STATES OF AMERICA

INTERNATIONAL CONVENTIONS

CHAPTER 1

Medical Negligence: The *Dunne* Principles and their Application

CIARÁN CRAVEN

INTRODUCTION

The starting point for any modern discussion of medical negligence must be considered to be the decision of the Supreme Court in *Dunne (an infant) v. National Maternity Hospital & anor.*[1] The cases which follow *Dunne* are replete with examples of the fairly straightforward application of the principles set out there in fairly unexceptional factual situations. Sometimes, however, issues arise in respect of the relationship between the first two principles, the application of the third principle and as to whether or not the principles should even apply at all.

THE *DUNNE* PRINCIPLES

In *Dunne*, it will be recalled, as a matter of policy and practice, the defendants, in the case of twin labour, only monitored one foetal heart. It was asserted on the part of the defendant hospital that the practice of seeking to identify one foetal heart only had been the practice of that hospital for 15 to 20 years at the time of the trial. The practice did not seek to identify one foetal heart only, it was a specific attempt to identify the foetal heart of the first twin, because of the extreme difficulty in obtaining what might be considered a reliable result from any attempt to monitor the second twin and the impossibility, since that twin is not the presenting twin, of carrying out further investigations on it. The clinical evidence adduced by the hospital was also to the effect that an attempt to monitor two foetal hearts could be so misleading as to be a dangerous practice. Thus, this was a standard practice in what was, at the time, the largest maternity hospital in Europe and which had outcomes for twin pregnancies comparable to hospitals which adopted a different approach. Although the practice adopted was challenged as being a "general and approved" practice, there was, in addition, evidence of its having been used elsewhere too and of its having professional support on the evidence recited in the judgment of Finlay C.J. In the instant

---

1 [1989] I.R. 91.

case, however, the plaintiff was severely brain damaged and his twin brother was stillborn. On the defendants' appeal from a jury award of damages in the sum of IR£1,039,334 (including general damages in the amount of IR£467,000.00) (Finlay C.J., for a unanimous Supreme Court, Griffin and Hederman JJ. concurring), one of the principal grounds of appeal related to whether the jury, on the evidence, if properly directed as to the legal principles applicable could have made a finding of negligence arising from failure to attempt to identify a second foetal heart. In this regard, a question of law arose on the argument as to the proper meaning and interpretation of the decision in *O'Donovan v. Cork County Council & ors.*[2] and "in particular, to the question of the appropriate directions which a court must give to a jury or, in the case of a trial by a judge alone, must follow, where questions of medical practice arise".[3] In allowing the appeal and ordering a re-trial (on the grounds that the trial judge had misdirected the jury as to the proper legal test to be applied in a case such as this), Finlay C.J., in relation to the applicable principles, stated:

> "The courts have consistently recognised certain features in the general law of negligence which have particular reference to allegations of negligence made against professional persons in the carrying out of their professional duties. These particular features applicable to allegations of medical negligence have been fully set out by this court in *O'Donovan v. Cork County Council*[4] which adopted and followed the decision of the former Supreme Court in *Daniels v. Heskin*.[5] The reasoning of *O'Donovan v. Cork County Council* was expressly followed by this court in *Reeves v. Carthy*.[6] It was again approved and applied to a case of professional negligence by a solicitor in *Roche v. Pielow*.[7]
>
> There was no argument submitted to us on the hearing of this appeal which constituted any form of challenge to the correctness of the statements of principle thus laid down, although there was controversy concerning their application to the facts of this case.
>
> The principles thus laid down related to the issues raised in this case can in this manner be summarised.
>
> 1. The true test for establishing negligence in diagnosis or treatment on the part of a medical practitioner is whether he has been proved to be guilty of such failure as no medical practitioner of equal specialist or general status and skill would be guilty of if acting with ordinary care.
> 2. If the allegation of negligence against a medical practitioner is

---

2 [1967] I.R. 173.
3 *Ibid.*, p.106.
4 *Ibid.*
5 [1954] I.R. 73.
6 [1984] I.R. 348.
7 [1985] I.R. 232.

based on proof that he deviated from a general and approved practice, that will not establish negligence unless it is also proved that the course he did take was one which no medical practitioner of like specialisation and skill would have followed had he been taking the ordinary care required from a person of his qualifications.

3. If a medical practitioner charged with negligence defends his conduct by establishing that he followed a practice which was general, and which was approved of by his colleagues of similar specialisation and skill, he cannot escape liability if in reply the plaintiff establishes that such practice has inherent defects which ought to be obvious to any person giving the matter due consideration.
4. An honest difference of opinion between doctors as to which is the better of two ways of treating a patient does not provide any ground for leaving a question to the jury as to whether a person who has followed one course rather than the other has been negligent.
5. It is not for a jury (or for a judge) to decide which of two alternative courses of treatment is in their (or his) opinion preferable, but their (or his) function is merely to decide whether the course of treatment followed, on the evidence, complied with careful conduct of a medical practitioner of like specialisation and skill to that professed by the defendant.
6. If there is an issue of fact, the determination of which is necessary for the decision as to whether a particular medical practice is or is not general and approved within the meaning of these principles, that issue must in a trial held with a jury be left to the determination of the jury.

In order to make these general principles readily applicable to the facts of this case, with which I will later be dealing, it is necessary to state further conclusions not expressly referred to in the cases above mentioned. These are:

(a) 'General and approved practice' need not be universal but must be approved of and adhered to by a substantial number of reputable practitioners[8] holding the relevant specialist or general qualifications.

(b) Though treatment only is referred to in some of these statements

---

8 Sometimes characterised as "a *responsible* body of medical men" or "a competent *reasonable* body of opinion" (see *Bolam v. Friern Hospital Management Committee* [1957] 2 All E.R. 118 at 122, [1957] 1 W.L.R. 583 at 587-588), or a "*respectable* body of professional opinion" (see *Maynard v. West Midlands Regional Health Authority* [1985] 1 All E.R. 635 at 639, [1984] 1 W.L.R. 634 at 639, *per* Lord Scarman).

of principle, they must apply in identical fashion to questions of diagnosis.

(c) In an action against a hospital where allegations are made of negligence against the medical administrators on the basis of a claim that practices and procedures laid down by them for the carrying out of treatment or diagnosis by medical or nursing staff were defective, their conduct is to be tested in accordance with the legal principles which would apply if they had personally carried out such treatment or diagnosis in accordance with such practice or procedure.

In order fully to understand these principles and their application to any particular set of facts, it is, I believe, helpful to set out certain broad parameters which would appear to underline their establishment.

The development of medical science and the supreme importance of that development to humanity makes it particularly undesirable and inconsistent with the common good that doctors should be obliged to carry out their professional duties under frequent threat of unsustainable legal claims.

The complete dependence of patients on the skill and care of their medical attendants and the gravity from their point of view of a failure in such care, makes it undesirable and unjustifiable to accept as a matter of law a lax or permissive standard of care for the purpose of assessing what is and is not medical negligence.

In developing the legal principles outlined and in applying them to the facts of each individual case, the courts must constantly seek to give equal regard to both of these considerations."[9]

A number of observations might be made at this point. Firstly, the principles are expressly stated to apply only to questions of diagnosis and treatment. No attempt was made in *Dunne* to deal with the equally (both then and now) vexed question of the pre-operative disclosure of operative risks and consent. Secondly, whereas, in many ways, it is appealing to regard *Dunne* as no more than an expression of "the test" set out in England by McNair J. in his direction to the jury in *Bolam v. Friern Hospital Management Committee*[10] as to the standard of care required of a medical practitioner, modified by the "inherent defects" qualification articulated ten years later by Walsh J. *O'Donovan v. Cork County Council & ors.*,[11] *Bolam* is not, in fact, cited in any of the cases in our courts, including *Dunne*. Thirdly, although *Dunne* is the case that sets out the principles to be applied in all subsequent cases involving allegations of medical negligence

9 [1989] I.R. 91 at 108-110.

10 [1957] 2 All E.R. 118, [1957] 1 W.L.R. 583.

11 *Loc. cit.*

and is, thus, of seminal importance, examination of the judgment of the Supreme Court does not reveal analysis of the limited authority that is relied upon.[12]

Looking at the principles as a whole, if a case is solely concerned with a deviation from a "general and approved" practice, the application of the second *Dunne* principle, to be followed by application of the third, if appropriate, ought to dispose of the matter. The fourth, fifth and sixth principles deal with evidentiary matters, in a manner wholly consistent with what has been set out since *Daniels*. The first principle, which Laffoy J., in *Mordaunt v. Gallagher & anor.*[13] considered was "the fundamental rubric", it seems, must stand alone, to be applied in those circumstances where there is no "general and approved" practice. One might have anticipated that the circumstances in which there would be no such practice, would, in modern evidence-based medicine, be very rare. However, the practice of medicine is probably more craft than science and common experience amply demonstrates that human disease can be complex in its manifestation. Whatever about a practitioner's defending his or her actions by invoking compliance with a "general and approved" practice representing the lowest common denominator of such practice and, thus, creating particular difficulties for a plaintiff in seeking to establish breach of the professional negligence standard, the terms of the first principle are cast in the terms of even a lower standard, i.e. such failure as *no medical practitioner* of equal specialist or general status and skill would be guilty of if acting with ordinary care (*emphasis* added). Therefore, it appears, it is sufficient to defeat liability on the first principle if there is evidence of *any* professional support for what the practitioner did.

In applying the principles, a question may be asked: must a court approach them sequentially? Given the ordinary language of the principles, it appears not. Where different views are expressed as to the propriety of a doctor's actions – none of which amount to stigmatising the conduct as deviation from a "general and approved" practice (because there is none) – that must be a simple matter of fact for the trier of fact, albeit with a very low threshold for a successful defence. In those cases where there is, in fact, evidence of a "general and approved" practice it also remains for the trier of fact to determine whether or not the doctor has fallen below an appropriate standard of care. This is consistent with what Kingsmill Moore J. set out in *Daniels & anor. v. Heskin*,[14] Walsh J. in *O'Donovan v. Cork County Council & ors.*[15] and Griffin J. in *Reeves v. Carthy & O'Kelly*.[16]

---

12 Craven, "Medical Negligence and the *Dunne* Principles: what do the first and second principles mean"? *Quarterly Review of Tort Law* (2006) 1 (3) 1 – 12.

13 [1997] IEHC 123.

14 *Loc. cit.*, p.85.

15 *Loc. cit.*, p.193.

16 *Loc. cit.*, p.365.

The first and second principles

The decision of the High Court in *Shuit v. Mylotte & ors.*,[17] however, flags an issue that may present a difficulty, in relation to the inter-relationship between the first three principles. The sole issue for determination in the case was, essentially, whether or not the defendant gynaecologist was negligent in carrying out a radical hysterectomy on the plaintiff on the basis of the information he then had before him. It was alleged, *inter alia*, that the gynaecologist proceeded to operate on the plaintiff without first having a full and clear radiological report in writing and when such a report was necessary for her proper treatment, and that he had failed to exhaust preliminary tests before embarking on the radical procedure that he did. In particular it was alleged that he had failed, contrary to best medical practice, to take a frozen section of the lymph nodes in the plaintiff's abdomen before continuing with the surgery despite persistent findings contrary to his initial expectations of a tumour. White J. found, on the evidence, that the plaintiff had failed to satisfy him that no gynaecologist of like skill, acting with ordinary care, would have performed the surgery carried out by the defendant gynaecologist. He was satisfied "that a number of reputable obstetricians would have done as [he] did." This seems, on its face, to be a fairly unexceptional application of the first *Dunne* principle.

However, the plaintiff submitted that if the defendant gynaecologist's case, or at least part of his case, was that he was following a "general and approved practice", the trial judge must, accordingly, also consider the third *Dunne* principle. In this regard, it was also contended that the plaintiff had proved that the practice met the inherent defects qualification and that the evidence established that the operation carried out on the plaintiff was unnecessary. White J., however, accepted as "well founded" the defendant's submission that it was never part of the defendant gynaecologist's case, nor had it been shown to be, that his defence was one of "general and approved" practice and dismissed the plaintiff's claim.

The only reasonable conclusion seems to be that the outcome was premised on the application of the first *Dunne* principle alone. Both that conclusion and the defence assertion as to its nature, however, seem difficult to harmonise with the specific finding by the trial judge that there were two "schools of thought" as to how to treat the plaintiff in her circumstances. The net effect, however, was that a finding having been made on the application of the first *Dunne* principle, consideration of the application of the third principle did not arise. Having said that, in *O'Gorman v. Jermyn & ors.*[18] the hospital defendants contended that the defendant consultant surgeon who carried out a total gastrectomy for cancer of the stomach on the 21 year-old plaintiff, in circumstances where the defendant's hospital's pathology laboratory had mis-labelled his pathology specimen and mistakenly reported that he had cancer, was in breach of the

---

17 [2006] IEHC 89.

18 [2006] IEHC 398.

first *Dunne* principle and also of the third principle too. It was argued that a practice of accepting, without question, biopsy results was a practice that had inherent defects, that should have been obvious to any person giving the matter due consideration. Having regard to the specific finding in *Shuit*, and the actual language of the first three *Dunne* principles, such an alleged breach (of the third principle) does not logically flow. The cases, illustrate, however, what may be pleading or evidentiary pitfalls.

The third principle[19]

Apart from *O'Donovan v. Cork County Council & ors.*[20] and *Dunne*, there are few other written judgments of the Superior Courts, dealing with medical negligence, which consider the third principle. Its evidentiary provenance has only occasionally been addressed and, therefore, only limited and tentative conclusions are possible in relation to its practical limits.

There is an understandable reluctance on the part of the courts to gainsay the reasonableness of how other professionals go about their work.[21] Nevertheless, the courts reserve the right to have the final say in all such matters. *Bolitho v. City and Hackney Health Authority*[22] seems to suggest that persuasive expert evidence will be necessary before a "general and approved" practice can be impugned to such an extent that it will not afford a defence to a medical practitioner's conduct. In our jurisprudence, the approach is different. Walsh J. in *O'Donovan v. Cork County Council & ors.*[23] seems to have been of the view that determining whether or not there is an inherent defect in any particular practice is a matter for the trial judge (when sitting with a jury). In that case, he expressly found that the defendant surgeon was not liable in entrusting to his senior house officer the carrying out of an appendicectomy on the plaintiff's husband when he himself was not within immediate call, being at home some 20 miles away. In *Collins v. Mid Western Health Board & anor.*[24] Keane J. did not expressly indicate his view one way or the other but his decision tends towards a conclusion that it is a matter for the trial judge.

Unlike in those cases, the question of the application of the third *Dunne* principle arose in *Griffin v. Patton & anor.*[25] in the context of a clinical practice. Although not expressed in those precise terms at first instance, it was a matter

---

19 For a more extensive consideration of the issues that arise, see, Craven, "Medical Negligence and the *Dunne* Principles: the third and later principles" *Quarterly Review of Tort Law* (2006) 1 (4) 12 – 20.

20 [1967] I.R. 173.

21 See, in particular, *Collins v. Mid Western Health Board & anor* [2000] 2 I.R. 154 at 158 *per* Keane J. and *Bolitho v. City and Hackney Health Authority* [1997] 4 All E.R. 771 at 778-779 *per* Lord Browne-Wilkinson.

22 [1997] 4 All E.R. 771 at 778-779 *per* Lord Browne-Wilkinson.

23 *Loc. cit.*

24 *Collins v. Mid Western Health Board & anor* [2000] 2 I.R. 154 at 156.

25 [2004] IESC 46 *aff'g* unreported, High Court, O'Donovan J., March 21, 2003.

considered expressly in the defendant obstetrician's unsuccessful appeal to the Supreme Court. The central liability question related to the leaving of a piece of foetal bone in the plaintiff's uterus after a surgical evacuation following a spontaneous intrauterine death at 17 weeks' gestation. It was conceded that small pieces of soft tissue can sometimes be left behind in such a procedure without any negligence on the part of the operator. The issue was: could a piece of bone 5.5 centimetres in length and probably a lower limb, be retained in the uterus without substandard care on the part of the operator and, even if it could, was the operator, in fact, guilty of substandard care?

Although O'Donovan J. was satisfied that the defendant obstetrician could not be faulted in relation to the allegation that leaving a large piece of foetal bone behind after the procedure constituted a want of care, he also considered that "... it is not as simple as that." The court was not persuaded, on the evidence, that the visual check carried out on the foetal remains was sufficient to identify the major bony structures, much less to satisfy the operator that the entire foetus had been removed: to that extent, therefore, the court concluded that the defendant had fallen below an acceptable standard of care. Given the difficulty of the procedure and that it was not routine, O'Donovan J. later stated:

> "In those circumstances, it seems to me to defy logic that it was not incumbent upon [the defendant obstetrician] to carry out an ultrasound scan because, whether or not she believed that she had removed the entire foetus, and even though it was not routine to conduct an ultrasound scan following [the] procedure if, as appears to be the case, it is difficult to visually confirm that every single part of the foetus has been removed, common sense would dictate that recourse should be had to an ultrasound scan so as to ensure that the foetus had been fully evacuated. . Accordingly, it seems to me that the reality is ... that the failure, in the particular circumstances, to carry out an ultrasound scan amounted to substandard care...".

This is as close to a judicial expression of the third *Dunne* principle as there has been, in a clinical context. In dismissing the defendant obstetrician's appeal, Geoghegan J., however, for a unanimous Supreme Court[26] identified a clear procedural limitation of the application of the third *Dunne* principle; he was satisfied that a finding of negligence on that ground could not be sustained and that there were "a number of problems" about it as follows:

> "... the non-routine aspect of the operation related essentially to the difficulties of removing the head. Secondly, ... there [wa]s [no]thing in the evidence to suggest that it would be medical practice to carry out an ultrasound scan unless either the doctor had himself or herself

---

[26] [2004] IESC 46.

> doubts as to whether everything had been removed because of some objective evidence or if the particular doctor was somewhat squeamish about "ticking off" the major parts such as limbs, spine etc and resorts to an ultrasound scan instead which would be perfectly effective as a checking device. But quite apart from those evidential points…counsel for the [defendant] objected at one stage during the hearing to having to meet a case that an ultrasound scan although not required as a matter of routine practice might be required in special instances other than in the[se] two examples…That case could only be made, in my view, within the parameters of the third principle…in *Dunne*…. .This would seem to me to be not altogether unlike the famous principle in *Bradley v. CIE*[27] established in a non-medical context. It is a particular case however which would have had to be made from the start and argued as such. I do not think it was. For all these reasons (which can be taken disjunctively) I believe that the finding…that the [defendant] was negligent in not carrying out an ultrasound scan cannot be supported."

For Geoghegan J., therefore, if the third *Dunne* principle is to be relied upon, it must be pleaded as such. The decision at first instance, and on appeal, also clearly suggests that it is a matter for the trial judge to determine whether or not there is an inherent defect in the general and approved practice followed. The decision of Johnson J. in *Gottstein v. Maguire & anor*,[28] where the third *Dunne* principle arose for consideration in what might be described as a mixed setting, is also to the same effect. Relying on what Walsh J. had stated in *O'Donovan v. Cork County Council & ors.*[29] Johnson J. was

> "… satisfied that the failure to have in the intensive care unit of the hospital a person, nurse or doctor, skilled in the replacement of a tracheostomy tube under the circumstances of the present case is an inherent defect in what appears to be the practice which ought to be obvious to any person giving the matter due consideration and having given it due consideration, it is obvious to me."

The evidentiary threshold, sufficient to invoke it, as required by Geoghegan J. in *Griffin v. Patton & anor.*,[30] on the face of the judgment, appears to have been met.[31]

---

27 [1976] I.R. 217.

28 [2004] IEHC 416.

29 *Loc. cit.*, p.193, *per* Walsh J: "Neglect of duty does not cease by repetition to be neglect of duty."

30 [2004] IESC 46 *aff'g* unreported, High Court, O'Donovan J., March 21, 2003.

31 A further case that should be noted for the sake of completeness is *Kelly v. Lenihan* [2004] IEHC 427, where the question of the application of the third *Dunne* principle arose in very specific circumstances. It was alleged that the practice apparently relied on by the

The fourth, fifth and sixth principles

The last three *Dunne* principles can most easily be considered together. The undoubted clinical reality is that medical practitioners may often disagree as to the most appropriate approach to be taken in a particular condition. This is often no more than an expression of a clear evidential limitation insofar as diseases and their treatment are concerned, in effect, a reflection of the limitation of the understanding of the human condition. These last principles also acknowledge that the courts are limited in their competence to decide the relative merits or demerits of a particular approach (subject to the courts' overriding application of the third *Dunne* principle). In effect, they give practical, evidential effect to the first two principles, in particular.

What, however, is an "honest difference of opinion between doctors", as set out in the fourth *Dunne* principle? In the fourth principle, the adjective "eminent" used by Kingsmill-Moore J. in *Daniels & anor. v. Heskin*[32] is omitted. Nor is there reference to a practice being "general and approved" in this context, as in *O'Donovan v. Cork County Council & ors.*[33] Read alone, therefore, if a difference of opinion, while honest, arises between doctors of different levels of specialisation and experience, there is no matter for decision (subject to the application of the third principle). But, the question of the eminence of the doctors who are disagreeing, or whether or not the practice is "general and approved" cannot be wholly irrelevant. Interpreting the fourth principle in that manner is difficult to harmonise with the second part of the fifth principle which specifies the function of the trier of fact, i.e. "merely to decide whether the course of treatment followed, on the evidence, complied with careful conduct of a medical practitioner of like specialisation and skill to that professed by the defendant" or, indeed, with the sixth principle.[34] Eminence – or, more particularly, equivalence of specialisation and skill (and, probably, experience) – must be material in applying the fourth principle.

The next question that arises is: what is the effect of an "honest difference of opinion"? In *Griffin v. Patton & anor.*[35] O'Donovan J. considered that there was "an honest difference of opinion between [the] doctors as to which is the better of two ways of treating [the] patient" in relation to the leaving in the plaintiff's uterus of a piece of bone, 5.5 centimetres in length and probably

---

defendant's hospital of not carrying out any (or virtually any) episiotomies except in cases where a perineal tear was virtually seen to be developing during delivery was a practice which had such inherent defects which ought to have been obvious to "a prudent and careful midwife". Abbott J., in imposing liability, was not convinced by the statistical import of the studies relied upon and it was not necessary, in the circumstances, to find that the third *Dunne* principle applied.

32 *Loc. cit.*, p.85.

33 *Loc. cit.*, pp.193-194 *per* Walsh J.

34 [1989] I.R. 91 at 109.

35 *Loc. cit.*

a lower limb, following surgical evacuation of the plaintiff's uterus after a mid-trimester intra-uterine death, and in relation to the failure to perform an ultrasound examination – to confirm complete evacuation of the uterus – after the procedure. The Supreme Court, on the defendants' unsuccessful appeal, was also critical of the approach taken to the application of the fourth *Dunne* principle generally. Geoghegan J. stated:

> "It is quite clear that the judge interpreted *Dunne* as holding that where medical experts honestly disagreed as to whether a doctor had fallen below an acceptable standard of care, the judge was not entitled to prefer one view rather than the other and make a finding of negligence. In my view, *Dunne* is not authority for such a proposition. The principle of the "honest difference of opinion between doctors" only arises in relation to diagnosis and ways of treating a patient. There is nothing in *Dunne* to support the view that if two medical experts express an honestly held opinion on the negligence issue to opposite effect, the judge is precluded from making a finding of negligence in relation to the way a particular treatment is carried out. The learned trial judge was perfectly entitled if the evidence supported it, to form a view that the [appellant] did not carry out the evacuation process properly there being no disagreement between the experts as to how such process should be done."

Geoghegan J. later continued:

> "The issue…was essentially a factual issue to which [the trial judge] had to apply the same principles as he would have done in any kind of negligence action whether professional negligence or otherwise. It was not complicated…by the special principles set out [in *Dunne*]. Where two professional expert witnesses have an honest difference of opinion of what ought to be done in, say, diagnosing or treating then the judge is not entitled to prefer one view to the other and if the defendant complied with one of those courses of action, he could not be found to be negligent. But that does not seem to me to be of the essence of the matter in this case. Here, it was common case among all the medical experts that a gynaecologist carrying out the procedure which the appellant did carry out had to take all the correct steps to ensure as far as possible that the uterus was properly evacuated and especially of the major bony structures. It was for [the trial judge] to decide on the issue of fact as to whether the [defendant obstetrician] did that or not. He found that she did not, as he was entitled to do… . The fact that one doctor may say in the witness-box that in his opinion, the [defendant obstetrician] was not to blame does not in any way oust the normal function of the trial judge on the issues of fact even if the judge takes the view that the doctor giving evidence was giving an honest opinion."

Geoghegan J. considered that, nevertheless, in that case, there was "no doubt that there was ample evidence" to support the finding of negligence against the defendant obstetrician. In *Kelly v. Lenihan*,[36] the application of the fourth principle was orthodox. There, Abbott J. concluded that he could not, on the evidence, choose between the competing schools of thought in relation to elective episiotomy in the plaintiff's case. Imposing liability, however, he found, on the evidence, that there had been non-compliance with the approach actually adopted. Factual matters are, accordingly, for the trier of fact when faced with apparently conflicting expert opinion, or "honest differences of opinion", other than in relation to diagnosis and treatment. Determination of negligence is not a matter of clinical hegemony.

Do the *Dunne* principles always apply?

In cases alleging medical negligence, the *Dunne* principles may not always apply.[37] In *Wolfe v. St. James's Hospital & ors.*[38] the primary liability issue centred on the defendants' alleged failure to diagnose a tumour of the adrenal gland from which the plaintiff's husband subsequently died at the age of thirty-three. On the defendants' successful appeal to the Supreme Court, Geoghegan J. observed that in respect of the second of the alleged failures to investigate the deceased's symptoms, the "test" set out in the first *Dunne* principle (on which the matter had been decided at first instance) was of "very little relevance." The deceased had been complaining of "panic attacks". For Geoghegan J., this "was a clear statement coming from the patient." It was, he noted,

> "...not a question of the deceased's medical advisors being obliged to use their professional skills and thinking up some test which ought to be carried out. At that stage the patient himself...was telling [the second defendant] that he was seeking treatment not for the abdominal pains but for the panic attacks...[which] had featured in earlier complaints and the medical records show that he had had them for some years. If this was his major concern...and that concern was expressed to his doctors I see no reason why one has to apply some artificial test as to what the doctor's duty was. Expert evidence is never necessary to prove the obvious. The learned trial judge was entitled to take the view that there was a clear

---

36 [2004] IEHC 427. See, fn.31, *supra*.

37 See, for example, administrative or managerial negligence: *O'Donovan v. Cork County Council & ors*. [1967] I.R. 173, *Collins v. Mid-Western Health Board & anor*. [2000] 2 I.R. 154, *Fitzpatrick* v. *Midland Health Board & anor.*, (unreported, High Court, Johnson J., May 1, 1997) and *Gottstein v. Maguire & anor*. [2004] IEHC 416. See, also, in this regard, Binchy and Craven (1998) *Doctors in the Dock* G.I.L.S. June 1998 Vol. 92, No 5, pp.18 - 21.

38 [2002] IESC 10 rev'g [2002] IEHC 83.

> duty on [the second defendant] to see to it that the panic attacks would be investigated as required by the patient."

Although Geoghegan J. was the dissenting judge, and the majority (Fennelly and Murray JJ.) concluded differently on the liability issue on this point, the passage, nevertheless, seems to suggest contemplating a re-casting of the application of the principles of professional negligence. It might usefully be noted that its thrust reflects the approach of the earlier Supreme Court decision in *Collins v. Mid-Western Health Board & anor.*[39] There, Barron J., when considering the role of a general practitioner, seemed to consider that patient-doctor consultation should be considered in the same manner as a client-solicitor consultation. That does not, however, reflect the reality of doctor-patient interactions and given the sometimes complex presentations of many, even common, conditions, such analysis and analogy, arguably, runs the very real risk of imposing a standard that it might not be possible to discharge.

Dunne principles in action

Having considered the *Dunne* principles, review of some of the cases that were determined after *Dunne* demonstrates those principles in action. Review by reference to specialty is probably the most convenient approach.

Physicians

Actions against physicians are comparatively less common than those against their surgical colleagues. That is not to suggest that physicians are inherently more careful – or that surgeons are naturally more careless – in the manner in which they fulfil their professional obligations. Rather, the nature of their respective crafts is different such that error, or momentary inattention, may have dramatically different consequences for their patients. Of central importance for all clinicians, including physicians, is the making of a diagnosis, which may present its own difficulties. The selection of cases that follow are illustrative of the issues that arise.

In *Coughlan v. Wheaton & anor,*[40] it was alleged that the two defendant consultant physicians had failed to diagnose the plaintiff's Hodgkin's disease. Having investigated the plaintiff's complaints, and all investigations being normal, no diagnosis at all was made. Lavan J. found that that could not constitute negligence and the plaintiff's claim was dismissed. In *Wolfe v. St. James's Hospital & ors.*[41] a similar question arose in relation to the failure to diagnose another tumour – although on this occasion it was fatal tumour of the adrenal gland and the patient died. In imposing liability at first instance, applying

---

[39] [2000] 2 I.R. 154.

[40] Prof. Neg. L.R. 456.

[41] *Loc. cit.*

the first *Dunne* principle, Barr J. found that some of the deceased's symptoms, which had remained as "loose ends", had not been followed up and that he had been negligently discharged from the care of the defendant consultant physician. The Supreme Court,[42] however, on the defendants' appeal, reversed. Fennelly J. (with whom Murray J. (as he then was) agreed) considered that the findings in the High Court were not supported by the evidence. The approach of the trial judge, in his view, went "well beyond the standard laid down in *Dunne*." However, as a general proposition, "loose ends" are always liable to trip the unwary, as *Lopes v. Walker*[43] in the solicitor's context demonstrates.

In *Cleary v. Cowley & anor,*[44] the allegation made against the defendant clinician, who was not a consultant but a medical senior house officer, was that he had failed to diagnose a pulmonary embolus (a clot in the lung) in a seventeen year old who had recently been discharged from the defendant's hospital following treatment for pneumonia. The obvious diagnosis, which was resolving pneumonia, although subsequently shown to have been wrong, was made, and the patient died a few days later. Carroll J. found that the defendant doctor came well within the standard required by the *Dunne* principles and was, accordingly, not negligent.

Surgeons

The potential for mishap with any invasive procedure is self-evident, not least because of the complexity of hospital systems necessary for the carrying out of highly technical procedures. In addition, adverse outcomes can eventuate, notwithstanding all due care having been taken. Against that background, actions against surgeons can arise under a multiplicity of headings. The outcomes are invariably fact-dependent and only a limited number of themes merit discussion for present purposes.

All surgery has risks

All surgery has risks intrinsic to the actual procedure itself. In addition, being subject to general anaesthesia, immobilisation, dependency etc. also exposes a patient to risk of injury unrelated to the reason for the surgery. For example, in *Doherty v. Reynolds & anor*,[45] the plaintiff was diagnosed as suffering a severe injury to his right brachial plexus following a procedure he underwent for heartburn and reflux (and, therefore, at a site remote from the injury). Although satisfied on the evidence that the operator had not been negligent, O'Donovan J. found that the plaintiff had suffered his injury while under the care of the defendant's hospital and imposed liability in that regard, even though there was

---

[42] *Loc. cit.*

[43] [1999] IESC 57.

[44] Unreported, High Court, Carroll J., December 20, 2002.

[45] [2004] IESC 42.

no evidence which identified any particular incident which gave rise to that injury and the mechanism of injury was unclear. The Supreme Court, although finding that there was evidence on which the trial judge might have concluded that the plaintiff was entitled to succeed, was satisfied that he had misdirected himself in law as to the approach he should adopt in determining the liability question (and in relation to the application of *res ipsa loquitur*) and ordered a re-trial.

Johnson J., in *Gottstein v. Maguire & anor.*,[46] imposed liability on the defendant ear, nose and throat surgeon, in relation to the death of the plaintiff's husband following the displacement of his tracheostomy tube after throat surgery in circumstances where he had sent the deceased to the defendant's hospital's intensive care unit where he knew there was no-one trained to re-insert such a tube if it did become displaced. Even though the surgeon had no control over the intensive care unit, and it was the anaesthetist who directed that the deceased should return there, Johnson J. found that because of his overall responsibility for the patient he was responsible, as a matter of law, for the hospital's failure to provide appropriate care. Liability was not imposed under the second *Dunne* principle – there was evidence that the ENT consultant had not departed from a practice that had general professional support – and the liability finding against the hospital, which was based on the "inherent defects" dictum of Walsh J. in *O'Donovan v. Cork County Council & ors.*[47] seems also to have informed the decision in relation to the ENT consultant too.

Complications must be properly managed

Liability may arise because of the manner in which an operative complication is dealt with such as occurred in *Quinn v. South Eastern Health Board.*[48] There, the plaintiff suffered severe pain and disability affecting her right leg (and attributable to irritation of a nerve behind the operative site) following an appendicectomy when she was 14 years old. Although conservative treatment produced temporary relief, within a number of months the treating surgeon proceeded to division of the nerve and removal of a segment to prevent regeneration. The plaintiff's condition deteriorated and she was left with disabling, permanent and essentially untreatable nerve damage. With evidence to the effect that 90% of cases of this nature settle within two years on conservative treatment alone, Ó Caoimh J. had "no hesitation" in accepting that the surgery carried out was the wrong treatment at the particular time when it was carried out and imposed liability.

Second-guessing surgeons is very difficult

In *Mordaunt v. Gallagher*[49] (a case involving the removal of surgical wires from

---

46 *Loc. cit.*

47 *Loc. cit.*

48 [2002] IEHC 43.

49 [1997] IEHC 123.

the plaintiff's hip), *Barrett v. Southern Health Board*[50] (another case involving the removal of fixing metal in orthopaedic surgery), *Lynskey v. Jervis Street Hospital*[51] (where the plaintiff's testis was removed after the testicular artery was divided during the course of the removal of epididymal[52] cysts) and *Conley v. Strain*[53] (where the amount of surgical packing used by a general surgeon in an attempt to stop haemorrhage in a head injury was in issue) the intra-operative decision of the operating surgeon as to the approach he took was sought to be impugned. In none of these cases was liability imposed. Each operator was found to have come well within the terms of what is set out in the first or second *Dunne* principles. These decisions reflect the marked difficulties often encountered in attempting to analyse critically a surgical intervention years after the event. Once most per-operative judgments are made, it is difficult for someone other than the surgeon involved to convince a court at a later stage as to what actually occurred. Such was the case, too, in *Egan v. Midland Health Board & anor.*[54] where the plaintiff suffered damage to his sciatic nerve during the course of a total hip replacement which was complicated by the occurrence of a spiral fracture of the femur that had to be stabilised before the procedure was completed. It was alleged that the nerve damage had to have been caused by contact with an instrument in or about the area of the greater trochanter, which was the area where the operator had identified the damage on exploration a couple of days after the index procedure. Johnson J. accepted the evidence of the operator, albeit challenged, that he did not apply any instrument near the region where the nerve was damaged but rather further down the shaft of the femur. Finding, accordingly, that the damage to the nerve was not caused by anything the operator had used, Johnson J. applied the first *Dunne* principle and dismissed the plaintiff's claim. Evidence of the nature and site of the injury – of which the operator gave evidence – disposed of the matter.

Pre-operative investigations must be adequate

Allegations may arise as to the adequacy of the pre-operative assessment that has been carried out by the operating surgeon. Such was the case in *O'Gorman v. Jermyn & ors.*,[55] where it was alleged that the plaintiff should have undergone further specific investigation (*viz* upper gastro-intestinal endoscopy) before a total gastrectomy was carried out on the then 21 year-old plaintiff for malignant disease which, following surgery, it was found had never been present. A biopsy, which had been carried out at earlier surgery, had been mixed-up in the defendant's hospital's laboratory with that of another, older patient whose

---

50 Prof. Neg. L.R. 211.

51 Prof. Neg. L.R. 468.

52 At either pole of the testis.

53 [1988] I.R. 629.

54 [2006] IEHC 227.

55 *Loc. cit.*

specimen arrived in the pathology laboratory in or about the same time. Lavan J., on the evidence, refused to impose liability on the operating surgeon on the first *Dunne* principle, accepting that an endoscopy was not necessary in the circumstances of the case. Both the High Court, and the Supreme Court, on appeal, reached a similar conclusion, albeit in different factual circumstances, in *Bolton v. Blackrock Clinic Ltd & ors*.[56] Inadequate assessment, however, can result in the imposition of liability, as in *Philp v. Ryan & anor.*[57] where Peart J., at first instance, also effectively applied the first *Dunne* principle.

Obstetricians and gynaecologists

Given the nature of their craft, it is, perhaps, not entirely surprising that actions against obstetricians and gynaecologists are not unusual – although relatively few give rise to written judgments. As in other areas, the outcomes are generally quite fact-specific.

Birth injury

Injury to an infant may arise because of the manner in which labour is managed. *Dunne* was one such case. In *O'Mahony v. Tyndale & anor*,[58] negligence was alleged in relation to the non-attendance of a consultant obstetrician or registrar during the plaintiff's mother's labour, and the subsequent delay in the delivery of the plaintiff after he developed signs that were compatible with foetal distress. However, the plaintiff was born with good Apgar scores and examination by a consultant paediatrician prior to his discharge from hospital indicated no abnormalities. It was initially alleged that the plaintiff suffered cerebral palsy, as a consequence of hypoxia-ischaemia during the last 30 minutes prior to his birth. Quirke J. was not satisfied that the standard of proof had been discharged in that regard. (Insofar as another cause was also proposed – hypoglycaemia, which had not been properly managed - he was not satisfied that the evidence was sufficient in that regard either). The plaintiff having failed on proof of both liability and causation, the Supreme Court affirmed on appeal.

Non-catastrophic, but nevertheless serious, injury may also occur, during delivery, as, for example, in *O'Sullivan (a minor) v. Kiernan & anor.*[59] – a case of Erbs' palsy. It cannot be gainsaid but injury may occur in this situation, absent established negligence, such as in *Keogh (a minor) v. Dowling & anor.*[60] – another case of Erbs' palsy. There, forceps delivery, after a failed "ventouse" extraction had produced an easy delivery with an infant in good condition. The central allegation was that a condition that manifests as obstruction to the

---

56 Unreported, Supreme Court, Hamilton C.J., Barrington and Murphy JJ. *nem diss,* January 23, 1997 (*aff'g* unreported, High Court, Geoghegan J., December 20, 1994).

57 *Philp v. Ryan & anor* [2004] IEHC 77 *aff'g* [2004] IESC 105, [2004] 4 IR 241.

58 [2001] IESC 62 *aff'g* [2000] IEHC 43.

59 [2004] IEHC 78 (assessment only, liability conceded) (O'Neill J.).

60 [2005] IEHC 359.

delivery of the infant caused by the impacting of a shoulder occurred and that it had not been properly dealt with. It was common case that in the majority of cases of Erbs' palsy this condition is an element. The delivering obstetrician was satisfied that had the condition been present, she would have (a) detected it and (b) recorded it and she did not consider it possible for it to occur without her recognising it. If present, a delay between the emergence of the plaintiff's head with the forceps and the delivery of the trunk would have occurred and there was no evidence of such a delay. Johnson J. dismissed the plaintiff's claim, being satisfied that the plaintiff's delivery fell within that group where obstruction to labour by the infant's shoulder is not a feature in the cause of Erbs' palsy. Thus, the mere fact that the two conditions are associated did not determine the liability issue.

At the most serious end of the scale of infant injury, in *Cunningham v. Coombe Hospital & ors.*,[61] liability was imposed in relation to the misdiagnosis of the type of twins the plaintiff was carrying, and as a consequence of which they were stillborn just before they were due to be delivered.

Obstetric injury

Quite apart from injury to an infant, injury may also be caused to the mother because of the manner in which labour is managed as in *Kelly v. Lenihan*.[62] Here, the plaintiff suffered a third degree perineal tear during the course of the otherwise uncomplicated delivery of her third baby. Although subsequently repaired, the plaintiff suffered significant faecal incontinence and had a permanent end-colostomy fashioned. She contended that had she been properly observed a mediolateral episiotomy – which it was maintained significantly reduced the risk of a third degree tear - should have been carried out. For Abbott J., eschewing application of the third *Dunne* principle, and having regard to the different "schools of thought" in relation to elective episiotomy, any case to be made on that basis had to fail. However, faced with the plaintiff's uncontroverted evidence as to what she was told to do by the student midwife who attended her during the course of her labour, he concluded that the defendant's hospital had deviated from the approach actually adopted and liability was imposed, essentially on the basis of the second *Dunne* principle.

Management of operative surgical risks

There is a risk of wound infection with all surgical interventions, including in respect of methicillin resistant *Staphylococcus aureus* (MRSA). If infection does occur, an issue may arise as to its management as in *Edwards v. Southern*

[61] [2005] IEHC 354 (September 5, 2005) (Macken J.). This decision deals solely with the question of liability, in respect of "the medical aspects of the case" as a preliminary issue.

[62] [2004] IEHC 427; in relation to the application of the third *Dunne* principle, fn. 31 *supra*.

Health Board & ors.[63] In that case, the High Court, in dismissing the plaintiff's claim, was satisfied that the doctors acted in accordance with accepted practice and that that practice did not have inherent defects and the Supreme Court affirmed on appeal.

Another surgical risk eventuated in *Russell v. Walsh*[64] where the plaintiff developed an uretero-vaginal fistula following an abdominal hysterectomy. The court was satisfied, on the evidence, that this could occur without operator negligence in up to 0.5% of cases. Expert opinion differed sharply on only one essential point – whether the ureter should be palpated during the course of the surgery so as to avoid causing it damage, or be visually inspected. Being satisfied, however, that an acceptable approach had been adopted by the defendant gynaecologist and that, as a matter of fact, he had not damaged the ureter,[65] Johnson J. found no specific proof of any failure on his part and he dismissed the plaintiff's claim in the express terms of the first *Dunne* principle.

In addition, it may be difficult to complete a particular procedure, for any of a number of reasons, e.g. simple mechanical difficulty.[66] *Griffin v. Patton & anor.*,[67] already discussed in a different context, is another such case, albeit, one where liability was imposed.

Paediatricians

Prompt diagnosis of childhood problems is important for a number of reasons, not least because future development may be affected if left undiagnosed or unremediated. In those circumstances, it might be considered that paediatrics and, more particularly, neonatal diagnosis, would be high risk areas. Nevertheless, cases alleging negligence against paediatricians are not particularly common for a variety of practical reasons.

One area that has given rise to negligence litigation against paediatricians, however, is that of diagnosis – or rather the non-diagnosis – of congenital dislocation of the hip. In two such cases *Goonan v. Dooley*[68] and *Buckley v. National Maternity Hospital*[69] the central allegation was of negligence in the examination of the plaintiffs' hips in the neonatal period, such that the diagnosis was delayed until significant damage had occurred. In the first of those cases, the plaintiff's hips had been examined in the couple of months after her birth

---

63 Unreported, Supreme Court (Finlay C.J., Egan and Denham JJ.) July 26, 1994 (*aff'g* Prof. Neg. L.R. 227 (O'Hanlon J) [1989] IEHC 36.

64 Unreported, High Court, Johnson J., April 3, 1995.

65 Johnson J. found that the ureter had not been severed by the incorrect placing of a clamp or encircled by an incorrectly placed suture. Such damage, as did occur, he was satisfied on the evidence, could occur without failure on the part of the surgeon to carry out the operation properly.

66 E.g. in *Mordaunt v. Gallagher, loc. cit.*

67 *Loc. cit.*

68 Unreported, High Court, Lynch J., March 23, 1994.

69 Unreported, High Court, Smith J., December 21, 1998.

on four separate occasions and all examinations had been reported as normal. Although Lynch J. considered that a medical practitioner might culpably fail to diagnose congenital dislocation of the hip, he considered that that was less likely where a normal examination was reported on four occasions by three separate medical persons. In this regard, it merits noting that the diagnostic method had, in any event, inherent limitations such that a properly carried out examination might non-culpably fail to reveal the presence of the condition. In the circumstances, Lynch J. was satisfied that it was not negligent not to have detected the plaintiff's condition sooner.

Similarly, in *Buckley v. National Maternity Hospital*,[70] Smith J. rejected the allegation that the doctor who examined the plaintiff three days after her birth had culpably failed to detect abnormalities in her hips, being satisfied on the evidence that he had used due care. Although not necessary for his ultimate determination, he also indicated that had he been obliged to resolve the question in the light of the evidence, he would have found, as a matter of probability, that the plaintiff's problem was developmental, rather than congenital,[71] which is an issue at the heart of cases of alleged non-diagnosis of hip dislocation in the neonatal period.

Psychiatrists

Insofar as psychiatrists are concerned, most litigation now relates to *habeas corpus* applications in the context of a person's involuntary detention. Allegations of negligence have arisen in a limited number of areas which are self-evidently high risk, i.e. in relation to failure to predict suicide or suicidal behaviour and to prevent the "escape" of a patient.

The first issue arose in *Healy v. North Western Health Board,*[72] where the plaintiff's father committed suicide four days after his discharge from the defendant's psychiatric hospital. It was not disputed that he was suffering a depressive illness or that there was a causal connection between his illness and suicide. The liability issue related to the adequacy of his assessment prior to his discharge. Flood J. refused to choose between the different approaches to such assessment commended by the experts who gave evidence; however, he was satisfied, on the evidence, that it was unlikely that an appropriate assessment was ever carried out and that the deceased had been negligently discharged when he was not in firm remission. This was a straightforward application of the second *Dunne* principle.

In *Armstrong v. Eastern Health Board*,[73] the doctor who assessed the plaintiff for admission, having been referred by her general practitioner for that purpose,

---

70 *Ibid.*

71 See, Byrne and Binchy, *Annual Review of Irish Law 1998* (Round Hall Sweet & Maxwell, Dublin 1999), p.619.

72 Unreported, High Court, Flood J., January 31, 1996.

73 Prof. Neg. L.R. 291.

did not admit her to hospital. Within an hour, the plaintiff had thrown herself from a balcony in the flats complex where she lived, sustaining serious physical injuries. Egan J., in imposing liability, was not satisfied that the defendant's doctor, in making her assessment, had had sufficient regard to all the information that was available to her, finding, specifically, and notwithstanding her evidence to the contrary, that she had not read the general practitioner's referral letter. Records available to the doctor, which she had not read although she had an opportunity to do so, indicated that the plaintiff had twice presented with psychotic symptoms and with suicidal threats within the previous six weeks. The court was satisfied that the plaintiff would have been admitted to hospital had the doctor been in possession of all the clinical information.

Once a patient has been admitted to a psychiatric facility, (s)he does not have quite the same freedom as a patient in a general hospital to leave as (s)he wishes. Even a patient who is admitted voluntarily may be detained involuntarily in certain circumstances.[74] Where such a patient escapes, liability questions may arise if harm is caused to a third party. That was the issue in *C v. North Western Health Board.*[75] Here, the patient, having been brought to hospital under Garda escort, was admitted as a voluntary patient. After assessment by a consultant psychiatrist, close supervision was not considered necessary and, later, while watching television with other patients, he suddenly jumped through a large window in the defendant's hospital's day-room, onto a veranda and disappeared. A short time later he forcibly entered the plaintiff's house and assaulted him and his wife before he was re-taken by the Gardaí back to the hospital where he was detained for some ten days. Judge White was satisfied that there was a duty owed to the plaintiff, but, applying the *Dunne* principles, he also found, on the facts, that the psychiatrist had discharged that duty and refused to impose liability.

General practitioners

As with paediatricians, cases involving general practitioners are relatively infrequent. Insofar as a number of themes arise, most are of general applicability.

Asking questions

In *Collins v. Mid Western Health Board & anor,*[76] the plaintiff's evidence was that she had telephoned the defendant general practitioner, before he saw her husband, to indicate that he was unwell. Although he suffered an intra-cranial haemorrhage (and subsequently died), the history obtained from him by the general practitioner, when he saw him at his first consultation, was suggestive of

---

74 Mental Health Act 2001, ss 23 and 24 (previously, Mental Treatment Act 1945, s.194).

75 [1997] Ir. L. Log Weekly 133 (Circuit Court Judge White).

76 [2000] 2 I.R. 154 (*rev'g* unreported, High Court, Johnson J., May 14 1996).

a minor respiratory problem only; thus, the patient was treated conservatively and not referred to hospital for further examination. Although the general practitioner had no recollection whatsoever of the plaintiff's telephone calls, the Supreme Court considered that the obligation on him to act was not confined to what he was told by his patient at the surgery visit. The circumstances under which he came to the general practitioner's surgery were also important. Barron J. was clearly of the view that the telephone calls from the plaintiff should not have been ignored and that "ordinary care" required the doctor to take into account everything which might bear on the patient's condition. The manner in which the consultation was conducted, he considered, might have been very well for a patient coming to a doctor's surgery in the ordinary way. Where, however, it was preceded by a telephone call which suggested urgency, in his view, the doctor should have had regard to the circumstances, and what was said in the course of the call, and liability was imposed accordingly.

Failure to diagnose pregnancy

The accurate diagnosis of pregnancy is important for a number of reasons, not least because negligently caused pre-natal damage to an unborn child is actionable.[77] In *Maguire v. Randals & ors*,[78] Lynch J. clearly considered that loss of a pregnancy, through negligence, was also actionable.[79] The essential allegation of negligence, in that case, related to the fitting of an intra-uterine device while the plaintiff – unknown to both the plaintiff and the general practitioner - was actually pregnant. The plaintiff subsequently miscarried. In refusing to impose liability, the court found that there was nothing on physical examination that might reasonably have indicated to the general practitioner that the plaintiff was, in fact, pregnant. On the facts, the court was satisfied that all reasonable steps had been taken.

Prescribing without seeing patient

One of the issues that arose in *Hughes v. Staunton & ors*,[80] was whether or not the plaintiff's general practitioner had been negligent in prescribing for the plaintiff without first seeing him personally. The risks in this area are self-evident. In this case, on his return to work following illness, the general practitioner was advised over the telephone by his colleague who had deputised for him of his treatment of the plaintiff, and the advice he had received in that regard, by

---

77 Civil Liability Act 1961, s.58. See, however, the provisions of the English Congenital Disabilities (Civil Liability) Act 1976 which provides that such an action is derivative, on damage having been caused to the mother.

78 Prof. Neg. L. R. 350.

79 See, also, for example, *Cunningham v. Governor and Guardians of the Coombe Lying-in Hospital & ors.* [2005] IEHC 354 (negligence leading to stillbirth of twins was actionable).

80 Prof. Neg. L.R. 244.

telephone, from the defendant consultant neurologist; he also indicated that the plaintiff was doing well on that treatment. Shortly thereafter, the plaintiff's family sought a further prescription for the drug which had been prescribed and they confirmed to the general practitioner that the plaintiff was doing well. In those circumstances, and given that the general practitioner already knew the plaintiff very well – and had been intimately involved in his management for over a year, including his earlier referral to the defendant consultant neurologist in the first instance – Lynch J. could not see how he could be validly criticised "for acting on all these assurances from apparently responsible caring and reliable informants."[81] Although there were, of course, particular factors in this case, the thrust of the underlying principle is clear.

Failure to visit

A vexed issue that may arise, in particular, in general practice relates to whether or not a general practitioner is under a duty to make a domiciliary visit when requested. In *O'Doherty v. Whelan,*[82] liability in negligence for failure to make such a visit was imposed, in the particular circumstances of that case. The plaintiff was a young mother with a dependant child. Having suffered two previous miscarriages in the first trimester of pregnancy, she was again pregnant and approaching the end of the first term, ill at first presentation at the doctor's surgery and sufficiently ill to have been prescribed antibiotics. Furthermore, she was known by the general practitioner to be nervous, highly-strung and excitable. Against that factual background, O'Hanlon J., applying the *Dunne* principles, found that the general practitioner had not responded adequately to the patient's requests for subsequent domiciliary visits. That said, he expressly did not go so far as to impose an obligation in every case where such a request is made which, he considered, would be wholly unreasonable. Thus, the court contemplated the existence of a *restricted duty*.

Conclusion

Whereas, at first blush, the *Dunne* principles seem relatively straightforward both in terms of their articulation and philosophical underpinning, their application in practice, though frequently anodyne, may be somewhat more problematic from time to time. Their inter-relationship, *inter se*, is far from clear. They may also be more limited in their application than might at first appear. Judicial scrutiny of those limits will set the future tone.

---

81 *Ibid.*, p. 277.

82 Prof. Neg. L.R. 440.

CHAPTER 2

Recent Judicial Approaches to "Loss of Chance" in Medical Negligence Cases

RAY RYAN AND DES RYAN

> "It is always likely to be much easier to resolve issues of causation on balance of probabilities than to identify in terms of percentage the effect that clinical negligence had on the chances of a favourable outcome. This reality is a policy factor that weighs against the introduction into this area of a right to compensation for the loss of a chance. A robust test which produces rough justice may be preferable to a test that on occasion will be difficult, if not impossible, to apply with confidence in practice."[1]

INTRODUCTION

This chapter seeks to consider an avenue of liability in medical negligence "which has divided courts and commentators throughout the common law world".[2] The aim of the chapter is to provide an analysis of recent judicial approaches towards the issue of "loss of chance" in medical negligence litigation. Apart from developments in this jurisdiction, we focus in particular on the recent landmark judgment of the House of Lords in the case of *Gregg v. Scott*,[3] assessing the different approaches taken by the judges in the House of Lords and then going on to consider how those approaches have been and are likely to be treated by the courts in this jurisdiction. The five opinions delivered by the law lords in *Gregg* reveal, at times, starkly diverging positions on what is the correct approach in cases involving "loss of chance of a better medical outcome" arguments, and the case generally raises at least as many questions as it answers. In *Gregg*, the claim (which we set out in greater detail below) was that a doctor's negligent failure to diagnose cancer had caused the patient to have his chances of beating the disease reduced by 17%. It is very important to appreciate that no claim was made before the House of Lords in *Gregg* for

---

1 *Gregg v. Scott* [2005] U.K.H.L. 2; [2005] 2 A.C. 176, *per* Lord Phillips para.170.

2 *Ibid.*, *per* Lord Nicholls, para.1.

3 Above n.1 (hereafter *Gregg*).

damages for pain and suffering caused by the late diagnosis (such as psychiatric damage); this claim, which may well have been viable, was not pursued. Thus the sole complaint made by Mr Gregg was that the doctor's late diagnosis had caused his chances of recovery to be diminished, a loss which should sound in damages (including damages for his lost years' income, but reduced to reflect the fact that he would have died anyway). The fact that Mr Gregg's claim was so narrowly framed makes the claim "peculiarly difficult to analyse".[4] The trial judge accepted that the chances of cure fell from 42% to 25% as a result of the negligence on the part of Dr Scott causing the delay in treatment. The House of Lords did not question this finding but ruled, by a bare majority, that this reduction in the patient's chances of survival was not actionable damage for which he could be compensated. In so doing, the House of Lords opted for a policy-based restriction on the ambit of recovery for loss of chance.

This chapter seeks to grapple with a number of the interrelated questions referred to above. What, if any, special principles have guided and continue to guide the courts in their assessment of "loss of chance" arguments in medical negligence cases? What are the peculiar difficulties which plaintiffs face in bringing such claims? Given that courts in recent years can be said to have espoused on occasion a more benevolent approach towards the question of causation in favour of plaintiffs in certain negligence actions, is it appropriate or desirable that such an approach be adopted in the sphere of loss of chance claims in medical negligence cases? Given that the majority in *Gregg* denied outright recovery for loss of chance in cases where the original chance had been estimated at less than 50%, does the judicial approach in loss of chance cases involve no more than a "numbers game"? As to broader issues of policy, what are the core policy grounds which weigh with courts in determining loss of chance claims? In short, in medical negligence, what does "loss of chance" mean and when can it sound in damages?

Our consideration of judicial developments in this sphere of loss of chance is divided into three parts, as follows:

(i) A general overview affording consideration to the meaning of a claim in loss of chance, identifying those elements of the doctrine which occasion difficulties for plaintiffs. In this Part, we seek to locate loss of chance doctrine in the context of tort law generally and to consider those features of tort law which appear to render a claim for loss of chance hard to sustain. We then go on to consider a number of classic – but non-medical – cases in which loss of chance arguments have succeeded, before assessing medical cases in which the claim has failed. We do this in an attempt to ascertain whether a principled distinction can be drawn between cases of medical negligence, where

---

4 *Ibid.*, *per* Lord Phillips in *Gregg*, para.177.

the claim for loss of chance has been greeted with hostility, and other cases, where it has succeeded.

(ii) An assessment of the difficulties which plaintiffs will likely hereafter face in mounting a claim for damages for "loss of a chance" in medical negligence cases, assessing the significance of the landmark decision of the House of Lords in 2005 in *Gregg* on this issue, and considering the different approaches taken by the majority and minority judges in *Gregg*. In this Part, we afford particular attention to the policy arguments which have traditionally weighed with the courts – and which exercised the majority in *Gregg* – in declining to permit claims for loss of chance. In order to do this, we consider the treatment in *Gregg* of the decisions of the House of Lords in *Fairchild v. Glenhaven Funeral Services*[5] *and Chester v. Afshar*[6] – cases which can be regarded as "pro-plaintiff" in adopting a more benevolent approach to the causation hurdle than strict orthodoxy would appear to mandate – so as to consider whether or not the recognition of *Fairchild* flexibility might be of assistance to plaintiffs seeking to fashion arguments based on the loss of a chance.

(iii) A consideration of recent cases at Supreme Court level in this jurisdiction, which are relevant in the context of loss of chance, *Philp v. Ryan*[7] and *Quinn v. Mid-Western Health Board*.[8]

The chapter concludes by outlining what are at present some open questions and by identifying those issues of loss of chance that are likely to prove problematic in future cases both in this jurisdiction and elsewhere.

I. Loss of Chance: An Overview

It has been said that the common law – predicated as it is upon the notion of a wrongdoer and victim, a winner and a loser – is reluctant to split the difference and declare a draw.[9] Rather, the common law will incline towards giving judgment *in toto* for one party or the other, "with a win on points counting as a knock-out".[10] Within such a paradigm, the doctrine of loss of chance – clearly demanding a more rigorous conceptual approach to causation than that which is possible in the winner/loser paradigm just described – occupies somewhat uncertain territory.

---

5 [2002] U.K.H.L. 22, [2003] 1 A.C. 32.

6 [2004] U.K.H.L. 41, [2005] 1 A.C. 134.

7 [2004] I.E.S.C. 105, [2004] 4 I.R. 241.

8 [2005] I.E.S.C. 19, [2005] 4 I.R. 1.

9 For an illuminating advancement of this argument see Weir, "All or Nothing" (2004) 78 *Tulane Law Review* 511.

10 *Ibid.*, p.513.

Other orthodoxies of the common law compound this situation and heighten the anomalous status of loss of chance arguments. Three such orthodoxies, in particular, stand out. First, there is the well-entrenched principle that the standard of proof in civil cases is on the balance of probabilities. Secondly, there is that classic litmus test deployed by the courts in establishing whether causation has been satisfied, namely the "but for" test,[11] which imposes a requirement that the negligence complained of must have caused the damage of which the plaintiff complains. The function of the law of torts is thus to provide a remedy for a plaintiff who has suffered harm that is *caused* by the defendant's breach of duty. Thirdly – and this is a point of particular importance in the context of medical negligence cases involving loss of chance arguments – there is the peculiar ingredient of the tort of negligence itself which must not be forgotten, namely that it is the essential constituent or "gist" of the tort that *damage* be suffered by the plaintiff as a result of the defendant's wrongful act. It is of course true that, in most negligence cases, the operation of these three principles causes little controversy. Problems quickly begin to set in, however, in those cases in which it is difficult or even impossible to determine just *what would have happened* in the absence of the defendant's negligence. Very often, such cases will be argued in terms of "loss of opportunity" or "loss of chance".

It will be immediately apparent that in a "loss of chance" claim, the above strictures of the common law and of the law of negligence appear incongruous. At a conceptual level, courts have difficulties in locating loss of chance claims either within the "balance of probabilities" paradigm of the common law, or within the requirement that a plaintiff establish causation. A more tangible difficulty for the courts is the operation of the damage requirement in negligence where the plaintiff's alleged *damage* is itself viewed as something ethereal and elusive, namely, the diminution of a chance. It is these difficulties with which the courts are confronted when presented with an argument of the loss of, for example, a chance of recovery from an illness due to a doctor's negligence. If the patient in such a case originally (that is, before the tort occurred) enjoyed x chance of recovery, and as a result of the negligence now enjoys $x-1$ chance of recovery, is such a diminution to be regarded as comprising "damage" so as to satisfy the "gist" of the tort of negligence?

Actionable loss of chance

Before considering these difficult questions, it should be noted from the outset that there are, however, well-established examples of cases in which the courts have permitted recovery for loss of chance. An orthodox textbook example is

---

11 Perhaps the best-known authority in this regard is the decision of Nield J. in *Barnett v. Chelsea and Kensington Hospital Management Committee* [1969] 1 Q.B. 428. See generally Schroeder, "Causation, Compensation and Moral Responsibility" in Owen (ed.), *Philosophical Foundations of Tort Law* (OUP, 2001), 347.

the case of *Chaplin v. Hicks*,[12] where a woman who was wrongly deprived (due to inadequate notification of an interview appointment) of the chance of being one of the winners in a beauty competition was awarded damages for loss of a chance. Crucially, the Court of Appeal in *Chaplin* did not attempt to decide on the balance of probabilities what would have happened if the plaintiff had been properly notified of her interview.[13] Rather, the Court was satisfied that the chance of attaining success at the interview was something of intrinsic value, the deprivation of which should sound in damages. This conclusion was memorably captured by the following passage in the opinion of Fletcher Moulton L.J.:

> "The contract gave the plaintiff a right of considerable value, one for which many people would give money; therefore to hold that the plaintiff was entitled to no damages for being deprived of such a right because the final result depended on a contingency or chance would have been a misdirection."[14]

Another famous, and more recent, application of loss of chance principles arose in the well-known decision of the majority of the House of Lords in *Spring v. Guardian Assurance plc*.[15] In that case, where an employer negligently supplied an inaccurate character reference, the employee did not need to prove that, but for the negligence, he would probably have been given the new job. The employee only had to prove that he lost a reasonable chance of employment, which the courts could – and the Court of Appeal[16] ultimately did – evaluate. In the course of his opinion in the House of Lords Lord Lowry commented as follows:

> "Once the duty of care is held to exist and the defendants' negligence is proved, the plaintiff only has to show that by reason of that negligence he has lost a reasonable chance of employment …He does not have to

---

12 [1911] 2 K.B. 786.

13 See in particular the opinion of Vaughan Williams L.J., pp.791-792, where Vaughan Williams L.J. took pains to disavow the proposition advanced on behalf of the appellant that "whenever the contingencies on which the result depends are numerous and difficult to deal with, it is impossible to recover any damages for the loss of the chance or opportunity". A similar approach was taken by the Court of Appeal in the case of *Kitchen v. Royal Air Force Association* [1953] 1 W.L.R. 563. There, a solicitor's failure to issue a writ in time precluded his client from exercising the opportunity of pursuing court proceedings. The Court of Appeal assessed what would have been the plaintiff's prospects of success in the proceedings which the solicitor's negligence prevented him from pursuing, rather than having to satisfy itself as a matter of probability that the plaintiff would have succeeded in those proceedings.

14 [1911] 2 K.B. 786 at 797.

15 [1995] 2 A.C. 296.

16 The effect of the House of Lords judgment in *Spring* was that the matter was remitted to the Court of Appeal for an assessment of damages appropriate to the chance lost.

prove that, but for the negligent reference, [the prospective employer] *would* have employed him."[17]

A final – and very significant – example from the non-medical line of caselaw is the decision of the Court of Appeal in *Allied Maples Group Ltd v. Simmons & Simmons*.[18] Here a solicitor's negligence deprived the plaintiffs of an opportunity to negotiate a better bargain in their purchase of the shares of a subsidiary company of a business rival. The Court of Appeal, upholding the approach of the judge at first instance, adopted the "loss of chance" approach, Stuart-Smith L.J. expressing his agreement with the approach taken by Lord Lowry in the above-quoted passage of his opinion in *Spring* and regarding the *Allied Maples* case as one where "the plaintiff's loss depends on the hypothetical action of a third party".[19] This decision has been regarded[20] as authority for the proposition that cases involving the actions of third parties will generate a more relaxed judicial inquiry on the issue of loss of chance.[21]

For present purposes, what must be considered is the extent to which (if at all) this loss of chance reasoning can be applied to medical negligence cases. In considering the question of whether loss of chance constitutes actionable damage in such cases, it is necessary to consider the line of English caselaw which predated the decision of the House of Lords in *Gregg v. Scott*. In particular, we draw attention to two cases which pre-dated *Gregg*. Both are decisions of the House of Lords. In this Part, we discuss these two cases and the backdrop which they formed to the approach of the House of Lords in *Gregg* itself, the subject of Part II. We then go on in Part III to examine two recent decisions of the Supreme Court in this jurisdiction which pertain to the issue of loss of chance in medical negligence actions.

Hotson v. East Berkshire Area Health Authority

Perhaps the most important of the pre-*Gregg* English cases is *Hotson v. East Berkshire Area Health Authority*.[22] The plaintiff was a boy who broke his hip when he fell out of a tree whilst playing during his lunch hour at school. The hospital negligently failed to diagnose the fracture for five days. The boy suffered avascular necrosis of the epiphysis, involving disability of the hip joint with the virtual certainty that osteoarthritis would later develop. He brought an action against, *inter alia*, the health authority, who admitted negligence in failing to diagnose and treat with sufficient promptness the boy's injury. The judge found

---

17 [1995] 2 A.C. 296 at 327 (emphasis in original).

18 [1995] 1 W.L.R. 1602.

19 *Ibid.*, p.1611.

20 Though the approach of the Court of Appeal in *Allied Maples* is not without controversy: see especially Stapleton (2005) 68 M.L.R. 996, 1005.

21 *Gregg v. Scott*, above n.1, particularly the opinion of Lord Hoffmann para.82.

22 [1987] A.C. 750.

that the rupture of the blood vessels caused by the fall had probably made the damage inevitable but there was a 25%. chance that enough had remained intact to save the joint if the fracture had been diagnosed at the time. Both Simon Brown J (as he then was) at first instance and the Court of Appeal held that the plaintiff should be awarded damages for loss of the 25%. chance of a favourable outcome, the Court of Appeal expressly identifying as actionable damage in negligence the loss of a chance of avoiding a damaging outcome. The approach of the Court is perhaps best captured in the following passage of the opinion of Dillon L.J.:

> [W]hen the plaintiff was taken to... hospital...he had, on the judge's findings a 25% chance that by prompt treatment the development of avascular necrosis... could be avoided. When he left the hospital...he had lost the chance as a result of the breach of duty...As a result of the doctor's negligence, there was no prompt treatment and so we can never know how the chance would have turned out had the examination of the plaintiff not been negligent.[23]

Dillon L.J. clearly took the view that the plaintiff's case in *Hotson* was comparable to that of the plaintiff in the *Chaplin v. Hicks* case. Dillon L.J. pointed out that in *Chaplin*, no one could ever know whether, but for the defendant's wrongful act, the plaintiff would have been successful in the competition. But for that wrongful act, however, she would have had the chance of competing; thus "by his act she was deprived of that chance and for that chance, and not for any probability of success, she was compensated by an award of damages".[24] The Court of Appeal took the view that a valid analogy could be drawn between the facts of *Chaplin* and those at issue in *Hotson* since in *Hotson*, when the boy was taken to hospital on the day of his fall, he enjoyed a 25%. chance that with prompt treatment the development of avascular necrosis could be avoided. However, when he left the hospital to return home he had lost that chance as a result of the breach of duty on the part of the doctor. As in *Chaplin*, it was impossible for the court to say how that chance of which the plaintiff was deprived would ultimately have turned out, but this was not a reason to deny the plaintiff compensation for the loss of that chance.

On appeal to the House of Lords, however, this decision was unanimously reversed and it was held that this conclusion was premature, since *Hotson* was not a case of hypothetical contingencies at all. Instead, the core question of fact was: what was the condition of the plaintiff's hip at the time of his being admitted to hospital? The House of Lords held, as a matter of fact, that the initial injury had, on the balance of probabilities, been so severe that the plaintiff was "doomed"[25]

---

[23] *Ibid.*, 763.

[24] *Ibid.*

[25] *Ibid., per* Lord Ackner p.792.

to develop necrosis of the hip joint at the time of his being admitted to hospital.[26] Accordingly, any treatment provided – delayed or otherwise – could not have been causative of his subsequent deterioration. On this basis, a case such as *Chaplin v. Hicks* could not avail the plaintiff, since in *Chaplin* the plaintiff had lost something of "value", which the Lords held could not be said of *Hotson's* case since the boy only stood a 25%. chance of recovery before he set foot in the hospital. The appeal was disposed of by Lord Bridge with crisp succinctness in the following passage summarising the position:

> "In a sentence, the plaintiff was not entitled to any damages in respect of the deformed hip because the judge had decided that this was not caused by the admitted breach by the defendants of their duty of care but was caused by the separation of the left femoral epiphysis when he fell some 12 feet from a rope on which he had been swinging."[27]

It may be worth pausing at this juncture to consider whether a principled distinction can be drawn between the *Chaplin* and *Hotson* cases. An obvious starting point is to note that *Chaplin* was a case premised on breach of contract, whereas *Hotson* was a case in tort. Commentators[28] considering the two cases have emphasised that in a negligence action, damage or loss is necessary to give rise to a complete cause of action, whereas in a claim for breach of contract the cause of action is complete the moment breach is committed – with damage only being afforded consideration in the context of assessing damages. Despite the superficially attractive simplicity of this distinction, it is submitted that it cannot adequately explain why *Chaplin* and *Hotson* should be decided differently in terms of the loss of chance claim. As was recognised by the Court of Appeal in *Hotson*, such a distinction becomes untenable when one bears in mind that its operation would have enabled an identical plaintiff to *Hotson*, but in a private hospital, to mount a claim (assuming the plaintiff in the private hospital would have a claim for breach of contract). As Reece[29] notes, such a consequence "represents an unprincipled distinction between contract and tort unless the plaintiff in a private hospital is regarded as having contracted to be protected against chances" She goes on to note that such a construction "seems highly unlikely. The private patient may have paid for a higher standard of care, but the standard of proof should surely remain the same".[30]

---

26 As Baroness Hale said of *Hotson* in the course of her opinion in *Gregg*: "the die was already cast by the time the claimant got to the hospital (or at least the claimant could not prove otherwise)" (*Gregg*, para.211).

27 Above n.22, 793.

28 See, for example, Lunney, "What Price a Chance?" (1995) 15 L.S. 1.

29 Reece, "Losses of Chances in the Law" (1996) 59 M.L.R. 188, 191.

30 *Ibid.* The same author suggests two further possible grounds of distinguishing *Chaplin* and *Hotson*: a distinction between past facts and future hypothetical outcomes (which

In *Hotson*, Lord Bridge expressly stated that he saw "formidable difficulties"[31] with the argument that the courts should accept an analogy with contractual damages for lost chances in a personal injury case where there is a claim for loss of chance. However, Lord Bridge went on to state that "I do not see this appeal as a suitable occasion for reaching a settled conclusion as to whether the analogy can ever be applied".[32]

The approach of the House of Lords in *Hotson* left a number of questions unanswered. Among the most important was whether a principled distinction could be drawn between *Hotson*, where the fate of the plaintiff was known at trial, and a case in which the plaintiff's fate remained unknown, that is, where the loss of chance of recovery had not yet resolved itself and thus the court in assessing the claim for a lost chance could not determine the result of the lost chance.[33] It was this species of unresolved or indeterministic case which presented itself in *Gregg*.

Wilsher v. Essex Area Health Authority

The second pre-*Gregg* English case of relevance for present purposes is the decision of the House of Lords in *Wilsher v. Essex Area Health Authority*.[34] The facts are well known but bear brief repetition. The plaintiff was born prematurely and was placed in a special care unit at the defendants' hospital. In order to survive, he needed extra oxygen; to ensure that the correct amount was administered it was necessary to insert a catheter into an umbilical artery so that his arterial blood oxygen levels would be accurately read on an electronic monitor. A junior doctor mistakenly inserted the catheter into the umbilical vein with the result that the monitor gave a lower reading The baby suffered rentrolental fibroplasia ("RLF"), a condition of the eyes which resulted in blindness. The plaintiff claimed damages from the defendant health authority for the negligent medical treatment he had received in their special care baby unit. The judge held that the defendants were liable since they had failed to prove that the plaintiff's condition had not been caused by the negligence of their employees. The Court of Appeal, by a majority, dismissed the defendant's appeal.

Once again, this decision of the Court of Appeal was reversed by the House of Lords. The Appellate Committee held that the baby's RLF was caused either by lack of oxygen or by something else or by a combination of causes. The defendant could be held liable only if the lack of oxygen caused or substantially contributed to the injury, a matter which had to be proved on a balance of

---

distinction Reece rejects); and a distinction between cases which are indeterministic and those which are deterministic (which she accepts and explores at length).

31 Above n.22, 782.

32 *Ibid.*, pp.782-783.

33 See above n.30.

34 [1988] A.C. 1074.

probabilities. As we discuss below, *Wilsher* featured prominently both in the House of Lords' ruling in *Gregg* and in the judgment of the Irish Supreme Court in *Quinn v. Mid-Western Health Board*,[35] considered in parts II and III of this chapter respectively. Moreover, the crucial message from *Wilsher* was that the courts would not be willing to apply a more relaxed approach to conventional rules on causation merely to assist a plaintiff who could elicit judicial sympathy. In the stern language of Lord Bridge in *Wilsher*:

> "[W]hether we like it or not, the law, which only Parliament can change, requires proof of fault causing damage as the basis of liability in tort. We should do society nothing but disservice if we made the forensic process still more unpredictable and hazardous by distorting the law to accommodate the exigencies of what may seem hard cases."[36]

II. *Gregg v. Scott*

The importance of the judgment of the House of Lords in 2005 in the case of *Gregg v. Scott*,[37] can scarcely be overstated. The decision has already generated a wealth of academic discussion and comment,[38] but from the perspective of Irish lawyers there are a number of reasons why it is worth setting out the background to the case and an analysis of the opinions of the Appellate Committee in some detail. In the first place, it will be of interest to Irish practitioners to note that Lord Hoffmann in his opinion in *Gregg* cited the Supreme Court decision in this jurisdiction in the case of *Philp v. Ryan*.[39] Moreover, given the uncertainty which currently surrounds the recoverability of damages for loss of chance in a medical negligence context in Irish law, a consideration of the approaches in *Gregg* seems particularly timely, since the very extensive treatment afforded in the opinions to the rationales for allowing or disallowing recovery in such cases may well prove highly persuasive to Irish courts in the not-too-distant future.

The decision of the House of Lords in *Gregg* was eagerly awaited, particularly since the case had divided the Court of Appeal. As in the Court of

---

35 Above n.8.

36 Above n.34, at 1092.

37 Above n.1.

38 See for example Foster, "Last Chance for Lost Chances?" (2005) 155 N.L.J. 248; Green, "Coherence of Medical Negligence Cases: A Game of Doctors and Purses" (2006) 14 Med. Law Rev. 1; Morgan, "A chance missed to recognise loss-of-a-chance in negligence" [2005] L.M.C.L.Q. 281; Peel, "Loss of a Chance in Medical Negligence" (2005) 121 L.Q.R. 364; Reid, "*Gregg v. Scott* and Lost Chances" (2005) 21 P.N. 78; Samuels, "Misdiagnosis Leading to the Loss or Diminution of the Chance of Recovery or Survival: Any Remedy?" [2005] M.L.J. 115; Spencer, "Damages for Lost Chances: Lost for Good?" [2005] C.L.J. 282 and Stapleton, "Loss of the Chance of Cure from Cancer" (2005) 68 M.L.R. 996.

39 Above n.7. On Lord Hoffmann's treatment of *Philp* see below, text preceding n.108.

Appeal, the case was one that weighed heavily with the judges who heard it. As Lord Hope revealed:

> [T]his is an anxious and difficult case. It is only after many months of deliberation that it has become clear that the majority view is that the appeal must be dismissed.[40]

Lord Nicholls, too, underlined at the very outset of his opinion the depth of the inquiry at issue in *Gregg* when he stated that:

> "This appeal raises a question which has divided courts and commentators throughout the common law world. The division derives essentially from different perceptions of what constitutes injustice in a common form type of medical negligence case. Some believe a remedy is essential and that a principled ground for providing an appropriate remedy can be found. Others are not persuaded."[41]

Background

The material background facts in the *Gregg* case were as follows. In November 1994 Mr Gregg presented to Dr Scott complaining of a lump under his left arm. Dr Scott told him that the lump was merely a collection of fatty tissues. In breach of the duty of care he owed to Mr Gregg, Dr Scott failed to refer him immediately for biopsy investigation; nor did Dr Scott arrange a subsequent appointment for Mr Gregg so as to ascertain whether the lump had resolved itself. Had he done so, it would have been discovered that the lump was cancerous and cancer treatment could have been commenced in April 1995. The breach of duty on the part of Dr Scott meant that the cancer remained undetected until November 1995 and cancer treatment did not commence until January 1996. Accordingly, Dr Scott's breach of duty had caused a nine-month delay in having treatment commenced. Meanwhile, the cancer spread to the left pectoral region.

It is essential from the outset to set out the details of treatment received by Mr Gregg. From January 1996, chemotherapy and radiotherapy were administered but, although the tumour responded to this treatment, it did so incompletely. As a result it was decided that aggressive high dose chemotherapy would be administered in August 1996. In early 1998, Mr Gregg suffered a relapse, with a new tumour being detected in the right axilla. The medical conclusion from this relapse was that he could not be "cured";[42] palliative therapy was administered. In April 1998 there was another suspected relapse and further palliative therapy was administered. From April 1998 onwards, there was no evidence of any recurrence

---

40 Above n.1, para.92.

41 *Gregg* para.1.

42 "Recovery" or "cure" in this context was taken by the expert witnesses – and accepted at all levels of court – as meaning survival for ten years.

of the disease, and Mr Gregg was in remission throughout this period.

It was accepted at trial that, on the day Mr Gregg presented to the doctor (both men of course being at that time unaware of the existence of the disease) Mr Gregg's chances of recovery were 42%. It was also accepted that because of the delay in getting the treatment (due to the misdiagnosis) Mr Gregg's chances of recovery had been greatly lessened – to about 25%. His claim (which was rejected at first instance and in the Court of Appeal, by a majority) was that he was entitled to damages for having been deprived of the original 42%. chance of recovery. The essence of his argument was that Dr Scott's breach of duty had reduced Mr Gregg's "prospects of a cure". Crucially for present purposes, Mr Gregg did not choose to advance the alternative claims in negligence against Dr Scott for having *increased* his injuries. As a result, the question of general damages for pain and suffering was not addressed by the trial judge. Rather, Mr Gregg's claim, as presented to the judge, was for damages to compensate him for the loss of, or diminution in, his expectation of life due to the doctor's negligence, that is, loss of chance. That the case was framed in such narrow terms was clearly to the regret of the Appellate Committee of the House of Lords in *Gregg*. As Lord Hope said: all "the appellant's eggs were . . . put in this one ['cure'] basket".[43]

It is of fundamental importance to note at this point that, unlike the situation which had pertained in the *Hotson* case, in *Gregg* the chance had not yet been determined, that is, the post-litigation prognosis was "unresolved" since it remained uncertain as to whether or not Mr Gregg would be cured. Indeed, the very fact that Mr Gregg remained alive at the date of the House of Lords decision, some eight and a half years after the commencement of treatment in 1996, is an important feature of *Gregg*. As Lord Phillips stated, "[t]he closer that Mr Gregg comes to being a survivor the smaller is the likelihood that the delay in commencing his treatment has had any effect on his expectation of life".[44] Mr Gregg did not, therefore, complain that he had been deprived of a cure; rather, he argued that he should be able to recover for being deprived of a *chance* of a cure. He sought to employ two alternative arguments for this proposition, neatly described by Stapleton[45] as "the conventional consequential-on-a-physical-injury argument" and the "radical "pure loss of a chance" argument". For convenience, each of these arguments will now be summarised briefly, before we proceed to consider the different approaches taken by the members of the House of Lords to these arguments.

The "conventional" argument

Mr Gregg argued that the delay in diagnosis and treatment had occasioned him physical injury, in the form of the spread of the cancer in late 1995 before

---

43 *Gregg*, para.97. See also the opinion of Baroness Hale, paras.206-207.

44 *Ibid*., p.169.

45 Stapleton, "Loss of the Chance of Cure from Cancer" (2005) 68 M.L.R. 996, 998-999.

his therapy began in 1996. The losses he had suffered, embracing his loss of a chance of cure, were simply consequential on this physical damage, just as loss of earnings and loss of life expectancy could be consequential on a broken leg. The argument has a nuanced sophistication. The risk of premature death is characterized as a future contingency, "parasitical upon past actionable damage in the form of the enlargement of the tumour".[46] Now, in loss of chance cases, what makes this line of argument particularly attractive to plaintiffs is that courts frequently are happy to take into account possibilities, even though they are not probabilities, in assessing the loss caused by the defendant's breach of duty.

For the purposes of considering this argument, it is important to distinguish between issues of causation and issues of quantification. In advancing this argument Mr Gregg accepted that issues of causation of damage must be decided on the balance of probabilities, but argued that consequential loss is essentially a matter of quantification and not causation; accordingly, the loss of the chance of a cure should be evaluated in the same way as, for example, an increased risk of arthritis arising from a broken leg.

It has been suggested that this is a sensible route for the law to go down in cases where the claim concerns a future contingency that has not yet occurred. To assuage fears of indeterminate liability and floodgates concerns, Reid argues that this approach does contain sufficient control mechanisms.[47] According to Reid, "it will be a rare case where future contingent harm has yet to take place and is sufficiently serious in magnitude as to justify litigation".[48]

The "radical" argument

Mr Gregg's alternative, and more ambitious, submission was that the reduction in the prospect of a favourable outcome (that is, loss of a chance) should of itself be a recoverable head of damage. The loss of a chance of averting premature death satisfies the requirement of minimum actionable damage; it is the gist of negligence.

We now turn to analyse how each of these arguments was dealt with by the House of Lords in *Gregg*.

Judicial treatment of these arguments in *Gregg*

The conventional argument

We turn first to the "conventional" argument by which Mr Gregg sought to hang the loss of chance claim on the "hook" of the physical injury.[49] As both Latham

---

[46] Reid, "*Gregg v. Scott* and Lost Chances" (2005) 21 P.N. 78.

[47] For discussion of "control mechanisms" in Irish negligence law, see the judgment of Geoghegan J. in *Fletcher v. Commissioners of Public Works* [2003] 1 I.R. 465, 487.

[48] Reid, *op. cit.*, p.84.

[49] Remembering that the trial judge and the Court of Appeal had accepted that the effect of the doctor's negligence and resultant delay was that the chances of long-term survival

and Mance L.JJ. said in the Court of Appeal, the delay in diagnosis caused the tumour to enlarge, invade neighbouring tissues and cause severe pain.[50] As Mance L.J. (as he then was) put it, the enlarged tumour was a clear physical consequence of the doctor's negligence.[51] On the judge's findings a conventional view of the case would be that the delay resulted in a physical injury which entitled the appellant to an award of damages for the consequences of that injury. Latham L.J. developed this point more fully in the following passage of his dissenting opinion in the Court of Appeal in *Gregg*:

> "It was the enlargement of the tumour which reduced the chances of successfully treating it. This aspect of the plaintiff's claim was never addressed by the judge. Nonetheless the judge's findings amply support the submission that the appellant had indeed suffered injury which entitled the appellant to general damages for the pain and suffering which were the physical consequence of the spread of the tumour, an assessment of the extent to which delay resulted in more intensive therefore damaging treatment, an assessment of the increased risk of relapse and the adverse effect on prognosis, involving an assessment of the consequences to the appellant's expectation of life."[52]

It was also accepted by Lord Hope in his opinion in the House of Lords.[53] Lord Hope characterised Mr Gregg's claim in the following terms:

> "It is, in essence, a claim for the loss and damage caused by the enlargement of the tumour due to the delay in diagnosis. It is for the loss and damage caused, in other words, by a physical injury which the appellant would not have suffered but for the doctor's negligence. The fact that there was a physical injury has been proved on a balance of probabilities. So too has the fact that, in addition to pain and suffering, it caused a reduction in the prospects of a successful outcome. I would hold that, where these factors are present, the way is open for losses which are consequential on the physical injury to be claimed too. I do not think that those consequences of the physical injury should be treated as if they were the product of a separate cause of action from the pain and suffering. I see the reduction in the prospects of a successful outcome as one element among several in the claim for which there is a single cause – the enlargement of the tumour. This was a physical injury, the avoidance

---

fell from 42%. (on initial presentation to Dr Scott) to 25%. (as at the date of trial).

50 [2002] E.W.C.A. Civ. 1471 and [2003] Lloyd's Rep. Med. 105, paras 21 and 47.

51 *Ibid.*, para.86.

52 *Ibid.*, para.21.

53 Above n.1, paras 93-94 and 117. Lord Nicholls, who also would have allowed Mr Gregg's appeal, focused his analysis on the second, "pure", loss of chance argument which, he held, was sufficient to constitute actionable damage.

> or minimisation of which was within the scope of the doctor's duty of care when the appellant consulted him."[54]

The majority of the House of Lords, composed of Lord Phillips of Worth Matravers, Lord Hoffmann and Baroness Hale, took a different view and rejected this "hook" argument. Lord Phillips regarded it as a "fallacy",[55] explaining that he could see no basis for establishing a nexus between the delayed diagnosis and spread of the cancer, on the one hand, and the deterioration in Mr Gregg's prospects of recovery, on the other. Lord Phillips conducted a comprehensive survey of the complex statistical evidence that had been led in the case, and questioned the veracity of certain assumptions made in the Court of Appeal with regard to that statistical evidence.[56] Once Mr Gregg had entered into remission in 1996, there was nothing to indicate that his prospects of recovery had been worsened as a result of the spread and, in particular, that they were any worse than they had been at the time of his first consultation with Dr Scott.

Baroness Hale, for her part, confessed that she "was for a long time attracted by [this argument]".[57] She ultimately determined, however, that the argument could not succeed in this case, on an application of the orthodox principle that consequential loss still has to be consequential upon – itself *caused by* – the injury that has been caused by the defendant's negligence. She drew some comfort from the fact that "on conventional principles",[58] this approach did not preclude all remedies to a plaintiff such as Mr Gregg, since the defendant in such a case remains liable for any extra pain, suffering, loss of amenity, financial loss and loss of expectation of life which may have resulted from the delay. So too should the plaintiff be entitled to damages if he can establish that, without the delay, the claimant would have achieved a longer gap before more radical treatment became necessary. If the pain and suffering he would have suffered anyway was made worse by the anguish of knowing that his disease could have been detected earlier, then he should be compensated, *inter alia*,[59] for that damage. Baroness Hale noted with some regret, however, that no such remedies were explored by the trial judge, "presumably because the focus before him had been on establishing that the claimant would otherwise have achieved a complete "cure"… [which] would have entitled the claimant to far more in the way of loss of earnings and cost of care…".[60]

---

54 Above n.1, para.117.

55 *Ibid.*, para.147.

56 *Ibid.*

57 *Ibid.*, para.200.

58 *Ibid.*

59 Baroness Hale also explored (para.207) the possibility of a claim for loss of life expectancy being made by a plaintiff such as Mr Gregg, a claim which she regarded as capable of being made out in appropriate cases. As with the other alternative remedies discussed by Baroness Hale, however, this argument was not raised by the appellant in *Gregg* itself.

60 Above n.1, para.208.

The remaining member of the majority, Lord Hoffmann, proferred another reason for rejecting the "conventional" argument using the physical injury as a hook upon which to hang the loss of chance claim. Lord Hoffmann noted that while a plaintiff with a tortiously injured joint can recover for the associated risk that the joint will later develop arthritis, if the joint does later develop arthritis there is usually no dispute that the arthritis was attributable to the tort rather than some pre-existing personal vulnerability. However, on the facts of *Gregg*, quite apart from a dispute about the link between the original tort (Dr Scott's negligence) and an increase in Mr Gregg's chance of dying early, there also existed doubt as to whether early death could properly be attributed to the said negligence, or whether it could be attributed to some personal idiosyncrasy such as the loss of expectation of life that would, even in the absence of the negligence, have been associated with the cancer. Lord Hoffmann concluded that, in *Gregg*, it was more likely to be the latter, so that the possibility of attributing the diminished prospects of survival to the negligence of Dr Scott was less than 50%.

Quite apart from the peculiar difficulties in the *Gregg* case, Lord Hoffmann regarded the "hook" argument generally as an "artificial limitation",[61] the boundaries of which would be "a fertile source of litigation", and which should, as a matter of principle, be rejected.

What conclusions can be drawn from the manner in which the majority approached this conventional "consequent upon a physical injury" argument? Perhaps the most important point to stress is that of the five Law Lords in *Gregg*, only Lord Hoffmann apparently rejected outright the possibility, as a matter of principle, of making out a loss of chance claim where physical injury is deployed as a "hook" on which to hang that claim. The difficulty identified by the remaining members of the majority[62] was that it could not conclusively be said that the loss of chance could accurately be characterised as a consequent loss flowing from the physical damage caused by Dr Scott's negligence.

The radical argument

Let us now turn to the treatment by the members of the House of Lords in *Gregg* of the more ambitious or "radical" pure loss of a chance argument. As noted at the outset of this Part, it was accepted at all levels of court that on first presenting before Dr Scott, Mr Gregg enjoyed a 42%. chance of recovery, whereas by the time of trial he enjoyed only a 25%. chance of recovery. Since medical opinion assessed Mr Gregg's recovery prospects in terms of percentages, should the law not follow suit and provide a remedy for the diminution in percentage value? This argument commended itself to Lord Nicholls, who explained his reasoning as to why the law should be developed to embrace just such a "radical" loss of chance argument as follows:

---

[61] *Ibid.*, para.87.

[62] See the opinion of Lord Phillips para.188 and that of Baroness Hale para.200.

> "The way ahead must surely be to recognise that where a patient is suffering from illness or injury and his prospects of recovery are attended with a significant degree of medical uncertainty, and he suffers a significant diminution of his prospects of recovery by reason of medical negligence whether of diagnosis or treatment, that diminution constitutes actionable damage. This is so whether the patient's prospects immediately before the negligence exceeded or fell short of 50%. 'Medical uncertainty' is uncertainty inherent in the patient's condition, uncertainty which medical opinion cannot resolve. This is to be contrasted with uncertainties arising solely from differences of view expressed by witnesses. Evidential uncertainties of this character should be resolved in the usual way."[63]

The above passage is clearly premised on the conviction that the law should not continue to insist on maintaining the fiction of a certain outcome when medical judgment accepts uncertainty of outcome as a day-to-day reality. Lord Nicholls registered his disagreement with such conventional legal fiction in particularly trenchant terms:

> "It cannot be right to adopt a procedure having the effect that, in law, a patient's prospects of recovery are treated as non-existent whenever they exist but fall short of 50%. If the law were to proceed in this way it would deserve to be likened to the proverbial ass."[64]

It has been noted that the other dissentient in *Gregg*, Lord Hope, would have allowed the appeal on narrower grounds than those proposed by Lord Nicholls; as discussed above, Lord Hope was satisfied that the "conventional" claim for loss of a chance consequent upon physical injury could be sustained on the appeal. For the members of the majority, who as we have seen rejected the "conventional" or "hook" argument in *Gregg*, Lord Nicholls's approach to the "pure" loss of chance claim did not prove convincing either. Quite apart from a comprehensive treatment of the statistical evidence in the case that was invoked to point to difficulties in recognising the loss of chance claim in Mr Gregg's case,[65] the majority invoked clear policy concerns as to why, as a matter of principle, the law should set its face against the recoverability of damages for "pure" loss of chance in Mr Gregg's case. From an Irish perspective, it is illuminating to consider in detail the policy considerations canvassed by the different judges.

At first glance, it might be concluded that for the majority, the matter could be reduced to something of a numbers game: recovery was permissible only if the initial chance of cure had been greater than 50%., because only then could the

---

63 Above n.1, para.44.

64 *Ibid.*, para.43.

65 See especially the opinion of Lord Phillips at paras 150 and 187 – 188.

claimant "come up to proof" and show that it was more likely than not that but for the negligent diagnosis, the illness would have been beaten. In *Gregg*, however, the initial chance had been less than 50%. and thus, according to the majority, the plaintiff failed to prove his case, and could not recover. The determining factor for the majority judges was that Mr Gregg had failed to establish that through his negligence, Dr Scott had caused him injury. With the majority, Lord Hoffmann revealed that the invitation that had effectively been extended to the House of Lords by counsel for the claimant to overrule its earlier decision in *Hotson v. East Berkshire Health Authority*[66] was not one which he was prepared to accept. Lord Hoffmann prayed in aid a judgment from the Supreme Court of Canada[67] on similar facts where recovery had been denied.

Lord Phillips attached great significance to the fact that the claim in *Gregg* was one for the reduction of the prospect of a cure, even though the long-term result of treatment was still unknown. He placed emphasis on the fact that at the time of the trial, Mr Gregg had survived about five years from commencement of treatment and by the time of the hearing in the House of Lords had survived a further three years, without relapse. According to Lord Phillips, this "must plainly have resulted in a dramatic improvement in his prospects of being a survivor".[68]

Policy considerations

Reading the majority judgments, one is struck by the underlying philosophy that to extend the law in this area would be too generous to plaintiffs. Consider the following passage from the judgment of Baroness Hale:

> "Almost any claim for loss of an outcome could be reformulated as a claim for loss of a chance of that outcome. The implications of retaining them both as alternatives would be substantial. That is, the claimant still has the prospect of 100% recovery if he can show that it is more likely than not that the doctor's negligence caused the adverse outcome. But if he cannot show that, he also has the prospect of lesser recovery for loss of a chance. If (for the reasons given earlier) it would in practice always be tempting to conclude that the doctor's negligence had affected his chances to some extent, the claimant would almost always get something. It would be a 'heads you lose everything, tails I win something' situation. But why should the defendant not also be able to redefine the gist of the action if it suits him better?"[69]

The argument advanced by counsel to the effect that control mechanisms could

---

66 [1987] A.C. 750.

67 Above n.22.

68 Above n.1, para.133.

69 *Ibid.*, para.224.

govern this area of law was stoutly rejected by Lord Hoffmann on the grounds that such a system of mechanisms would be unprincipled.[70]

It is important to note that Lord Hoffmann identified a *Fairchild*[71] type claim as being at the core of the argument in *Gregg*. It will be recalled that in *Fairchild* the House of Lords greatly extended the approach it had taken some thirty years earlier in the famous case of *McGhee v. National Coal Board*.[72] In *Fairchild*, employees had developed mesothelioma after exposure to asbestos dust while employed by numerous different employers. Breach of duty was established against all the employers. However, the claimants could not prove on a balance of probabilities that the onset of the disease was caused by any one particular exposure or cumulative exposures. Given that each employer's wrongdoing had materially increased the risk of contracting the disease, the House of Lords held that a modified approach to proof of causation was justified.[73] Lord Nicholls had expressly proceeded on the basis that the ordinary "but for" standard of causation was not satisfied, but endorsed the application of "a different and less stringent test".[74] Lord Bingham in his opinion in *Fairchild*[75] quoted the following passage from the opinion of Lord Hoffmann in *Kuwait Airways Corporation v. Iraqi Airways Co (Nos 4 and 5)*:[76]

> "There is therefore no uniform causal requirement for liability in tort. Instead there are varying causal requirements, depending upon the basis and purpose of liability. One cannot separate questions of liability from questions of causation. They are inextricably connected. One is never simply liable; one is always liable *for* something and the rules which

---

70 Lord Hoffmann drew support for this conclusion from the current state of English law on liability for negligently inflicted psychiatric injury, citing the decision of the House of Lords in *Alcock v. Chief Constable of the South Yorkshire Police* [1992] 1 A.C. 310. From an Irish standpoint, it will be recalled that Geoghegan J in the course of his opinion in *Fletcher v. The Commissioners of Public Works in Ireland* [2003] 1 I.R. 465 stated, at 503, that "there are great problems arising out of [*Alcock*] and I am not in any way intending either to approve or disapprove of it" For recent consideration of *Fletcher* see the judgment of the Supreme Court in *Devlin v National Maternity Hospital* [2007] I.E.S.C. 50 (unreported, Supreme Court, November 14, 2007).

71 *Fairchild v. Glenhaven Funeral Services Ltd*, above n.5. For discussion of the potential relevance of *Fairchild* in an Irish context see Ryan and Ryan, "A Lost Cause?": Causation in negligence cases – recent Irish developments" (2006) 24 I.L.T. 91 (Pt I) and (2006) 24 I.L.T. 107 (Pt II).

72 [1973] 1 W.L.R. 1.

73 On the difficulties in identifying precisely the nature of the rule laid down by the House of Lords in *Fairchild* see further *Barker v. Corus (UK) plc (formerly Barker v. Saint Gobain Pipelines plc)* [2006] U.K.H.L. 20, [2006] 2 A.C. 572.

74 Above n.5, para.45.

75 *Ibid.*, para.12.

76 [2002] 2 W.L.R. 1353, para.128.

> determine what one is liable for are as much part of the substantive law as the rules which determine which acts give rise to liability."

The appellant's attempt to invoke *Fairchild* in *Gregg* was explained in the following passage of the opinion of Lord Hoffmann:

> "In effect, the appellant submits that the exceptional rule in *Fairchild* should be generalised and damages awarded in all cases in which the defendant may have caused an injury and has increased the likelihood of the injury being suffered. In the present case, it is alleged that Dr Scott may have caused a reduction in Mr Gregg's expectation of life and that he increased the likelihood that his life would be shortened by the disease."[77]

In a crucial passage, that both echoes the conservative approach that had prevailed eighteen years previously in *Wilsher v. Essex AHA*,[78] and emphasises the undesirable ripple effects of permitting recovery in this case, Lord Hoffmann insisted that:

> "a wholesale adoption of possible rather than probable causation as the criterion of liability would be so radical a change in our law as to amount to a legislative act. It would have enormous consequences for insurance companies and the National Health Service."[79]

The attempt at invoking *Fairchild* was also rejected by Lord Phillips, who adverted to the danger that "if special tests of causation are developed piecemeal to deal with perceived injustices in particular factual situations, ... the coherence of our common law will be destroyed."[80] Baroness Hale, for her part, alluded to *Fairchild* as an example of the common law's flexible approach to causation in difficult cases, but apparently regarded it as of no application in a case such as *Gregg*.[81]

Given that the House of Lords had regarded itself as enjoying the power to relax traditional causation rules in *Fairchild*, it is not immediately obvious why the majority in *Gregg* was not equally comfortable with taking such an approach so as to assist the appellant. After all, just weeks prior to *Gregg*, a majority of the House of Lords had decided that the claim in the important case of *Chester v. Afshar*[82] could be upheld notwithstanding apparent difficulties of causation in that case. The background to *Chester* may be briefly stated. Miss Chester

---

77 Above n.1, para.84.

78 [1988] A.C. 1074.

79 Above n.1, para.90.

80 *Ibid.*, para.172.

81 *Ibid.*, para.192.

82 Above n.6.

had suffered repeated episodes of lower back pain. After conservative treatment which proved ineffective, she was referred to Dr Afshar, a distinguished consultant neurosurgeon with much experience of disc surgery. Dr Afshar advised her to undergo an elective lumbar surgical procedure. This procedure entails a 1% – 2% risk of serious neurological damage, a condition known as cauda equina syndrome (CES) In breach of the common law duty of care, Dr Afshar failed to inform the Miss Chester of the risk. She reluctantly agreed to undergo the operation, which was carried out three days later. Unfortunately, the risk, about which Miss Chester should have been but was not warned, eventuated and she sustained CES. At trial and in the Court of Appeal it was accepted that, had the plaintiff been fully informed of the risks attendant upon the procedure in question, she would merely have postponed undergoing the procedure to some later date, as opposed to deciding *never* to subject herself to a procedure in which such a risk inhered. The question thus arose as to whether Miss Chester could establish causation. By a majority of three to two, the House of Lords, upholding the Court of Appeal decision, found for Miss Chester. Crucially for present purposes, certain of their Lordships in the majority had regard to *Fairchild* flexibility as a justification for their approach.[83] In light of this, it does seem surprising that four out of five law lords "completely ignored"[84] *Chester* in their opinions in *Gregg*; while Baroness Hale did refer to *Chester*, the reference was a brief one:

> "Well settled principles may be developed or modified to meet new situations and new problems: the decisions in *Fairchild v. Glenhaven Funeral Services Ltd* and *Chester v. Afshar* are good examples. But those two cases were dealing with particular problems which could be remedied without altering the principles applicable to the great majority of personal injury cases which give rise to no real injustice or practical problem."[85]

Perhaps Baroness Hale's reference to "no real injustice or practical problem" indicates a concern on the part of the majority in *Gregg* that to find for the appellant would have far-reaching implications for future cases of a nature that could not apply to the approach taken by the majority in *Chester*'s case;[86] yet it is difficult to argue with the conclusion that *Chester* was "unconvincingly distinguished"[87] in *Gregg*.

---

83 For more detailed commentary on the treatment of *Fairchild* in the opinions of the majority in *Chester v. Afshar*, see Ryan and Ryan, "A Cause Wrapped up in a Duty: Causation and Informed Consent to Medical Treatment" (2005) 27 D.U.L.J. 260, 273-274.

84 Amirthalingam [2005] C.L.J. 32, 35.

85 Above n.1, para.192 (citations omitted).

86 A point made by Spencer [2005] C.L.J. 282, 284-285.

87 Morgan, "A chance missed to recognise loss-of-a-chance in negligence" [2005] L.M.C.L.Q. 281, 285 (n.32).

Stapleton[88] identifies as another reason for the majority's reluctance to uphold the "pure" loss of chance claim in *Gregg* the concern that such an approach might have been apt to undermine the authority of the earlier decision of the House of Lords in *Wilsher*, discussed above, which had been approved so recently in *Fairchild*. She points out that, had the "pure" loss of chance claim been accepted in *Gregg*, could it not then be said that at the moment after the breach of duty by the junior doctor in *Wilsher*, the baby would have had a loss of a chance claim of the sort contemplated by Lord Nicholls because his premature condition gave rise to a "significant medical uncertainty"?[89]

Unresolved questions after *Gregg*

Before leaving our analysis of the approach of the House of Lords in *Gregg* and turning to recent Irish jurisprudence on loss of chance in the context of medical negligence claims, some final points should be made.

The first concerns the rather puzzling treatment of the earlier authority of *Hotson* by the majority in *Gregg*. Baroness Hale[90] clearly regarded the facts of *Gregg* as not covered by *Hotson*. Of the facts in *Hotson* she offered the graphic analogy that by the time of the boy's entering the hospital, the "coin had already been tossed, and had come down heads or tails".[91] She distinguished *Hotson* from *Gregg* on the grounds that in the latter case, "[t]he coin is in the air [and] is whipped out of the air before it has been able to land".[92] As a result *Gregg* was "a new case, not covered precisely by previous authority".[93] Lord Hoffmann, on the other hand, apparently regarded *Hotson* as being dispositive of the issue in *Gregg*[94] This apparent conflict of opinion as to the status of *Hotson* in the *Gregg* appeal can be explained when one considers that, had the claim in *Gregg* been allowed, this may well have rendered untenable the position espoused in *Hotson*. Since Mr Gregg had not died, were his case to succeed, then he would only have had to prove a lost chance. However, had he died, then under *Hotson* the case would have to have been made out on the balance of probabilities. Accordingly, when Lord Hoffmann spoke[95] in *Gregg* of a favourable outcome for Mr Gregg requiring that *Hotson* be overruled, it is submitted that he was alluding to the anomalous situation which would result if *Hotson* were to remain good law but Mr Gregg could nonetheless recover.

---

88 Stapleton, "Loss of the Chance of Cure from Cancer" [2005] M.L.R. 996, 1003.

89 Indeed, Stapleton goes on to argue that even if the majority had adopted the narrower and more conventional "consequent-upon-a-physical-injury" claim for loss of chance in *Gregg*, this would have undermined the authority of *Wilsher*: Stapleton, *supra*, p.1003.

90 See in particular *Gregg*, para.211.

91 *Ibid.*

92 *Ibid.*

93 *Gregg* at para.212.

94 *Ibid.*, para.85.

95 *Ibid.*

Another point to be made about *Gregg* concerns the "conventional" or "hook" argument, whereby physical injury, which the plaintiff can prove on the balance of probabilities, opens the door for consequential injury. As we have seen, the majority in *Gregg* adopted a strict approach to the question of what can constitute consequential injury. Another key point which should not be overlooked in this context, however, is the ongoing debate about what precisely constitutes "actionable damage" for the purposes of negligence. In this regard, attention is drawn to the recent decision of the House of Lords in the case of *Rothwell v. Chemical & Insulating Co Ltd.*[96] The case is significant in an Irish context given the parallels between it and the Supreme Court decision in *Fletcher v. The Commissioners of Public Works in Ireland.*[97] The claimants in the *Rothwell* litigation had established that their employers had, in breach of the duty of care in negligence, caused them to be exposed in the course of their employment to asbestos dust. This negligent exposure to dust caused three foreseeable consequences. The employee developed pleural plaques; he was at risk of developing one or more long-term asbestos related diseases; and he suffered anxiety at the prospect that he might suffer such disease. The arguments advanced on behalf of the claimants had a nuanced sophistication. Whilst it was accepted that the benign scarring of the lung was not sufficient "damage", it was argued that such scarring coupled with one or both of the other consequences meant that sufficient damage could be demonstrated to found a cause of action. Effectively, the argument being advanced was that the existence of pleural plaques was the "hook" on which the claimants could successfully hang their claim for "fear of disease", or for the mere fact that the scarring might possibly cause a serious disease to develop. The House of Lords unanimously rejected this argument and, affirming the approach taken by the majority of the Court of Appeal, held that minimum actionable damage for negligence could not be made out. It will be recalled that the Supreme Court in *Fletcher* declined to determine whether or not benign pleural plaques could constitute actionable damage, but it is submitted that it is likely that Irish courts would follow the approach taken by the House of Lords and the majority of the Court of Appeal in *Rothwell*[98]

After *Gregg v. Scott*, then, the law in England remains as it was stated in 1987 in *Hotson v. East Berkshire Health Authority*. However, the door was not as firmly shut on claims for loss of chance in medical negligence as it might have

[96] [2007] U.K.H.L. 39, affirming [2006] E.W.C.A. Civ. 27, [2006] 4 All E.R. 1161 (sub nom *Grieves v. FT Everard & Sons*), noted Ryan and Ryan, "Damage in negligence: getting the gist?" (2006) 1(2) Q.R.T.L. 20 (C.A.) and "Asbestos Litigation and the Requirements of the Negligence Action: New Developments in Irish and English Law" (2007) 2(3) Q.R.T.L. 10 (H.L.).

[97] [2003] 1 I.R. 465.

[98] This prediction may be strengthened by a consideration of the *ex tempore* judgment of the Supreme Court in *Packenham v. Irish Ferries Limited (formerly known as B & I Limited)* (unreported, Supreme Court, January 31, 2005 (*ex temp*); on which see Canny, (2005) 10 Bar Rev. 138).

been. Lord Nicholls's dissenting opinion is a powerful call for recovery to lie for "pure" loss of chance claims. And Lord Phillips's opinion with the majority is in essence based, as we have seen, on the insistence that the continuing survival of Mr Gregg – and the flaws in the statistical evidence – meant that this case was not a "suitable vehicle"[99] through which to sanction recovery for a lost chance in the context of clinical negligence. Consider, in particular, the following passage in the opinion of Lord Phillips:

> "Where medical treatment has resulted in an adverse outcome and negligence has increased the chance of that outcome, there may be a case for permitting a recovery of damages that is proportionate to the increase in the chance of that outcome."[100]

It is submitted that of crucial importance in the above paragraph are the words "has resulted in an adverse outcome", a requirement that was clearly lacking in Mr Gregg's case. An even greater chink of hope might be thought to have been allowed in when one considers the following reflection of Lord Phillips on the "pure" loss of chance argument accepted by Lord Nicholls in *Gregg*:

> "I can envisage the application of this approach once the adverse outcome, which the exercise of due care might have averted, has occurred. I find it less easy to see the basis on which the claim is established where the adverse outcome is still prospective."[101]

Baroness Hale, too, placed great emphasis on the proposition that the law of torts is concerned with outcomes, not with chances of outcomes, and there are passages in her opinion in *Gregg* which apparently leave the door open for recovery for loss of chance in a case where death has occurred.[102]

III. Loss of Chance in an Irish Context

In Ireland arguments relating to "loss of chance" in medical negligence actions may in the future be advanced with greater frequency. Of particular interest to Irish practitioners are two separate judgments of the Supreme Court delivered in very close proximity of each other. In this part, we set out the background to each of these two judgments before considering the approach of the Supreme Court in each case to the issue of loss of chance.

---

99 Above n.1, para.190.
100 *Ibid.*
101 *Ibid.*, para.188.
102 *Ibid.*, para.226.

Quinn v. Mid-Western Health Board

The important recent decision of the Supreme Court in *Quinn v. Mid-Western Health Board*[103] constitutes a significant contribution to Irish jurisprudence on causation in the context of claims of medical negligence and merits close analysis.

The plaintiff, Anne Marie Quinn, was born on May 4, 1990 in Limerick Maternity Hospital at a gestational age of 39 weeks and one day. At birth, she had severe brain damage attributable to a condition subsequently diagnosed as periventricular leukomalacia (PVL). Instituting proceedings through her mother and next friend, the plaintiff claimed in the High Court that she ought to have been delivered not later than week 35 of her gestation, contending that had this been the case, she would have avoided all, or substantially all, of the brain damage which occurred. The defendants[104] did not dispute that there had been negligence in the management of the pregnancy and that the plaintiff should have been delivered earlier than she was. However, the defendants contended that the plaintiff's brain damage was sustained as a result of an acute episode which occurred between 28-30 weeks of the pregnancy and that the outcome would not have been any different had she been delivered at any earlier time than she was. Thus, the action turned upon whether the plaintiff was capable of demonstrating causation.

It is to be noted at the outset that here we see a familiar pattern in terms of the case law where plaintiffs have sought a more flexible approach to causation. We find the defendants admitting that they have breached their duty of care in negligence to the plaintiff, and we also find the manifestation of the harm against which the existence of that duty is designed to protect. However, the defendants in *Quinn* contended that even if there had been no negligence, the plaintiff would still have been born suffering from the brain damage from which she did in fact suffer, and her claim was consequently unwinnable on the grounds that she had failed to discharge the burden of proof and make out the requisite causation.

In the High Court, O'Sullivan J. dismissed the plaintiff's claim, holding that the plaintiff had failed to establish, on the balance of probabilities, that she would have avoided her catastrophic injuries had she been delivered by the 35th week of gestation. The plaintiff appealed unsuccessfully to the Supreme Court.

A point to be noted in analysing *Quinn* is that counsel for the plaintiff/appellant did not pursue the "loss of chance" line of argument. Although Kearns J in delivering the judgment of the Supreme Court was thus not called upon to assess the correctness of *Gregg v. Scott* in an Irish context, it is noteworthy that reference was made to the approach taken by the majority in *Gregg*. Consider,

---

[103] Above n.8.

[104] The first named defendant had responsibility for the Limerick Maternity Hospital at the material time. The second named defendant was the consultant obstetrician and gynaecologist who had responsibility for the obstetric management of the plaintiff's gestation and subsequent delivery.

for example, the following passage of the judgment of Kearns J.:

> "It may be noted en passant that this decision of the House of Lords is also the most recent authority in support of the proposition that actionable claims for loss of chance do not lie. A useful resumé of the relevant policy considerations suggesting why this is the preferred approach appears in the judgment of Baroness Hale of Richmond. Given that the decision of Peart J. in *Philp v. Ryan* was referred to in the judgment of Lord Hoffmann, it is perhaps appropriate to comment that that judgment, containing as it does an excellent analysis of the facts on which that particular case turns, does not purport to address the underlying legal principles."[105]

This passage is significant for a number of reasons. First, it is interesting to note that Kearns J did not refer to the approach of the minority in *Gregg*. Can the minority approaches of Lords Nicholls and Hope in *Gregg* not also be said to provide a "useful resumé of the relevant policy considerations" suggesting why their approach is to be preferred over that of the majority? Any conclusions as to the precise stance of the Supreme Court in *Quinn* on this question would, however, be highly tentative, and it remains for the loss of chance doctrine to be analysed in a fully argued case before one can venture a synopsis of the Supreme Court's thinking in this regard.

Secondly, the reference by Kearns J to *Philp v. Ryan* is significant. Lord Hoffmann in the relevant paragraph of his opinion in *Gregg*[106] cited, *inter alia*, *Philip* as an example of the *contrary approach* to that being taken by the majority in *Gregg*. It is worth revisiting the relevant passage in Lord Hoffmann's opinion:

> "Academic writers have suggested that in cases of clinical negligence, the need to prove causation is too restrictive of liability. This argument has appealed to judges in some jurisdictions; in some, but not all, of the States of the United States and most recently in New South Wales and Ireland: *Rufo v. Hosking* [2004] N.S.W.C.A. 391; *Philp v. Ryan* [2004] IESC 105. In the present case it is urged that Mr Gregg has suffered a wrong and ought to have a remedy."[107]

It seems clear that Lord Hoffmann was here citing authorities – among them the approach of the Supreme Court in *Philp* – which had adopted a more generous or "pro-plaintiff" approach to loss of chance claims; Lord Hoffmann thus apparently interpreted the approach in *Philp* as comprising recognition of the recoverability of a "pure" loss of chance claim. Indeed, Fennelly J. in *Philp*

---

105 Above n.8, 18-19 (citations omitted).

106 Above n.1, para.84.

107 *Ibid.*

used language regarding the status of loss of chance that is undoubtedly more in keeping with the sentiments of the minority of the law lords in *Gregg* than the majority. That is to say, the judgment of Fennelly J in *Philp* is altogether more enthusiastic about the "loss of chance" argument, and appears to permit general recovery for such a loss at Irish law.[108] In *Philp*, the first defendant's negligent failure to diagnose prostate cancer led to an eight-month delay in the provision of appropriate treatment for that condition. Let us consider the following passage from the judgment of Fennelly J. (Murray C.J. and McCracken J. concurring) in *Philp*:

> "The plaintiff claims an entitlement to be compensated for the loss of an opportunity to elect for treatment of his cancer on the basis of correct diagnosis and appropriate medical advice. Assuming such correct diagnosis, he claims that there was a possibility that his life could have been prolonged to some extent. It is common case that the chances of successful treatment were, at best, problematical. There is no dispute as to the trial judge's view that medical academic opinion was divided on the benefits of hormone therapy. The defendants argued that this type of lost opportunity was not valuable in the sense that it should not attract compensation unless it could be proved that the postulated treatment would *probably* have been successful. ... Counsel for the defendants went so far as to submit that a 49% chance of successful treatment would not confer an entitlement to damages, though a 51% chance would. Asked how this was reconcilable with the universal practice of allowing for percentage risks below fifty of the future development of conditions such as arthritis or epilepsy, he sought to distinguish these examples as being on the debit side only. These were negative possibilities for an injured person, whereas, in the present case, the plaintiff seeks compensation for the loss of a beneficial opportunity."[109]

Loss of chance in *Philp v. Ryan*

Crucially, Fennelly J. then proceeded to state his view that "loss of chance" was actionable at Irish law. In an important passage in his judgment in *Philp*, Fennelly J. appears to have indicated that he may not accept the assertion of the majority in *Gregg* that only a 50%. or greater chance that the desired result in question could have successfully materialised would enable the plaintiff to succeed. Given the lack of certainty that now exists on this point in Irish law following the Supreme Court judgment in the *Quinn* case, it is worth setting out the relevant passage from the judgment of Fennelly J. in *Philp in extenso*:

---

[108] For discussion see Byrne and Binchy, *Annual Review of Irish Law 2004*, (Thomson Round Hall), p.500.

[109] Above n.7, 248-249.

> "[I]t seems to me to be contrary to instinct and logic that a plaintiff should not be entitled to be compensated for the fact that, due to the negligent diagnosis of his medical condition, he has been deprived of appropriate medical advice and the consequent opportunity to avail of treatment which might improve his condition. I can identify no contrary principle of law or justice. It is commonplace that allowance is made in awards and in settlements for the *risk* that an injured plaintiff *may* in the future develop arthritis in an injured joint. The risk may be high or low - a 15% risk is often mentioned – but damages are paid. I cannot agree that this is any different from what is sought in the present case. It does not matter that the damage suffered by the plaintiff consists of the loss of an opportunity to avail of treatment. It might, with equal logic, be described as an increased risk of shorter life expectancy. It seems to me as illogical to award damages for a probable future injury as if it were a certainty, as to withhold them where the risk is low on the basis that it will not happen at all."[110]

It is submitted that it is important to distinguish between a case where the "harm" has manifestly been caused by the breach of duty – such as the risk of arthritis consequent upon the injury to the joint in Fennelly J.'s example – with the loss of a chance *simpliciter* where the prospects of that "chance" manifesting itself are under 50% To put it another way, a 1%. risk of arthritis ought in principle to be recoverable in the situation envisioned by Fennelly J., but, consistent with this, the law could simultaneously say that loss of a 49%. chance of cure is irrecoverable; the crucial distinction between the two being that in the first case causation is established, whereas in the second the balance of probabilities test is not satisfied. This, as we have seen, was a key point taken up by the majority in the *Gregg* appeal. Or more simply still, the only reason the arthritis might occur is because of the established breach of duty; the reason individuals like Mr Gregg do not enjoy a cure is because the chance of them being cured was less than 50%. in the first place. Thus the difficulty with the 15%. risk of arthritis is one of *quantification*; the difficulty in the loss of chance cases where the chance is under 50%. is one of *causation.* Ultimately, before recovery can be permitted, the plaintiff must be able to show causal connectedness, to a probability standard, between the breach of duty and the harm complained of. In a case where the chance is less than evens, recovery can only be permitted through a modified approach to causation which would stretch markedly beyond *Fairchild* itself.

Fairchild considered in *Quinn*

It was noted in part II of this chapter that Lord Hoffmann in his opinion in *Gregg* insisted that *Fairchild* was of no application in *Gregg* – concluding that

---

110 *Ibid*, p.249.

the *Fairchild* rule was "restrictively defined in terms which make it inapplicable in this case"[111] – and so too did both Lord Phillips[112] and Baroness Hale[113] regard *Fairchild* as of no application in disposing of the *Gregg* appeal. It is instructive to consider the approach of the Supreme Court in *Quinn* to the rule in *Fairchild.* The key passage in the judgment on this point is the statement by Kearns J. that he:

> "[w]ould be firmly of the view that this decision turns on its own unique facts and it was expressly confined by the House of Lords to a particular set of circumstances where it would be patently unjust not to allow the appeal… Those considerations do not arise in the present case."[114]

Kearns J. was fortified in this stance by the approach of the House of Lords to *Fairchild* taken in *Gregg*. Kearns J. drew on a passage from the judgment of Lord Hoffmann in *Gregg* in which Lord Hoffman alluded to "all the qualifications and restrictions"[115] with which the House in *Fairchild* had etched out the exception allowed in that case to general principles of causation.

The caution evinced by the Supreme Court in *Quinn* to the so-called *Fairchild* exception was entirely vindicated by the judgment of the House of Lords delivered in May 2006 in *Barker v. Corus UK (plc) (formerly Barker v. Saint Gobain Pipelines plc)*.[116] In that case, speaking of the approach of the majority in *Gregg* in regard to the *Fairchild* argument, Lord Scott of Foscote observed that:

> "*Fairchild* was treated as an exception to the normal requirement of a proved causative link between the breach of duty and the damage for which tortious damages are claimed. *Fairchild* is explained as a pragmatic judicial response to what would otherwise have been an unjust and unsatisfactory denial of a remedy to a mesothelioma sufferer whose disease had been caused by one or other of a number of wrongdoers (in the sense of persons shown to have been in breach of duty) each of whose breach of duty may have caused the disease, and could not be shown not to have done so, but could not be shown to have done so. *Fairchild* cannot, therefore, be taken to have established an overarching principle in the law of tort. Its narrow scope was, in my respectful opinion, rightly recognised by Lord Hoffmann in his comments in *Gregg v. Scott*...".[117]

---

[111] Above n.1, para.78.
[112] *Ibid.*, para.172.
[113] *Ibid.*, para.192.
[114] Above n.8, 17.
[115] Above n.1, para.85, cited by Kearns J. at [2005] 4 I.R. 1, 18.
[116] [2006] U.K.H.L. 20, [2006] 2 A.C. 572.
[117] *Ibid.*, para.57.

The Supreme Court in *Quinn* has therefore indicated with firmness its view that the *Fairchild* exception cannot be lightly expanded to assist plaintiffs in medical negligence cases. This is in line with the approach of the majority in *Gregg*, but the approach of both courts leaves the same unanswered questions, so that it remains difficult to predict when the courts will permit *Fairchild* flexibility to avail a plaintiff in crossing the causation hurdle. A good example of these difficulties is manifested by the differences of opinion expressed in the opinions in *Gregg*. Lord Nicholls, for example, in his dissenting opinion, laid emphasis on the fact that Mr Gregg faced even greater difficulties of proof than those faced by the plaintiff in *Hotson*, and Lord Nicholls appeared to regard these difficulties of proof as warranting an extension of the *Fairchild* principle to assist Mr Gregg. As we have seen, the majority in *Gregg* took a diametrically opposed approach to *Fairchild* flexibility. And in both *Fairchild* and *Gregg* – not to mention *Chester v. Afshar* – policy arguments were advanced so as to illuminate the course being taken by the court. It is indeed "difficult to see why such arguments are convincing in some cases but not others".[118] One possible justification is that cases such as *Gregg* and *Quinn v. Mid-Western Health Board* are redolent of a *Wilsher* type situation; the insuperable problem of proof is not due to the limits of medical science (as in *Fairchild*) but simply due to the fact that it cannot be shown that the breach complained of was causative of the injury (here loss of a chance). Lord Hoffmann encapsulated this in the following memorable passage of his judgment in *Gregg*:

> "There is no inherent uncertainty about what caused something to happen in the past or about whether something which happened in the past will cause something to happen in the future. Everything is determined by causality. What we lack is knowledge and the law deals with lack of knowledge by the concept of the burden of proof."[119]

As one commentator says ominously of the above passage: "This is stern stuff. It will be beautiful music to the ears of insurers."[120] As against this, it is important to bear in mind that the defendant in a case such as *Gregg* could still be liable for, *inter alia*, damages for extra pain and suffering arising from the delay. This point was stressed by Baroness Hale in her opinion in *Gregg*.[121]

Clearly the issue of whether Irish law permits recovery for loss of a chance that is "less than evens" – recovery countenanced with apparent endorsement by Fennelly J. in *Philp*[122] – awaits authoritative resolution. It is suggested that the

---

[118] Morgan, "A chance missed to recognise loss-of-a-chance in negligence" [2005] L.M.C.L.Q. 281, 285.

[119] Above n.1, para.79.

[120] Foster, "Last Chance for Lost Chances" (2005) 155 N.L.J. 248, 249.

[121] Above n.1, para.206.

[122] The approach in *Philp* was subsequently considered by Clarke J in the (non-medical) case of *Vavasour v. O'Reilly* [2005] IEHC 19 (unreported, High Court, January 28, 2005).

issue is likely to surface again soon at superior court level in this jurisdiction, upon which occasion the opinions in both *Gregg v. Scott* and the *Fairchild*-type argument seem most likely to be canvassed.

Conclusion

It has been said that the common law – predicated as it is upon the dual paradigm of a wrongdoer and victim, a winner and a loser – is reluctant to go halves and declare a draw.[123] Rather, the common law will incline towards delivering judgment *in toto* for one party or the other, or, in Weir's graphic apothegm, "with a win on points counting as a knock-out".[124] Such a Procrustean formula of right and wrong, focused on arriving at a clear and definite result, poses problems for the law as it grapples with claims for "loss of chance". While permitting such claims in cases of economic loss, the courts have insisted on cleaving to "policy" concerns so as to disallow the actionability of such claims in cases of medical negligence. Although Irish law on the point remains unsettled, this trend of denying recovery for "pure" loss of chance in medical negligence has recently been exemplified by the approach of the majority of the House of Lords in the *Gregg* case. In the Court of Appeal in *Gregg*, Simon Brown L.J. noted the existence of "powerful policy arguments for not extending the scope of liability within the field of health treatment".[125] This concern was to be later echoed by the majority in the House of Lords.

Inherent malleability and unpredictability surrounds any recourse to "policy" in support of fashioning approaches to causation in negligence. After all, it was "policy" concerns which weighed with the courts in both *Fairchild* and *Chester v. Afshar*, two cases in which, as we have seen, the House of Lords invoked policy concerns as a justification for adopting a pro-plaintiff approach to causation. When considered alongside the "policy" concerns ventilated by the majority for disallowing recovery for loss of chance in *Gregg*, it becomes obvious that "policy" is frequently a driving force which serves to mask, rather than to clarify, the underlying judicial reasoning in a given case.

It has been said that after judicial developments in the last five years, "the only thing which can be predicted with confidence about future developments in causation is that they will continue to be unpredictable".[126] As a result of the approach of the majority in *Gregg*, it might be thought that the possibility of successfully bringing a claim for loss of chance in medical negligence cases

---

[123] See above, text to n.9.

[124] Weir, above n.9, at 513.

[125] [2002] E.W.C.A. Civ. 1471; [2003] Lloyd's Rep. Med. 105, at [102]. For comment on the Court of Appeal decision see, for example, Peel, "'Loss of a Chance' Revisited: *Gregg v. Scott*" (2003) 66 M.L.R. 623; Jones, "Another Lost Opportunity?" (2003) 19 P.N. 542.

[126] Morgan, "A chance missed to recognise loss-of-a-chance in negligence" [2005] L.M.C.L.Q. 281, 285.

has been firmly closed off. As we have suggested in this chapter, however, it may be that such an interpretation of the majority opinions in *Gregg* will prove too narrow. Certain passages in the opinions of the majority appear to suggest that the loss of a chance argument may be open to a plaintiff in a future medical negligence case.[127]

There is, perhaps, an irony about the approach of the majority of the House of Lords in *Gregg* when compared with approaches taken to difficult issues of causation in other recent cases. It was noted above, for example, that the approach of the majority of the House of Lords just weeks earlier in *Chester v. Afshar* was anchored in a concern about the paramount importance of individual autonomy and the imperative that the courts should vindicate that autonomy through a robust doctrine of informed consent to medical treatment. As a result, the majority of the House of Lords concluded in *Chester* that to absolve the defendant surgeon from liability – even in a case where the claim could not be sustained on orthodox causation principles – would be to dilute the surgeon's duty of its content, with a consequent undermining of patient autonomy. In *Gregg*, however, the majority of the House of Lords recognised that recovery for loss of a chance may lie in cases of loss of a chance of an economic outcome, but denied recovery for loss of a chance of a cure from a fatal disease. The principle of autonomy – which appears to include respect for bodily integrity – could drive the majority to uphold the claim in *Chester*, but no similar principle or interest in bodily integrity prevailed in *Gregg* – on the contrary, one implication of the majority decision is the unhappy conclusion that the law of torts provides, in this respect, more vigorous protection for pecuniary interests than for bodily integrity. Such a conclusion begs the graphic but inevitable question: why is it that the chance of negotiating a better bargain is regarded as something of intrinsic and compensatable value by the law of torts, while the very chance of living is not? Will it be that the starkness of such a question will galvanise the courts in this jurisdiction to adopt a more pro-plaintiff approach than that evinced in *Gregg*?

[127] See Pt II *supra*, text to nn.99 -101.

CHAPTER 3

Issues of Proof in Medical Negligence Litigation: New Questions Posed in the Irish Courts

WILLIAM BINCHY

The challenges facing plaintiffs in medical claims are formidable. The professional negligence standard protects all customary practices save those involving inherent defects which ought to be obvious to anyone giving the matter due consideration.[1] The limitation period has been reduced to two years[2] and the courts retain a power to dismiss a claim, taken within the statutory period, where permitting it to continue would be unjust to the defendant having regard to the lapse of time, even in cases where the plaintiff is guilty of no culpable delay in prosecuting the claim.[3] Causal issues can prove problematic in these claims, as Des and Ray Ryan have described in chapter 2.

In this chapter I shall be dealing with problems of proof. Of the nature of things, proving negligence in the context of medical care can be difficult. A patient who has been the victim of negligent treatment may simply not have the expertise to appreciate that negligence has occurred. Often the negligence will have taken place at a time when the patient was unconscious The body is a complex instrumentality and it may be hard to discern exactly what caused a negative outcome. Many, if not all, treatments have a downside even where the doctor has taken all due care. Identifying negligence can be a difficult task.

This is where the *res ipsa loquitur* doctrine can offer some hope for patients. The doctrine came into being in 1863, in the course of legal argument in the English decision of *Byrne v. Boadle*[4]. The plaintiff had been injured by a barrel of flour which had fallen from a window on the first floor of the defendant's

---

1 *Dunne v. National Maternity Hospital* [1989] I.R. 91. Ciaran Craven has already analysed recent developments in relation to the *Dunne* test in chap.1 *supra*.

2 Civil Liability and Courts Act 2004, s.7.

3 *Toal v. v Duignan (No. 1)* [19991] I.L.R.M. 135, *Kelly v. O'Leary,* unreported, High Court, Kelly J, June 22, 2001, *Feehan v. Doyle*, unreported, High Court, April 23, 2004, *Manning v. Benson and Hedges Ltd,* [2004] I.E.H.C. 316, *Kearney v McQuillan* [2006] I.E.H.C. 186, *Faughnan v. Maguire* [2006] I.E.H.C. 282.

4 2 H. & C. 722, 159 E.R. 299 (1863). See Webb "Note: The Law of Falling Objects: *Byrne v. Boadle* and the Birth of *res ipsa loquitur*", 59 Stanford L. Rev. 1065 (2007).

warehouse. The defendant gave no evidence to explain how the accident occurred. The defendant had succeeded at trial. On appeal to the Court of Exchequer, counsel for the defendant argued that the plaintiff "was bound to give affirmative proof of negligence. But there was not a scintilla of evidence, unless the occurrence is of itself evidence of negligence". Pollock C.B. responded that "there are certain cases of which it may be said *res ipsa loquitur* and this seems one of them ..." In his judgment Pollock C.B. stated that:

> "The learned counsel was quite right in saying that there are many accidents from which no presumption of negligence can arise, but I think it would be wrong to lay down as a rule that in no case can presumption of negligence arise from the fact of an accident."

Whilst there was nothing amiss in Pollock C.B.'s making the Latin remark in *Byrne v. Boadle*, it was very shortly afterwards elevated to the status of a principle,[5] in respect of which some courts have been guilty of very loose language and lack of conceptual clarity.

Two fundamental questions arise in relation to the principle: when will it apply and what is its procedural effect?

When Will The Principle Apply?

In *Scott v. London & St Katherine Docks Co*,[6] Erle C.J., in a passage that has been very influential in subsequent decisions,[7] stated:

> "There must be reasonable evidence of negligence. But where the thing is shown to be under the management of the defendant or his servants, and the accident is such as in the ordinary circumstances does not happen if those who have the management use proper care, it affords reasonable evidence, in the absence of explanation by the defendants, that the accident arose from want of care."

These elements require specific elucidation, bearing in mind the shadow of uncertainty cast by the decision of *Hanrahan v. Merck Sharp & Dohme*

---

5 *Cf Ballard v. NB Ry* (1923) S.C. 43 at 56 (*per* Lord Shaw): "If it had not been in Latin nobody would have called it a principle". See also Prosser, "*Res ipsa loquitur* in California" (1949) 37 Calif. Rev. 183 at 215.

6 (1865) 3 H. & C. 596 at 601, 159 E.R. 665 at 667.

7 In *Flannery v. W & L Ry Co* (1877) I.R. 11 C.L. 30 at 38 (Exch), Palles CB described *Scott* as being "distinguished from the chaos of authorities depending on particular facts by an attempt at the application of something in the nature of principle to cases of this class". He "entirely subscribe[d]" (at 39) to the doctrine laid down in the decision.

(Ireland) Ltd,[8] whose implications I shall examine after setting out the traditional understanding of the principle.

Management or control of defendant

According to the principle of *res ipsa loquitur* as widely understood in the cases and as mentioned by Erle C.J., "the thing" must be "under the management of the defendant or his servants." A clear case of management of the thing being under the control of the defendant arises where a barrel rolls out of premises to which only the defendant and his "employees" have access.[9] Another clear case may arise in relation to the operation of a motor vehicle,[10] although much will depend on the circumstances.[11] Airplanes are also normally capable of being regarded as being under the management of their proprietors.[12] So also guns may be regarded as under the management of those who use them.[13] Conversely, an electric lamp in a student dormitory was held not to have been under the control of the school at the time of the accident.[14]

Courts have been uncertain as to whether they should limit the application of *res ipsa loquitur* to cases in which the "thing" was under the actual management of the defendant or the defendant's "employees". Some courts have done so.[15] Others have taken the view that the concept of management or control should be broadly understood, so as to extend beyond physical custody or possession to

8 [1988] I.L.R.M. 629 (SC).

9 *Cf Byrne v. Boadle* (1863) 2 H & C 722, 159 E.R .299; *Scott v. London & St Katherine Docks Co* 3 H & C 596 at 60, 159 E.R. 665 at 667. In *Mullen v. Quinnsworth Ltd t/a Crazy Prices* [1990] I.R. 59 (SC) a supermarket floor on which colourless cooking oil had been spilled, causing the plaintiff a 74-year-old customer to slip and fall, was held to be under the management of the proprietors. Cf. *Black v. CB Richard Ellis Management Services Ltd.,* [2006] Scot S.C. 7, *Drake v. Harbour* [2007] E.W.H.C. 1670 (TCC).

10 *Cf Corcoran v. West* [1933] I.R. 210 (HC); *Halliwell v. Venables* (1930) 99 L.J.K.B. 353; *Doxtator v. Burch* (1973) 41 D.L.R. (3d) 768; *Jackson v. Millar* [1976] 1 S.C.R. 225.

11 *Cf Wing v. London General Omnibus Co* [1909] 2 KB 652 (CA); *Webster v. Paragon Bus Co* [1934] I.R. 448 at 455 (SC), *Yarrabee Coal Co Pty Ltd. v. Lujons* [2007] N.S.W.C.A. 342.

12 *Cf Fosbroke-Hobbes v. Airwork Ltd* [1937] 1 All E.R. 108. As regards boats, see *Ross v. Dunphy*, unreported, High Court, February 13, 1978 as explained in *McDonagh v. West of Ireland Fisheries Ltd*, unreported, High Court, December 19, 1986, Blayney J.

13 *Cf O'Regan v. Willis* (1936) 71 I.L.T. & Sol. J. 117 at 118 (HC).

14 *Scrimgeour v. Board of Management of the Canadian District of the American Lutheran Church* [1947] 1 W.W.R. 120 (Sask, CA).

15 *Cf Bloom v. Creed & Consumers' Gas Co* [1937] O.R. 626 (CA).

include cases of former possession[16] - most importantly in relation to products liability[17] - or the right to control.[18]

It is clear, however, that a former right to control the "thing" that causes the damage will not be sufficient to give rise to the application of the *res ipsa loquitur* concept where the "thing" is no longer in the condition in which it was when the control was exercised. In *Tracey v. Hagen*,[19] the Supreme Court held that the case had correctly been withdrawn from the jury where the plaintiff had been injured when he was servicing a machine used to make plastic bottles. The machine had been manufactured by the defendant and supplied to the plaintiff six months previously, the servicing of the machine being carried out by the plaintiff. Walsh J. considered that *res ipsa loquitur* was not applicable:

> "on the ground that the machine, not being under the control or management of the defendant, had not been proved to have been in the condition in which he provided it".[20]

Let me mention some of the difficulties attaching to the notion of the "thing" being under the management or control of the defendant.

First, there may be no actual "thing", other than the plaintiff himself or herself. This is especially the case in health care contexts. The plaintiff is usually complaining, not that some "thing" such as a scalpel, under the control of the defendant, injured him or her, but rather the defendant (or those for whom the defendant is responsible) injured the plaintiff. Of course, there is often a relationship between the parties which can often be described as involving the management or control of the patient but treating the patient as a "thing" is curious, and not all *res ipsa* claims in hospitals depend on a significant element of control. Rather is the relationship one of reliance and dependency, generally accompanied, but not constituted, by control.

A second difficulty with the control test is its lack of clarity. A person may have management or control of a situation in the sense that he or she has legal

---

16 *Cf Collen Bros v. Scaffolding Ltd* [1959] I.R. 245 (HC).

17 *Cf Kirby v. Burke and Holloway* [1944] I.R. 207 (HC); *Fleming v. Henry Denny & Sons*, unreported, Supreme Court, July 29, 1955; *cf Denniston v. McNamara Maxwell & Co* (1950) 84 I.L.T.R. 168 (CC) and *Sin Leng Industries Plc Ltd v. Ong Chai Teck* [2006] S.G.H.C. 25.

18 *Cf Mandeville v. PJ Carroll & Co Ltd*, DPIJ: Hilary and Easter Terms 1993 p.198 (High Court, May 13, 1993) where a chair broke under an employee; *per* O'Hanlon J. at 200: "[C]hairs provided for the use of the workers should not normally collaps[e] when used in the orthodox and ordinary manner unless [they have] been allowed to get into a dangerous condition ..".

19 Unreported, Supreme Court, March 6, 1973. See also *Williamson v. Rover Cycle Co* [1901] 2 I.R. 615 (CA) affg [1901] 2 I.R. 189 (Q.B.).

20 P.4 of Walsh J.'s judgment. See *McDonagh v. West of Ireland Fisheries Ltd*, unreported, High Court, December 19, 1986.

responsibility for exercising control in respect of it while in no sense exercising, or being capable of exercising, actual hands-on control over every thing or person falling within the remit of that control.[21] A hospital has control of the wards and the patients within them but clearly does not, cannot and should not act in such a way as to prevent patients (or visitors) from exercising control over their immediate environment. Is it meaningful to enquire whether the hospital is in control of the patient's bed, for example? In one sense, it undoubtedly is: the hospital certainly will have a responsibility if the bed collapses through inadequate maintenance. In another sense, the hospital is not in control of the bed since it cannot prevent a patient with a mechanical bent from taking a ratchet to it, if that is the patient's predilection. The same applies to a vast range of property situated, and of conduct occurring, within a hospital. Of course there will be particular contexts where, in the exercise of control, the hospital may be under a duty to take strong steps to prevent the exercise of control by anyone else. Thus, for example, a hospital must ensure that drugs such as morphine are kept under a rigorous system of exclusive control. But most situations of control where *res ipsa loquitur* falls for consideration will be a good deal more attenuated than this. The hospital may be regarded as being in control of the entire operation but not in any meaningful sense of every object on their premises.

Accident is such as in ordinary circumstances does not happen with the use of care by those in control of the thing

This is really the key ingredient in the operation of the maxim. Certain accidents suggest that those who were in control of the thing that did the injury were not exercising due care. Trains run by the same company do not normally[22] collide without negligence on the part of someone in the company's employment;[23] a barrel of flour does not usually drop from a warehouse[24] or a bale from a lorry,[25] nor does scaffolding normally collapse[26] without carelessness on the part of those in control. Of course there may be a perfectly innocent explanation for the accident, but too heavy a burden should not be placed on the plaintiff to disprove

---

21 There is a further difficulty with the notion of control. What should a court do in cases where the defendant had indeed such a right but was not in fact exercising it? *Res ipsa loquitur*, in its original formulation at least, was conceived as a rule of evidential inference from facts, not of imposition of liability based on the existence of certain legal entitlements or obligations.

22 The test is not whether or not the event happens rarely but rather whether, if the event happens, it rarely happens without negligence on the part of someone in control: *Cf Brannon v. Wood* (1968) 251 or 349, 444 P 2d 558.

23 *Skinner v. LB & SC Ry* (1850) 5 Exch. 787. See also *Moore v. Atchison Topeka & Santa Fe Railway* (1961) 28 Ill App. 2d 340n, 171 NE 2d 393.

24 *Byrne v. Boadle* (1863) 2 H & C 722, 159 E.R. 299 and *Hake v. George Wiedemann Brewing Co* (1970) 23 Ohio St 65, 262 NE 2d 703 (SC).

25 *Bellizia v. Meares* [1971] V.R. 641.

26 *Collen Bros (Dublin) Ltd v. Scaffolding Ltd* [1959] I.R. 245 (HC).

such a possibility. On the other hand, experience tells us that a fire may spread from an ordinary domestic grate without negligence on anybody's part.[27]

The courts formerly evinced some reluctance to go beyond the experience of ordinary persons[28] in determining whether the happening suggested negligence on the part of those in control of the object that caused the damage.[29] This is no longer the position. A plaintiff may introduce expert evidence to show that the inference of negligence should be drawn. Thus, in relation to medical negligence, where the judge's knowledge of the intricacies of medical practice is necessarily limited, the plaintiff can invoke the assistance of medical witnesses to show that the injury of which he or she complains does not normally result from the treatment given in the absence of negligence on the part of the doctor treating the patient.[30]

---

27 *Sochacki v. Sas* [1947] 1 All E.R. 344. Other types of fires may give rise to an inference of negligence: *cf Farrell v. Alliance & Dublin Consumers' Gas Co* [1939] Ir Jur 41 (CC). For United States cases see, *Anon.*, 'Note: *Res ipsa loquitur* in Actions Against Owner or Occupant of Premises for Personal Injury Death or Property Damage Caused by Fire' (1966) 8 A.L.R. (3d) 974.

28 As to what an ordinary member of the jury might be expected to know see *Coughlan v. Marks* [1918] 2 I.R. 306 at 324-325 (*per* Sir Ignatius J. O'Brien C) and at 342-343 (*per* Ronan L.J.), (CA affg KB).

29 *Cf Mahon v. Osborne* [1939] 2 K.B. 14 (CA Scott L.J.'s judgment; Goddard L.J. dissenting on this question).Courts in the United States of America still evince such reluctance: see, e.g., *Hayes v. Peters*, 645 S.E. 2d 846 (N.C. App., 2007).

30 *Cassidy v. Ministry of Health* [1951] 2 KB 343; *Roe v. Ministry of Health* [1954] 2 Q.B. 66; *Watson v. Davidson* [1966] N.Z.L.R. 853; *Raza v. Sullivan* (1970) 432 F 2d 617 - tooth extraction resulting in fracture of jaw; *Mayor v. Dawsitt* (1965) 240 Or. 196, 400 P 2d 234 (SC) - paralysis after use of anaesthetic during child-birth. *Cf Daniels v. Heskin* [1954] I.R. 73 (SC) discussed below; see also *Lindsay v. Mid-Western Health Board* [1993] 2 I.R. 147 (SC 1992 reversing HC 1991) analysed by Symmons, "Medical Negligence and the Doctrine of *Res ipsa loquitur* in Ireland" (1992) 9 Prof. Neg. 17; *Maitland v. Swan and Sligo County Council*, unreported, High Court, April 6, 1992; *Barrett v. Southern Health Board*, unreported, High Court, December 5, 1988; *Duffy v. North Eastern Health Board*, unreported, High Court, November 3, 1988; *Russell v. Walsh and Mid-Western Health Board*, unreported, High Court, April 3, 1995, *Kelly v. Lenihan*, unreported, High Court, July 2, 2004, *Griffin v. Patton*, unreported, Supreme Court, July 27, 2004, *Quinn v. South Eastern Health Board*, unreported, High Court, March 22, 2002 and *Doherty v. Reynolds and St. James's Hospital*, unreported, Supreme Court, July 14, 2004. In a number of these cases the court held that the doctrine of *res ipsa loquitur* did not on the evidence apply or that the defendant had discharged the burden of proof. See generally Renswick, "*Res ipsa loquitur* Hospital and Malpractice Cases' (1960) 9 Clev-Mar L.R. 179; Rossen, "Defense Against *Res ipsa* in Medical Malpractice" 13 Clev-Mar L Rev. 128 (1964); Louisell & Williams, "*Res ipsa loquitur*- Its Future in Medical Malpractice Cases" (1960) 48 Calif. L. Rev. 252; Fricke, "The Use of Expert Evidence in *Res ipsa loquitur* Cases" (1959) 5 Vill. L. Rev. 59, Haag, "*Res ipsa loquitur*: A Step along the Road to Laibility without Fault," 42 Brandeis L.J. 149 (2002) and BIB, "Note: The Use

In *Ratcliffe v. Plymouth and Torbay Health Authority*,[31] Hobhouse L.J. made the following helpful observations on the use of expert evidence to bolster a claim for the application of the *res ipsa loquitur* doctrine in medical negligence litigation:

> "If the facts of the present case had been that the plaintiff had gone into the operating theatre to have an arthrodesis to his right ankle and had come out of the theatre with his right ankle untouched and an arthrodesis to his left ankle, clearly no expert evidence would be required to support an inference of negligence on the part of the defendants. 'In the ordinary course of things' that does not happen if those conducting the operation have used proper care. But if on the other hand all that one knows is that a baby has been born with some brain defect, more needs to be proved and expert evidence is required to raise an inference of negligence on the part of those in charge of the management of the birth. The cases of *Cassidy v. Ministry of Health* [1951] 2 KB 343 (the plaintiff went into hospital to be cured of two stiff fingers and he came out with four stiff fingers) and *Roe v. Ministry of Health* [1954] 2 AER 131 (routine operations followed by complete paralysis from the waist down) were apparently treated by at least some members of the Court of Appeal as coming into the first category. The vast majority of medical negligence cases will come into the second category and require the plaintiff to adduce some expert evidence before an inference of negligence can be raised.
>
> In practice, save in the most extreme cases of blatant negligence, the plaintiff will have to adduce at least some expert evidence to get his case upon its feet. This is the more so because probably before he commences his action and delivers his pleading he will have seen some record of what occurred and obtained some explanation from the defendants. But, even if he has to rely upon some fairly broadly based inference at the outset, by the time he gets to trial he will both be expected to and should be able to make some more specific allegations, supported by expert evidence, as to why he says the defendant was negligent. The essential role of the doctrine of *res ipsa loquitur* is to enable the plaintiff who is not in possession of all the material facts to be able to plead an allegation of negligence in an acceptable form and to force the defendant to respond to it at the peril of having a finding of negligence made against the defendant if the defendant does not make an adequate response. But once the defendant has responded then the question for the court is whether, in the light of that response, that is to say upon all the evidence that has been placed before it at the trial both by the plaintiff and by the defendant, the court

of Expert Evidence in *Res ipsa loquitur* Cases" (1958)106 U. Pa. L. Rev. 731. *Cf Ybarra v. Spangard* (1944) 25 Cal. 2d 486, 154 P 2d 687.

[31] [1998] Lloyd's L.R.: Med. 162.

is satisfied that the defendant has been negligent and that his negligence caused the plaintiff's injury."

The courts have been less than forthcoming about how they determine whether the particular accident is "such as in the ordinary circumstances does not happen if those who have the management [of the thing causing the injury] use proper care.".[32] They generally eschew on overt statistical calculus[33]. In *Daniels v. Heskin*,[34] however, Lavery J. went some way towards doing so. The case involved a home birth, which took place in 1951. The defendant doctor and a midwife were in attendance. While the defendant was stitching the mother after the birth, a needle broke. One of the issues in the case was whether this breakage constituted negligence on the defendant's part.

Counsel for the mother (and her husband) conceded that the case was one where the *res ipsa loquitur* principle did not apply and that the needle might have broken through a flaw in itself not discoverable by the defendant or otherwise without negligence on his part. Three doctors gave evidence to this effect. The trial judge directed a verdict in favour of the defendant and the Supreme Court, by a four-to-one majority,[35] held that he had been right to do so.

Counsel for the appellants submitted that, as there was evidence that the breaking of needles in the course of a surgical operation was more often due to an imperfection of technique on the part of the operator than to a defect in the instrument, it would have been open to the jury on the balance of probabilities to find that it had been caused by negligence. Lavery J. considered that this amounted to a claim to apply the *res ipsa loquitur* principle in another form:

> "It is certainly not open to a jury, in my opinion, in th[e] state of facts [established in the instant case], to hold that the breaking was caused by imperfection of technique, on the ground that say in 60 per cent of cases of broken needles it is so caused, and the same is true of any other statistical record of such happenings until the point is reached where the preponderance is such as to make it a case of *res ipsa loquitur* shifting the burden of proof to the defendant to give an explanation and to establish that the mishap was not due to his negligence."[36]

The suggestion here appears to be that the doctrine is to be applied only where

---

32 *Scott v. London & St Katherine Docks Co* (1865) 3 H & C 596 at 60, 159 E.R. 665 at 667 (*per* Erle C.J.).

33 For consideration of the complex mathematics, see Kaye, "Probability Theory Meets *Res ipsa loquitur*", 77 Michigan L. Rev. 1456 (1979), Farley Thorne, "Comment: Mathematicas, Fuzzy Negligence and the Logic of *Res ipsa loquitur*", 75 NW U. L. Rev. 147 (1980), Ablin, "Note: *Res ipsa loquitur* and Expert Opinion Evidence in Medical Malpractice Cases: Strange Bedfellows", 82 Va. L. Rev. 325, at 338-344 (1996).

34 [1954] I.R. 73 (SC).

35 Murnaghan, O'Byrne, Lavery and Kingsmill Moore JJ.; Maguire C.J. dissenting.

36 [1954] I.R. 73 at 79.

the preponderance of statistical unlikelihood of the accident occurring without negligence on the part of the person in charge of the harmful agency is well over 60%.

In *Griffin v. Patton*,[37] the Supreme Court affirmed a finding by O'Donovan J. of liability in negligence against a consultant obstetrician and gynaecologist who, when removing the remains of a deceased unborn baby of seventeen weeks' gestational age from its mother's uterus, had failed to retrieve a piece of bone over five centimetres in length. Geoghegan J. addressed the issue of the limits of statistical evidence. Referring to Lavery J.'s approach in *Daniels v. Heskin* and using the same percentage example, Geoghegan J. accepted that, if the evidence before O'Donovan J. had established that 60 per cent of all instances where a limb of a foetus was mistakenly left behind in the uterus involved fault on the part of the operating surgeon, there could not on that evidence alone be a finding that as a matter of probability there had been negligence. Geoghegan J. ventured the opinion that percentages of that kind 'would probably have to be disregarded altogether. But that did not mean that, in a case where the evidence established that it would be rare in the extreme for a piece of isolated bone to be left behind, this fact would not be relevant, combined with all the other evidence in the case, in a judge arriving at a finding of negligence.

What appears to be underlying the judicial thinking here is the need for a plaintiff in civil litigation to establish his or her case by more than resort to statistical evidence of a general kind.[38] It would not be sufficient, for example, for the victim of a traffic accident late at night to establish that most drivers who crash their car at 2 a.m. are intoxicated. The plaintiff would have to go further and produce evidence relating to the particular circumstances of the case which connects this general statistical evidence with the facts of the fateful night. It seems that, in *Daniels v. Heskin* and *Griffin v. Patton*, there was a willingness to move from general statistical data to imposition of an onus of proof on the defendant under the *res ipsa loquitur* doctrine, but only where the percentage was very high. Geoghegan J.'s analysis appears to conflate the question of the infrequency of the damaging occurrence, on the one hand, with the infrequency of its occurrence without negligence relative to its occurrence with negligence, on the other.

Other judgments have not generally[39] reflected a similar approach. Perhaps the courts are reluctant to commit themselves to any particular statistical

---

[37] Unreported, Supreme Court, July 27, 2004.

[38] More generally, see Tribe, "Trial by Mathematics: Precision and Ritual in the Legal Process", 884 Harv. L. Rev. 1329 (1971).

[39] *Cf Barrett v. Southern Health Board*, unreported, High Court, December 5, 1988 where Blayney J, in a case alleging negligence in an operation on fractures on the plaintiff's arm in which a nerve was damaged, observed:

> "Th[e] doctrine [of *res ipsa loquitur*] has no application in the context of an operation which necessarily involved risk and where the evidence is that in more than 7% of the cases some nerve damage is sustained. Where such damage could

> occur without any negligence on the part of the surgeon the mere fact that there was damage is not evidence of negligence."

It may respectfully be suggested that this analysis is incomplete. For the *res ipsa loquitur* principle to apply, the accident must have been such as does not ordinarily happen without negligence on the part of those in control. The test is thus *not whether an accident of this type happens frequently or rarely* but rather *whether, on those occasions when it does happen (regardless of how often this may be), it rarely happens without negligence.* Thus, in *Barrett*, if it had been asserted and established that six of the seven cases out of every hundred in which nerve damage was sustained involved negligence on the part of the doctor then *Daniels v. Heskin* would appear likely to support the invocation of the *res ipsa loquitur* principle. The fact that the operation involved some inevitable risk of failure would not of itself be a reason for automatic exclusion of the principle. (It scarcely needs to be added that nothing in the case suggests that any proportion of the 7% involving nerve damage could be attributed to negligence). In a recent decision of the New South Wales Supreme Court, *Marko v. Falk* [2007] N.S.W.S.C. 14, Hislop J. adopted an approach similar to that favoured in *Barrett*.

Another decision which deals somewhat unsatisfactorily with the *res ipsa loquitur* issue is *Duffy v. North Eastern Health Board*, unreported, High Court, November 3, 1988. In *Duffy*, the plaintiff, who had been admitted to the defendant's hospital for an operation on his knee, found afterwards that, during his stay there, he had sustained damage to the ulnar nerve of his right arm, probably caused by pressure on the nerve. Hamilton P. withdrew the claim for negligence from the jury.

The plaintiff's expert witnesses gave evidence establishing that, in cases such as this, great care should be taken, particularly during the course of the operation, to prevent an injury of this type from occurring. One of these witnesses stated that the risk or danger of injury of this type could not be completely eliminated and that damage could occur even where every possible precaution was taken. Hamilton P. noted that "[n]o evidence" had been adduced on behalf of the plaintiff in regard to want of such care.

The plaintiff unsuccessfully relied on the principle of *res ipsa loquitur.* Hamilton P. said:

> "In the absence of any evidence with regard to want of care on behalf of the defendant, and the evidence of [one of the expert witnesses] that, even if every possible care was taken, an injury of this type could occur, I considered that the principle of *res ipsa loquitur* did not apply and, there being no evidence of any negligence on the part of the defendant, I withdrew the case from the jury."

It is of course true that, if the plaintiff's injuries could just as easily have been caused without negligence as with negligence, (or, a *fortiori*, more easily without than with negligence) the plaintiff could not succeed. But in *Duffy* the expert witness apparently said no more in favour of the defendant than that the risk of an injury of the type suffered by the plaintiff *could not be completely eliminated* even where every precaution was taken. On this basis it may be argued that the plaintiff's case was not excluded from the application of the *res ipsa loquitur* principle. That principle was first articulated in order to refute the suggestion that, in cases where the evidence of negligence is circumstantial, the plaintiff must exclude every possibility of a non-negligent explanation as a precondition of entitlement to get his or her case to the jury. On the basis of the evidence of the expert witness, it is hard to see how the accident was other than one which "in the ordinary circumstances does not happen if those who have the management of the thing causing threshold in order to preserve their flexibility in the application of the *res ipsa loquitur* principle, as well as to disguise the fact that there can be formidable methodological difficulties in defining the parameters of the category of accident in respect of which the statistical analysis should be effected. To take a simple example: if the driver of a motor vehicle brakes suddenly, so that a passenger is slightly injured, how narrowly or broadly should the category of accident be formulated for the purposes of the, *res ipsa loquitur* principle?[40] Does it depend on the size or function of the vehicle? The speed at which it was travelling? The character of the location - urban, suburban or rural? The time of day at which the braking took place? The truth of the matter is that the court retains considerable elasticity in its characterisation.[41] In most instances, it relies not on sharply measured statistical empirical data, but on a common-sense robust assessment of "how things are" in the real world. No doubt such common-sense lies at the heart of adjudication in negligence litigation but one can question whether it should be the linchpin for the application or non-application of a technical doctrine with potentially massive implications for the parties, so far as it determines which party is to have to discharge the burden of proof.

---

the plaintiff injury] use proper care …". *Scott v. London & St Catherine's Docks Co.*, 3 H & C. 596, at 601; 159 E.R. 665, at 667 (1865). In *Dully,* the plaintiff had introduced no *direct* evidence of negligence, but circumstantial evidence need not be considered as its poor relation. As Fleming observed, `the facts of an accident may speak in a whisper or shout aloud' the defendant's negligence: *The Law of Torts*, (7th ed., 1987) 300. *Cf. Bowie v. Argyll & Clyde Health Board*, [2007] C.S.O.H. 39.

40 *Cf Millington v. CIE* (1974) 108 I.L.T.R. 61 (SC).

41 In *Mullen v. Quinnsworth Ltd t/a Crazy Prices (No.1)* [1990] 1 I.R. 59 (SC) where an elderly customer of a supermarket slipped on some colourless cooking oil that had been knocked onto the floor of the aisle, the Supreme Court held that the *res ipsa loquitur* principle applied. Griffin J. (Finlay C.J. concurring) observed that "the floor was under the management of the defendant ... and the accident was such as in the ordinary course of things would not happen if floors were kept free from spillages of this nature." This is a curious way of applying the test unless supermarket proprietors are under a strict obligation to keep the floors free of spillages rather than (as traditionally understood) an obligation to take reasonable care to keep the floors free of them. Since it was acknowledged that supermarkets have an inevitable risk of items breaking and spilling, Griffin J.'s test and surrounding analysis tilt towards the conclusion that supermarkets should not escape liability for falls by customers by mere proof of a system to monitor and remove spillages. No such system, however intensive, could remove completely the risk to customers. McCarthy J. (Finlay C.J. concurring) actually toyed with the idea of imposing what he termed "absolute liability", using the rule in *Rylands v. Fletcher* as an inspiration. When the case returned to the Supreme Court (*Mullen v. Quinnsworth Ltd t/a Crazy Prices (No.2)* [1991] I.L.R.M. 439) McCarthy J.'s enthusiasm for this approach had abated. See further O'Higgins, "Strict Liabilty for Supermarket Spillage Cases …?, 9 Ir.L.T. (n.s.) 134 (1991).

THE PROCEDURAL EFFECT OF *RES IPSA LOQUITUR*[42]

One of the most difficult and unsatisfactory aspects of the operation of the *res ipsa loquitur* principle arises in relation to its procedural effect. If the plaintiff has established that *res ipsa loquitur* applies, this could have one of a number of consequences. These consquences can best be understood in the context of jury trial, bearing in mind that juries in personal injuries litigation were replaced by judges as fact finders in 1988. First, establishing *res ipsa loquitur* could mean no more than that the plaintiff's case was sufficiently strong to go to the jury. The jury would be free to find for either plaintiff or defendant, but the plaintiff would have the assurance that he or she would at least get the case to the jury for its consideration. In some (albeit rare) cases, the evidence which merits the application of the *res ipsa loquitur* principle might be sufficiently strong to entitle the plaintiff to a directed verdict in the plaintiff's favour.[43] Secondly, it could mean that the defendant is obliged to establish either that he or she was not negligent or to provide a reasonable explanation, equally consistent with negligence and no negligence on his or her part. On this interpretation (in contrast to the first), if the defendant elects not to give evidence, the plaintiff must (not may) win his or her case. Thirdly, it could shift the onus onto the defendant to establish affirmatively that the accident was not caused by his or her negligence.

The courts have been somewhat remiss in the language they have used to describe the law on this question. One even finds decisions[44] in which inconsistencies are apparent within the same judgment.

---

[42] See Prosser, "The Procedural Effect of *Res ipsa loquitur*" (1936) 20 Minn. L. Rev. 241; Kauffman, "Comment: *Res ipsa loquitur* - An Analysis of Its Application and Procedural Effects in Nebraska" (1962) 41 Neb. L. Rev. 747 and Harlow, "*Res ipsa loquitur* - A Progress Report' (1972) 3 Kingston L. Rev. 1.

[43] With the abolition of the jury in personal injuries litigation the judge takes on the responsibility of trier of fact. Experience in other common law jurisdictions is that this first interpretation of the procedural effect of *res ipsa loquitur* tends to give way to the second or third once the judge assumes this responsibility. There is no logical necessity for this change, however. *Cf* Fleming, *The Law of Torts* (9th ed., 1998):

> "Since the virtual disappearance of civil juries in England, the temptation has been strong to blur what, on the one hand, would *justify* and, on the other, *compel* a verdict for the plaintiff, since it is no longer so important to distinguish between questions of law and fact when both issues are decided by the trial judge himself. Hence it was easy to mistake for a principle of law what was merely intended to be the view of that court as to what the defendant in a particular case had to do, if he wished to protect himself by way of rebutting evidence against a probably adverse verdict."

[44] Including the decision of *Byrne v. Boadle* (1863) 2 H & C 722 which started the whole problem! See also *Lindsay v. Mid-Western Health Board* [1993] 2 I.R. 147 (SC revg HC) where O'Flaherty J. appeared to adopt the third interpretation whilst expressly approving of a quotation from Fleming, *loc. cit.* (7th ed., 1987), p.291 which advocated acceptance

There is much to be said in favour of the first interpretation, which has won favour in courts in the United States,[45] Canada,[46] Australia,[47] and, it seems, New Zealand.[48] Why should one species of circumstantial evidence (which is referred to as *res ipsa loquitur*) have greater evidential weight than direct evidence? To regard *res ipsa loquitur* as merely having the effect of ensuring that the plaintiff gets the case before the jury[49] means, however, that it ceases to be a distinctive doctrine and such concepts as "control" of the object that causes the danger lose their crucial significance.

The tendency in the Irish courts, especially in recent years, is not to favour the first interpretation (although a few decisions[50] in the past seemed to give some support to it). The second[51] had some support but today it is the third[52]

---

of the first interpretation. *Cf* Byrne & Binchy, *Annual Review of Irish Law 1992*, (Round Hall Press) pp 594-595. Fleming (9th ed., 1998), pp.360-364 maintained advocacy for the first interpretation.

45 *Cf* Prosser & Keeton, *loc. cit.*, pp.257-258.

46 *Cf* Fleming, *loc. cit.*, p.361; *Nominal Defendant v. Haslbauer* (1967) 117 C.L.R. 448; *Government Insurance Office of New South Wales v. Fredrichberg* (1968) 118 C.L.R. 403; *Schellenberg v. Tunnell Holdings Pty Ltd* (2000) 170 A.L.R. 594 and *Lanfranchi v. Transport Accident Commission*, [2006] V.S.CA. 81. See Schulz, "*Res ipsa loquitur* in Australia – The Maxim Remains", 26 Monash U. L. Rev. 379 (2000).

47 *Hawkes' Bay Motor Co Ltd v. Russell* [1972] N.Z.L.R. 542.

48 The Supreme Court of Canada, in *Fontaine v. British Columbia (Official Administrator)* [1998] 1 S.C.R. 424, frustrated by the confusion surrounding the *res ipsa loquitur* concept, held (at 435) that "the law would be better served if the maxim was treated as expired and no longer used in negligence actions. After all, it was nothing more than an attempt to deal with circumstantial evidence." See McInnes, "The Death of *Res ipsa loquitur* in Canada"(1998) 114 L.Q. Rev. 547.

49 Or, since 1988, that a defence motion to dismiss the claim at the conclusion of the plaintiff's case will fail.

50 *Cf O'Rourke v. McGuinness* [1942] I.R. 554 (SC); *Palmer v. Bateman* [1908] 2 I.R. 393 at 399 (KB); *Coughlan v. Marks* [1918] 2 I.R. 306 at 319 (CA 1917, *affg* KB 1917) *Tracey v. Hagen*, unreported, Supreme Court, March 6, 1973, (Walsh J.) and *Millington v. CIE* (1974) 108 ILTR 61 at 67 (SC).

51 *Cf Farrell v. Alliance & Dublin Consumers' Gas Co* [1939] Ir. Jur. 41 (CC). *Fleming v. Henry Denny & Son Ltd*, unreported, Supreme Court, July 29, 1955 (*semble*) and *O'Loughlin v. Kearney* [1939] Ir. Jur 39 (CC) (*semble*).

52 This support was evident even in some decisions many years ago. *Cf Coughlan v. Marks* [1918] 2 I.R. 306; *Flannery v. Waterford & Limerick Ry Co* (1877) I.R. 11 C.L. 30; *Corcoran v. West* [1933] I.R. 210; *Collen Bros (Dublin) Ltd v. Scaffolding Ltd* [1959] I.R. 245; *Palmer v. Bateman* [1908] 2 I.R. 393, *Millington v. CIE* (1974) 108 I.L.T.R. 61 (SC) (Fitzgerald J.'s judgment) and *Mullen v. Quinnsworth Ltd t/a Crazy Prices* [1990] I.R. 59 (SC) (Griffin J.'s judgment, Finlay C.J. concurring). In *Kelleher v. Tipperary (North Riding) Board of Health and Public Assistance* [1938] I.R. 43 (SC) FitzGibbon J., (with whom Sullivan C.J. concurred), favoured the third view. He said (p.62):

> "In actions founded upon negligence the principle embodied in the maxim *res ipsa loquitur* is called in aid to shift the onus of proof, and to relieve the

interpretation that is dominant.[53]

If it is accepted that the Irish courts have committed themselves to the view that an onus rests on the defendant, once the *res ipsa loquitur* principle applies, the question arises as to what precisely the defendant must do to avoid liability. The Supreme Court addressed the issue in *Lindsay v. Mid-Western Health Board*.[54] The case concerned a girl who, nine years before the trial, when she was aged eight, had been admitted to the defendant's hospital with suspected appendicitis. An alternative diagnosis of mesenteric adonitis was also considered by the medical staff. The plaintiff was operated on. She appeared initially to be recovering consciousness after the operation but had a sudden epileptic-form attack and lapsed into a deep coma from which she had not regained consciousness at the time of the litigation.

The plaintiff's action for negligence against the hospital involved the invocation of the *res ipsa loquitur* doctrine. The expert witness called on her behalf, a highly qualified and experienced anaesthetist, identified three possible causes for the plaintiff's condition: sub-arachnoid haemorrhage, hypoxic insult and "miscellaneous possibilities" Morris J. held in favour of the plaintiff on the basis that the defendant's hypothesis of a viral explanation was speculative, but the Supreme Court reversed.

O'Flaherty J. (Finlay C.J. and Egan J. concurring) was of the view that, in

---

> party who relies upon the maxim from the necessity of producing any evidence other than the bare occurrence of an accident. Where the maxim is applied, the mere occurrence of an accident of a particular kind is treated as casting upon the defendant, without any further evidence on behalf of the plaintiff, the onus of showing that the accident was not caused by his negligence."

Meredith J., dissenting, favoured the second approach. He said (pp.67-68):

> "[W]here th[e] *res ipsa loquitur* principle is the sole foundation of the allegation of negligence, an explanation merely consistent with the evidence, though not affirmatively substantiated as the actual explanation, and consistent also with the absence of negligence may be relied upon to show that the principle does not apply."

In *Daniels v. Heskin* [1954] I.R. 73 at 79 (SC) Lavery J. proffered a hybrid test, which can perhaps best be interpreted as tilting more towards the third than the second approach. See also *Moore v. Fox (R) & Sons* [1956] 1 Q.B. 596 and *Henderson v. Jenkins (Henry) & Sons* [1970] A.C. 282. For more recent examples of judicial support for the third interpretation see, e.g. *Lindsay v. Mid-Western Health Board* [1993] 2 I.R. 147 (SC *revg* HC); *O'Reilly v. Lavelle* High Court, 2 April 1990 (Johnson J); *Merriman v. Greenhills Foods Ltd* [1997] 1 I.L.R.M. 46 (SC) and *O'Shea v. Tilman Anhold and Horse Holiday Farm Ltd*, unreported, Supreme Court, October 23, 1996, analysed by Glanville, "Litigation and Evidence: Speaking up for the Maximum *Res ipsa loquitur*," 15 I.L.T. (ns) 121 (1997).

53 *Collen Bros (Dublin) Ltd v. Scaffolding Ltd* [1959] I.R. 245 (HC); *Kelly v. Gilmore*, unreported, Supreme Court, July 28, 1970 and *Murray v. Gilmore*, unreported, Supreme Court, December 20, 1973.

54 [1993] 2 I.R. 147 (SC *revg* HC) analysed by Byrne & Binchy, *Annual Review of Irish Law 1992*, pp.593-597.

the instant case, the most that the defendant should be required to do was to show that it had exercised all reasonable care; it should not be required to take the further step of proving, on the balance of probabilities, what had caused the plaintiff's brain damage.

The effect of this holding[55] is that a defendant can escape liability in a case where *res ipsa loquitur* applies even where a mystery remains as to the cause of the accident. Once the defendant has established that, whatever the actual cause, it can not be attributed to his or her negligence, then the defendant has done enough. Of course, if the defendant can establish the actual cause of the plaintiff's injury, he or she will also escape liability, in spite of having been guilty of negligence, if that negligence was not the cause of the injury.

The *Hanrahan* restatement of the *res ipsa loquitur* doctrine

We now must consider the implications of the restatement of the *res ipsa loquitur* doctrine in the Supreme Court decision of *Hanrahan v. Merck Sharp & Dohme (Ireland) Ltd*[56] The plaintiffs had claimed damages for negligence and nuisance and under the rule in *Rylands v. Fletcher*. They contended that the injuries which they had suffered - in regard to their health, their farm animals and plant life - had been caused by noxious emissions which they alleged had been discharged from the defendants' factory, where pharmaceutical products were processed. The central issue was one of causation, though the question of the quantum of the injuries was also a matter of dispute.

Keane J. dealt with the claim as essentially one of nuisance. Since no appeal had been taken alleging that this was erroneous, the Supreme Court was content to treat the claim similarly. This did not, however, prevent Henchy J. (for the Court) from proferring an important observation on the *res ipsa loquitur* doctrine:

> "The ordinary rule is that a person who alleges a particular tort must, in order to succeed, prove (save where there are admissions) all the necessary ingredients of that tort and it is not for the defendant to disprove anything. Such exceptions as have been allowed to that general rule seem to be confined to cases where a particular element of the tort lies, or is deemed to lie, pre-eminently within the defendant's knowledge, in which case the onus of proof as to that matter passes to the defendant. Thus, in the tort of negligence, where damage has been caused to the plaintiff in circumstances in which such damage would not usually be caused without negligence on the part of the defendant, the rule of *res ipsa loquitur* will allow the act relied on to be evidence of negligence in the absence of proof by the defendant that it occurred without want

---

55 Supported by Johnson J.'s decision in *Callaghan v. Gleeson*, unreported, High Court, July 19, 2002.

56 [1988] I.L.R.M. 629 (SC).

> of due care on his part. The rationale behind the shifting of the onus of proof to the defendant in such cases would appear to lie in the fact that it would be palpably unfair to require a plaintiff to prove something which is beyond his reach and which is peculiarly within the range of the defendant's capacity of proof."[57]

Central to this analysis is the notion of the defendant's superior knowledge of how the tort was caused: it would be "palpably unfair" to require the plaintiff to prove that which is "peculiarly within the range of the defendant's capacity of proof". This approach gives rise to difficulty.[58] It is not the case that *res ipsa loquitur* may be invoked only where the evidence is more accessible to the defendant. Of course, proof of the elements of a case based on *res ipsa loquitur* frequently shows superior or exclusive knowledge on the part of the defendant as to how the accident occurred: of the nature of things, those in control of the instrumentality causing the injury are generally more likely to have such knowledge than their victims. However the *res ipsa loquitur* doctrine is neither reducible to, nor dependent on, this element.

Henchy J.'s statement that *res ipsa loquitur* applies "where damage has been caused to the plaintiff in circumstances in which such damage would not usually be caused without negligence on the part of the defendant" involves an unfortunate elision of the separate elements of the doctrine. In fact the plaintiff does not have to discharge such an onus. The whole point of the doctrine is to permit the making of an inferential conclusion that the defendant's negligent conduct caused the plaintiff's injury from the fact that (a) the thing causing the injury was under the defendant's control, and (b) accidents such as the one befalling the plaintiff do not ordinarily happen if those in control exercise due care. Under Henchy J.'s approach, the inferential conclusion has become, in effect, a premise. In *Hanrahan*, the issue at the core of the case was whether in fact the "thing" that was under the control of the defendants was the "thing" which caused injury to the plaintiffs. Unless it could be proven on the balance of probabilities that it was, the plaintiffs could not succeed. The *res ipsa loquitur* doctrine would not assist in providing this proof.

The *Hanrahan* restatement has a somewhat contested status, though it has not been dislodged. Curiously, the Supreme Court made no reference to it in

---

57 *Ibid.*, pp.634-635.

58 *Cf Prosser & Keeton on the Law of Torts* (5th ed., 1984), pp.254-255:

> "If the circumstances are such as to create a reasonable inference of the defendant's negligence it cannot be supposed that the inference would ever be defeated by a showing that the defendant knew nothing about what had happened, and if the facts give rise to no such inference, a plaintiff who has the burden of proof in the first instance could scarcely make out a case merely by proving that the plaintiff knew less about the matter than the defendant."

Lindsay v. Mid-Western Health Board[59] or *Merriman v. Greenhills Foods Ltd.*[60] In *O'Shea v. Tilman Anhold and Horse Holiday Farm Ltd*,[61] Keane J. noted that "the recent restatement of the doctrine by this court in *Hanrahan* ... has been criticised[62] and may need to be reconsidered at some stage." He preferred to use the "classic formulation"[63] of *res ipsa loquitur*, contained in the famous passage of Erle C.J.'s judgment in *Scott v. London & St Katherine Docks Co*,[64] O'Flaherty J. merely referred to his own earlier judgment in *Lindsay*, which had derived no apparent inspiration from *Hanrahan*. Hamilton C.J. expressly reserved his position with regard to Keane J.'s suggestion that the *Hanrahan* restatement be reconsidered.

In *Rothwell v. Motor Insurers Bureau of Ireland*,[65] Hardiman J. noted that the *Hanrahan* rationale had been subject to academic criticism but observed that it appeared to him to be "authoritative unless and until specifically considered in a case where its reversal is sought". He emphasised that the *Hanrahan* rationale applied, not where the matter in question was merely within the exclusive knowledge of the defendant, but where furthermore it was also peculiarly within the range of the defendant's capacity of proof.

It remains to be seen whether the Irish courts will take the entirely different course, favoured by the Supreme Court of Canada[66] and finding certain sympathy

---

59 [1993] 2 I.R. 147 (SC 1992 *revg* HC 1991).

60 [1997] 1 I.L.R.M. 46 (SC). It is true that a central paragraph in Blayney J.'s judgment (with which O'Flaherty J. concurred) appears to place much weight on the plaintiff's lack of knowledge of the cause of the accident, and on the extent to which the defendant may have exercised due care. He was "satisfied that to enable justice to be done, the [*res ipsa loquitur*] doctrine should be applied to throw the onus on the [defendant] to prove that it was not negligent." There are perhaps resonances here of the *Hanrahan* restatement. As against this Blayney J. made no reference to it and instead relied on the *locus classicus* of *Scott v. London & St Katherine Docks Co* (1865) 3 H & C 596 at 601; 159 E.R. 665 at 667.

61 Unreported, Supreme Court, October 23, 1996, p 5 of Keane's judgment.

62 Citing the second edition McMahon & Binchy, *Irish Law of Torts*, (Butterworths, 1990), pp.142-144.

63 P.5 of Keane .'s judgment.

64 *Supra.*

65 [2003] 1 I.L.R.M. 521.

66 *Fontaine v. British Columbia (Official Administrator)* [1998] 1 SCR 424. See also the *obiter* observations of May L.J. in *Fryer v. Pearson* C.A., *The Times*, April 4, 2000, noted by Witting, "*Res ipsa loquitur*: Some Last Words", 117 L.Q.R. 392 (2001). It is interesting to note that the Supreme Court of Appeal of South Africa in *Wagener v. Pharmacare Ltd.*, 2003 (4) 285, declined to transform product liability from negligence to strict liability in the light of the constitutional mandate to protect bodily integrity. It envisaged that in future courts might be willing to extend the scope of *res ipsa loquitur* where expert evidence was extremely difficult for the plaintiff to acquire. See further Christopher J. Roederer, *The Transformation of South African Private Law after Ten Years of Democracy: The Role of Torts (Delicts) in the Consolidation of Democracy* (Bepress Legal Series, Paper 740,

in the High Court of Australia,[67] of announcing the demise of the *res ipsa loquitur* doctrine, leaving negligence litigation involving circumstantial evidence to be resolved simply on the weight of that evidence. Such a development could only contribute to clarity in our law.

Analysis of certain Irish decisions on *res ipsa loquitur*

Let us now look in a bit more detail at some of the Irish decisions which address the question of *res ipsa loquitur*.

In *Lindsay v. Mid-Western Health Board*,[68] as has been noted, a patient who went into hospital with suspected appendicitis, regressed into a deep coma after the operation. The Supreme Court, reversing Morris J., held that the defendants had the onus of disproving negligence, not the more expansive onus of explaining the cause of the plaintiff's post-operative condition. The defendants discharged that obligation to the satisfaction of the Supreme Court.

O'Flaherty J.[69] agreed with Morris J. that the *res ipsa loquitur* doctrine applied:

> "It is true that a precise circumstance of negligence cannot be pointed to – such as in the classical cases of bags of sugar falling on a passing pedestrian (*Scott v. London & St Katherine Docks Co.*)[70] or a motor car driven onto a footpath [71]- but it seems to me that if a person goes in for a routine medical procedure, is subject to an anaesthetic without any special features, and there is a failure to return the patient to consciousness, to say that that does not call for an explanation from defendants would be in defiance of reason and justice."

This passage raises some interesting issues as to the application of *res ipsa loquitur* in particular cases. It may be argued that in neither *Scott* nor *Murray* could the plaintiff point to "a precise circumstance of negligence", if by that concept is envisaged the precise identification of the particular mode of negligent conduct of which the defendant was guilty. What both plaintiffs could do was to raise a commonsense inference that the defendant was negligent, how precisely did not matter. Of course it is possible to describe the defendant's conduct in both cases by a formula that points the finger of negligence at the defendant: the defendants in *Scott* were (inferentially) guilty of negligent control of the bags of sugar on their premises and the defendant in *Murray* was (inferentially) negligent

---

2005), pp.47-48. This frank admission as to the capacity of the *res ispa loquitur* doctrine to be manipulated to serve constitutional goals is significant.

67 *Schellenberg v. Tunnell Holdings Pty Ltd* (2000) 170 A.L.R. 594, at 629 (*per* Kirby J.).

68 [1993] 2 I.R. 147.

69 Finlay C.J. and Egan J. concurring.

70 (1865) 3 H. & C. 596, 159 E.R. 665.

71 *Murray v. Gilmore,* unreported, Supreme Court, December 20, 1973.

in the manner in which he drove his car. But what do these formulae really tell us about what happened? Nothing very much, it would seem. Equally, in *Lindsay*, the plaintiff could not point precisely to a specific act of negligence on behalf of the defendants but she was entitled to say that the facts raised an inference of negligent treatment. Far from being an embarrassment in the invocation the *res ipsa loquitur* doctrine, this lack of specificity can be a potent characteristic of a case based on *res ipsa loquitur*.

It is interesting that O'Flaherty J. did not refer to Henchy J.'s rationale for the *res ipsa loquitur* doctrine in *Hanrahan v. Merck Sharp & Dohme (Ireland) Ltd*[72] only four years previously, which based the doctrine on the defendant's superior capacity of proof. Undoubtedly in the context of medical operations, where the patient is rendered unconscious, the defendant will almost invariably have just such a superior capacity of proof. Indeed, this superior capacity so tilts the balance in favour of the defendant that the California Supreme Court, more than sixty years ago, in *Ybarra v. Spangard*,[73] extended the principles of vicarious liability, under the guise of the *res ipsa loquitur* doctrine, to ensure that a plaintiff who is injured when under anaesthetic will not find himself or herself in the situation of knowing that someone of those involved in his or her treatment must have been guilty of negligence, without being able to find out who that person was.[74]

O'Flaherty J. went on to express the view that, in the instant case, the most that the defendant should be required to do was to show that it had exercised all reasonable care and that it should not be required to take the further step of proving, on a balance of probabilities, what had caused the plaintiff's brain

---

72 [1988] I.L.R.M. 629.

73 25 Cal 2d 486, 154 P 2d 687 (1944). See Seavey, "*Res ipsa loquitur*: Tabula in Naufragio", 63 Harv. L. Rev. 643 (1950).

74 One commentator (Adamson, "Medical Malpractice: Misuse of *Res ipsa loquitur*", 46 Minn. L. Rev. 1043, at 1047 (1962)) has criticised the decision in the following terms:

> "The *Ybarra* case is a classic example of the old cliché that 'hard cases make bad law' which really means that 'bad cases make hard law.' It is true that Joe Ybarra was in a difficult position. He had a disability and he, personally, apparently did not know how he acquired it. If he was 'wronged,' in the legal sense of the word, he was entitled to a remedy. He, and people like him, are natural objects of concern and sympathy. But it must be recognized that every harm is not a 'wrong,' and that 'remedy' means a remedy against the wrongdoer, not against the blameless. The law, as uttered by the pens and via the predilections of appellate judges, is justifiably troubled with people like Joe. But it should be equally concerned with people like defendants A, B, C, D, E and F - most of whom logically must have been innocent of any wrongdoing" and most (if not all), of whom were as incapable as Joe of showing just how Joe was harmed. The conscience of the law is hardly salved by affording an innocent man a remedy against another innocent man. This is especially true in the context of the defendant's activity - the activity of trying to cure the physical ills of man within the limitation of man's admitted lack of omnipotence and omniscience."

damage. He observed that "[t]he distinction between a negligent act and causation requires to be emphasised".

O'Flaherty J. adopted as "an apt description of the scope of the [*res ipsa loquitur*] maxim" the following passage from John Fleming's *Law of Torts*[75]:

> "In some circumstances, the mere fact that an accident has occurred raises an inference of negligence against the defendant. A plaintiff is never obliged to prove his case by direct evidence. Circumstantial evidence is just as probative, if from proof of certain facts other facts may reasonably be inferred. *Res ipsa loquitur* is no more that a convenient label to describe situations where, notwithstanding the plaintiff's inability to establish the exact cause of the accident, the fact of the accident by itself is sufficient in the absence of an explanation to justify the conclusion that most probably the defendant was negligent and that his negligence caused the injury. The maxim contains nothing new; it is based on common sense, since it is a matter of ordinary observation and experience in life that sometimes a thing tells its own story. Unfortunately, the use of a Latin phrase to describe this simple notion has become a source of confusion by giving the impression that it represents a special rule of substantive law instead of being only an aid in the evaluation of evidence, an application merely of 'the general method of inferring one or more facts in issue from circumstances proved in evidence'."[76]

Fleming advocated that *res ipsa loquitur* should be understood as no more and no less than a convenient label for a case based on circumstantial evidence which (in the days of a jury) was sufficiently strong to get to the jury, without a non-suit. It did *not* shift the onus onto the defendant to disprove negligence on his or her part. Nor did it require the defendant to adduce exculpatory evidence: on Fleming's approach a jury would be quite entitled to find in favour of a defendant in some cases where the doctrine applied and the defendant elected not to adduce any evidence. All that the doctrine involved was the process of identifying the case as being of sufficient strength to ensure that the trial judge would not withdraw it from the jury. There always was a certain range within which a reasonable jury could find negligence or the absence of negligence. Obviously, at the higher range of the register, there were and are cases where a verdict for the defendant would be perverse, but there are many *res ipsa loquitur* situations falling well short of such a coercively strong case for the plaintiff. It is curious that Fleming should be quoted with apparent approval when no member of the court in *Lindsay* appears to have interpreted the *res ipsa loquitur* doctrine as Fleming does.

O'Flaherty J. adopted the reasoning of Andrews J., in the British Columbia

---

[75] 7th ed., p.291.

[76] Citing *Davis v. Bunn,* (1936) 56 C.L.R. 246 at 268.

decision of *Girard v. Royal Columbian Hospital*,[77] that medical science had not yet reached the stage where the law ought to presume that a plaintiff must come out of an operation as well as or better than he or she went into it. In that case, the evidence indicated that the kind of injury the plaintiff suffered could have occurred without negligence on anyone's part. Andrews J. had concluded that, since he could not infer that there had been negligence on the part of the doctors, the maxim of *res ipsa loquitur* did not apply.

O'Flaherty J. accepted that in the circumstances of the instant case an answer was clearly required from the defendant:

> "That answer could be provided in two ways. [The defendant] could have proved, on the balance of probabilities, that the plaintiff met her injuries in a particular manner that caused her condition but which was not connected with the administration of the anaesthetic. This [it] failed to do. The furthest the defendan[t] got was to suggest as possibilities other means by which the plaintiff sustained her injuries. I believe this evidence is not, however, to be regarded as totally inadmissible. It was legitimate, I believe, for the defendan[t] to adduce evidence of possibilities, remote though they might be, as an explanation; in contradistinction to saying that [it] could not offer *any* explanation of any description whatsoever. It went to provide some corroboration, as well, that there was no negligence on [its] part in the administration of the anaesthetic. The other course was for the defendan[t] to establish that from beginning to end of this anaesthetic procedure there was no negligence on [its] part. This [it] did decisively and, in those circumstances, it appears to me that [it] rebutted the burden of proof that rested on [it] to displace the maxim *res ipsa loquitur* and so the case returned to the plaintiff's bailiwick to prove negligence."

O'Flaherty concluded as follows:

> "I believe that it is necessary to ensure that the rule embodied in the maxim does not put a burden on defendants which is so onerous as to produce an unjust result. Each case must, of course, be dealt with in accordance with its own particular facts but, as I have said, I believe that in the circumstances here the defendan[t] ha[s] met the *prima facie* case made against [it] as fully as could be expected. It would be an unjustifiable extension of the law to say that in the absence of an explanation that could be proved, on the balance of probabilities, negligence on the part of the defendant must be inferred. It has often been said that medical science is not an exact one and it is safe to prophesy that medical science and its technology will advance past frontiers which are not within anyone's

---

[77] (1976) 66 D.L.R. (3rd) 676 at 691.

> contemplation at this time and so matters at present not amenable to explanation will be capable of resolution."

O'Flaherty J.'s conclusion that the *res ipsa loquitur* doctrine no longer applies where a defendant establishes that he or she acted without negligence emerges clearly from this analysis. His discussion of the defendants' alternative explanation for the plaintiff's injuries in the instant case is somewhat less clear. There is a difference between the admissibility and the efficacy of such evidence. English courts are somewhat indulgent to defendants in relation to the potency of the evidence of possible other explanations for the plaintiff's injuries. Reading O'Flaherty J.'s analysis in its totality, it seems that he is demanding that evidence of this kind, to exempt the defendant, must meet the standard of the balance of probabilities.

In *Maitland v. Swan and Sligo County Council*[78], the defendant surgeon had removed the plaintiff's right ovary in circumstances where this resulted in interference with the plaintiff's procreative capacity on account of the failure of her left ovary. Barr J. held that the surgeon was negligent in failing to have prior recourse to a gynaecologist for assistance and advice. The plaintiff invoked the judgments of Henchy J. (for the Court) in *Hanrahan v. Merck Sharp and Dohmne (Ireland) Ltd*[79] and Morris J. in *Lindsay v. Mid-Western Health Board*.[80] In *Hanrahan*, as has been noted, Henchy J. had observed:

> "The rationale behind the shifting of the onus of proof to the defendant in such cases would appear to lie in the fact that it would be palpably unfair to require a plaintiff to prove something which is beyond his reach and which is peculiarly within the range of the defendant's capacity of proof."

In *Lindsay*, Morris J. had relied on this passage and had also quoted with approval the following passage from Denning L.J.'s judgment in *Cassidy v. Minister for Health*:[81]

> "If the plaintiff had to prove that some particular doctor or nurse was negligent, he would not be able to do it. But he was not put to that impossible task: he says, `I went into the hospital to be cured of two stiff fingers. I have come out with four stiff fingers and my hand is useless. That should not have happened if due care had been used. Explain it, if you can."

---

78 Unreported, High Court, April 6, 1992.

79 [1988] I.L.R.M. 629.

80 [1993] 2 I.R. 147 (reversed by the Supreme Court subsequent to Barr J.'s judgment in *Maitland v. Swan and Sligo County Council*).

81 [1951] 2 KB 343, at 356.

Barr J. perceived crucial differences between the facts of *Lindsay* and *Cassidy* on the one hand and the instant case on the other. In *Lindsay*, the plaintiff patient had failed to recover consciousness after routine surgery. These circumstances seemed to Barr J. to be precisely within the ambit of Henchy J.'s *dictum* in *Hanrahan* that "it would be palpably unfair to require a plaintiff to prove something which is beyond his reach and which is particularly within the range of the defendant's capacity of proof" In contrast, in the instant case there was no immediate unexplained damage arising out of or contemporaneously with the operation performed by the surgeon on the plaintiff. The plaintiff's case was not that the surgeon had been negligent *per se* in removing the plaintiff's right ovary but rather that in a wider context of professional responsibility the removal constituted negligence. In making the case of negligence in this wider context the plaintiff had all the information that was known to the defendant, who had no recollection of the operation and was forced to rely on his documentation made shortly after the operation. In these circumstances, the plaintiff was not required to prove something which was `beyond [her] reach and which [was] within the defendant's capacity of proof'. Furthermore, the defendant's removal of the right ovary was not in itself evidence of negligence on his part; it would be so only if the cyst affecting the plaintiff's right ovary had not destroyed all functional ovarian tissue. If it had done so, then the removal of the ovary would not have caused the plaintiff further harm.

Barr J. was of course bound to follow the Supreme Court decision in *Hanrahan* and might reasonably have considered himself obliged to address *res ipsa loquitur* in terms of the defendant's superior access to knowledge of how the injury occurred. This is in striking contrast to High Court judges in subsequent cases involving *res ipsa loquitur*, whose failure even to refer to *Hanrahan* suggests that they interpreted it, not as altering the content of the *res ipsa loquitur* doctrine but rather as merely seeking to address its underlying rationale.

In *Doherty v. Reynolds and St. James's Hospital*,[82] the plaintiff, who went to hospital for an operation to deal with his acid reflux and heartburn, emerged with a "frozen shoulder", which caused him intense pain. The hospital records failed to record adequately this fact but, in a conflict of evidence on the matter between the plaintiff, his wife and a priest, on the one hand, and certain witnesses on behalf of the defence on the other, O'Donovan J. held in favour of the plaintiff and, on appeal, Keane C.J. (Murray and Fennelly JJ. concurring) had not 'the slightest doubt' that O'Donovan J. had been entitled to do so. The Chief Justice commented that the absence of any records of the plaintiff's complaints of severe pain in his shoulder area by any of the hospital staff was "certainly remarkable and reflect[ed] at best, from their point of view, a singularly inadequate system of record keeping."

As to the cause of shoulder pain, there was a dispute. The plaintiff's expert

---

[82] Unreported, Supreme Court, July 14, 2004.

witnesses maintained that it was a traction injury. The defendants' expert witness argued that it was the result of brachial neuritis. He said that surgery or anaesthesia could precipitate the condition in 1 in 10,000 cases. Early recovery would occur in 90% to 95% of cases; this case must have been one of 5% to 10% where it had not. The essence of this evidence, therefore, was that the plaintiff had suffered an injury such as would occur only once in 100,000 to 200,000 cases.

O'Donovan J. preferred the plaintiff's expert evidence and held that the pain was attributable to traction injury. Accordingly the *res ipsa loquitur* principle applied. He was not greatly impressed by the fact that the thrust of the evidence adduced by the defendants was that, while the witnesses could not recall the day in which the operation had occurred, the treatment given to patients was of a high standard. O'Donovan J. observed:

> "In this case, the defendants have not established precisely how and when the plaintiff sustained the injury of which he complains and, accordingly, have not demonstrated that it cannot be attributed to any blame on their part and, although they have purported to lead evidence to establish that, from the beginning to the end of the procedure to which the plaintiff was subjected on 13th December, 1996, there was no negligence on their part, the fact of the matter…is because the persons responsible for caring for the plaintiff during that period have no actual recollection of what occurred, all that has been proved is what should have happened in an ideal hospital situation; not what actually occurred. Accordingly,…I am not persuaded that the defendants have excluded the likelihood on the balance of probability that the injury suffered by [the plaintiff] was occasioned by sub-standard care on their part. Accordingly, it is my judgment that the plaintiff is entitled to succeed in his claim here against the second named defendant."

The Supreme Court reversed, for two reasons. First, O'Donovan J., when determining whether the plaintiff's 'frozen shoulder' was attributable to a traction injury or brachial neuritis, should have weighed in his assessment the evidence by members of the hospital staff of their general good treatment of patients. Secondly, O'Donovan J. when addressing the *res ipsa loquitur* issue, had not given sufficient weight to that evidence. Keane C.J. stated:

> "The trial judge held that because, as he put it, no-one was in a position to state positively that their admittedly safe system had been implemented in the case of the plaintiff, he could not exclude the possibility that an incident did occur as a result of which the plaintiff sustained the traction injury Such an incident, he held, could not have happened without negligence on the part of the hospital.
>
> That approach seems to me difficult to reconcile with the law as stated

> in *Lindsay v. Mid-Western Health Board*. The fact that, for the most part, the anaesthetist, surgeon and nursing staff were unable to recall, at that remove of time, the specific details of what transpired during the operation itself or the peri-operative period generally did not have, as its necessary consequence, as the trial judge appeared to assume, that they could not discharge the burden of proof resting on them of establishing that there was no negligence on their part. In my view, that would be to impose a burden of proof on defendants in a case such as this which is unfair and unreasonable. The fact that the staff of the hospital cannot, at a particular remove of time, give honest evidence that they recall how a particular patient was dealt with is, of course, a fact to which the court must have regard. But it must also give the appropriate weight to evidence, such as was adduced in this case, as to the procedures which would normally be applied, the inferences that can properly be drawn from the hospital records and the evidence, if it exists, as it did in this case, of those concerned that, while they did not recall the specific operation, they had no recollection in any operation of the procedures being departed from with the consequences alleged to have resulted in this case."

It has to be said that this analysis seems indulgent to the defendants. The effect of the *res ipsa loquitur* rule is to place the burden on a defendant of proving, on the balance of probabilities, that he or she has not been guilty of negligence (or has not caused the injury). Evidence that one recollects nothing specific about the occasion in question but one's day-to-day practice is of a high standard scarcely discharges that onus. O'Donovan J. did not impose liability because the defendants could not remember the occasion: he found that this forgetfulness, in combination with evidence as to day-to-day practice, did not suffice to discharge that burden.

In *Quinn v. South Eastern Health Board*,[83] Ó Caoimh J. applied the *res ipsa loquitur* doctrine where an appendectomy carried out on the fourteen-year-old plaintiff resulted in meralgia parasthetica. Evidence was given on behalf of the plaintiff that the incidence of this condition in young people was very low. Ó Caoimh J. noted that '[w]hile [the expert witness giving evidence on behalf of the plaintiff] did comment on the location of the incision, he was not prepared to criticize the procedure carried out. He indicated that the location of the incision was such as was likely to present a risk of damage to the particular nerve in question in this case.' The defendants did not go into evidence.

Ó Caoimh J. was satisfied on the evidence that the condition of meralgia parasthetica had resulted from the appendectomy. In reaching this conclusion, he was:

> "mindful of the evidence of [the expert witness] as to the location of

[83] Unreported, High Court, March 22, 2002.

> the incision and the fact that it was unusually low and in an area with greater risk of damage to the lateral femoral cutaneous nerve. I believe the fact that rarely can the nerve be affected during appendectomy and the fact that the evidence shows that it was in the instant case … brings into play the doctrine of *res ipsa loquitur* and that the plaintiff is entitled to succeed against the defendant in respect of the appendectomy also as no explanation has been forthcoming from the defendant in whose care the plaintiff was at the relevant time."

Perhaps the finding can best be understood as a simple process of inferential reasoning from the evidence, in the absence of direct evidence adduced by the defendants, rather than what might be called a pure application of the *res ipsa loquitur* doctrine. Although Ó Caoimh J. referred earlier to the submission by counsel for the plaintiff that "meralgia parasthetica is not something that results in the ordinary course of things if those who have the management exercise reasonable care", he did not expressly endorse it and the basis of his holding seems more easily referable to the enhanced risk of damage to the nerve associated with the particular location of the incision. Had the *res ipsa loquitur* doctrine never been developed, such a conclusion would appear unexceptionable as it does not depend on any artificial manipulation of the onus of proof.

In *Kelly v. Lenihan*,[84] Abbott J. observed that "the doctrine of *res ipsa loquitur* does not apply to medical negligence as stated in the judgment of the Supreme Court in *Beatrice Lindsay v. Mid-Western Health Board*[85]". Perhaps this odd statement can best be interpreted as indicating that Abbott J. saw no place for application of the doctrine to the facts of the case. Clearly, as *Lindsay* itself makes plain, the doctrine does indeed apply to medical negligence claims.

Conclusion

The *res ipsa loquitur* doctrine is in poor shape. All of its crucial ingredients are problematic. The concept of management or control has no clear boundaries, especially in cases where the legal entitlement (or duty) to control does not coincide with factual realities or where control has recently been given up. The concept of accidents such as the one that happened not usually occurring without negligence on the part of those in control suffers from a double weakness: the scope of characterisation of the type of accident is entirely elastic and the degree of rarity of non-negligent occurrences relative to negligent occurrences is completely opaque. The procedural effect of *res ipsa loquitur* seems clear enough in Ireland but the principle on which it is based is not easy to defend. Why should only plaintiffs who succeed in pushing the two buttons necessary to activate the *res ipsa loquitur* doctrine obtain such a litigious advantage? The

[84] [2004] IEHC 427.
[85] [1993] 2 I.R. 177.

Hanrahan rationale for the doctrine may have some justification but, if so, this is entirely unconnected with the two ingredients traditionally considered to activate *res ipsa loquitur*, which are associated with the process of inferential thinking rather than the question of relative access to information.

In the specific context of medical negligence litigation, the shift in 1988 from juries to judges for personal injuries claims has presented a difficulty for patients which courts are unlikely to acknowledge publicly. A jury, having heard evidence from defence witnesses that they had treated the patient with all due care, might come to the robust conclusion not to place a great deal of weight on this evidence. A trial judge has no such luxury. He or she must adorn gut instincts as to credibility or weight of evidence with some justificatory prose. This can be a difficult task. When it comes to an appeal, the appellate court may not be impressed. The effect of this is that, in cases where there is a fog of uncertainty as to what happened at the crucial particular time, the onus that rests on the defendant may not be quite as intimidating as it appears.

My suspicion – impossible to verify – is that the *res ipsa loquitur* doctrine has probably resulted in a greater number of justified outcomes for patients than unjustified outcomes for the medical profession. But, even if this is so, it will have been on a hit-and-miss basis.

The logical solution would be to abolish *res ipsa loquitur* as a distinctive doctrine and let judges form such inferences as appear appropriate in any case. My hesitation about recommending this step is based on a sense that, with all its incoherence, the doctrine probably protects the interests of patients in particularly vulnerable positions. This is a difficult issue, probably best addressed by the Law Reform Commission, backed by empirical research.

CHAPTER 4

Suing Hospitals and Health Boards

NEVILLE COX

INTRODUCTION

This chapter deals with the occasionally difficult question of whether and when a hospital or health board will attract liability as a result of the acts or omissions of persons operating within its premises or under its auspices. In theory at least, this is a very important question in that if, for example, a nurse causes damage by virtue of his or her negligence, then it will be pointless to sue him or her because of the likelihood that he or she will not have the funds to meet any award of damages. Rather it will be far more profitable to seek compensation from the comparatively wealthy hospital. Moreover, in general the distributitive view of justice that underpins aspects of our tort system means that such recovery is generally possible – even if it can be difficult in any given case to explain precisely *why* it is possible.

As will be seen, it is long accepted that a hospital may be sued for the negligence of its employees, although there is some uncertainty as to who exactly a "hospital employee" is; whether and when, for example a private consultant working in a private clinic can legitimately be seen as an employee of the clinic. In reality, moreover, the impact of professional indemnity insurance means that in most cases, tricky instances of vicarious liability need only be addressed where a patient is injured by the negligence of a person who may be outside or only on the periphery of the hospital staff and has no, or limited insurance cover. Nonetheless the claim (both legal and ideological) is often made that a hospital should take responsibility for *everything* that goes on in its premises and irrespective of who is involved. Typically this claim is made by reference to the perceptions of the average patient, who goes to hospital in order to be healed and with no knowledge or interest as to the various legal relationships between the institution and the persons working on the premises.

This chapter considers three issues:

- First and briefly, it considers the statutory obligations of the hospital in respect of the general safety of the premises and the system of work in place.
- Secondly, it considers the question of when a hospital can be deemed to be vicariously liable for acts or omissions of healthcare personnel.

Specifically this involves assessing in any case (a) whether the negligent party can be seen as an employee of the hospital and (b) whether such negligence arose in the course of his or her employment.

- Finally, it assesses the possible circumstances in which a hospital may be deemed to owe a *primary and non-delegable duty of care* to its patients, whereby it is essentially and directly responsible for all instances of negligence on its premises that cause harm.

Statutory Liability of Hospitals and Health Boards

It is perhaps somewhat out of place in a book on medical negligence to refer to the statutory obligations of a hospital in respect of its premises, system of work, equipment and so on, and such reference will therefore be brief. Essentially under the Occupiers Liability Act 1995 and the Safety, Health and Welfare At Work Act 2005 obligations in this regard are owed to all persons present in the hospital premises – employees, patients, visitors and independent contractors. Such obligations entail ensuring that there is a safe premises (that is to say an obligation to take reasonable care to ensure that persons are not injured as a result of the state of the premises), a safe system of work, safe equipment and competent staff. It is entirely arguable that it is the 2005 Act which provides the more fertile ground for a would be plaintiff in this context and so its terms deserve some brief consideration.

The Safety, Health and Welfare at Work Act 2005

The employer's obligations under the 2005 Act relate to the manner in which the undertaking is carrying its business and extend beyond the obligation to ensure that "employees" are acting safely. In other words, from the standpoint of the hospital manager, these obligations relate to the way in which business is carried out in the hospital and not merely to the way in which employees are conducting themselves. Moreover, the duties which are owed are not merely to employees but rather to *all* persons on the premises. Thus section 12 of the Act provides that:

> 12.–Every employer shall manage and conduct his or her undertaking in such a way as to ensure, so far as is reasonably practicable, that in the course of the work being carried on, individuals at the place of work (not being his or her employees) are not exposed to risks to their safety, health or welfare.

As will be clear, the obligations of the employer are conditioned by two factors. First, an employer (like any occupier) is not an insurer of the well being of persons entering onto his property. If legal action, either civil or criminal, is to arise out of a situation where someone suffers harm in the workplace, then the employer must have causal responsibility for such harm. On the other hand, the essence of what the employer is required to do is contained in the notion which appears throughout the statute of "reasonable practicability" – a term which had previously appeared in the 1993 Safety, Health and Welfare at Work Regulations. In other words, whereas the employer is required to ensure that the particular obligations are met, s/he will only be required to fulfil such obligations as far as is reasonably practicable.

Under the 2005 Act, furthermore, the notion of reasonable practicability is given definition. Thus under section 2(6) of the Act it is provided that:

> "For the purposes of the relevant statutory provisions, "reasonably practicable", in relation to the duties of an employer, means that an employer has exercised all due care by putting in place the necessary protective and preventive measures, having identified the hazards and assessed the risks to safety and health likely to result in accidents or injury to health at the place of work concerned and where the putting in place of any further measures is grossly disproportionate having regard to the unusual, unforeseeable and exceptional nature of any circumstance or occurrence that may result in an accident at work or injury to health at that place of work".

It seems likely that what is provided for here is a standard which is in excess of the "reasonableness" standard at common law. What is unclear, however, is to what extent it is so in excess. Professor Binchy has argued that in fact, in as much as the employer must exercise all due care *by putting in place* the necessary measures, rather than exercise all due care *to put* the measures in place, the standard imposed under the act is effectively one of strict liability[1] After all it would seem that even if the employer *has* exercised all due care, yet s/he does not succeed in putting the measures in place, then s/he will not have complied with the reasonable practicability test.

Whether or not this is the case, the standard under the 2005 Act is plainly a high one. What it entails is that the duty of the employer operates at a two stage level. Thus s/he must:

(a) identify the hazards and assess the risks to safety and health likely to result in accidents or injuries to health at the place of works concerned, and
(b) put in place the necessary protective and preventative measures.

Moreover, and whereas irrespective of expense, the employer must put the

---

1 Binchy, "The Health, Safety and Welfare at Work Act 2005: How Does it Expand the Scope of Employers' Obligations?" Paper Given at a TCD Conference on "Litigation Against Employers" December 10, 2005.

necessary protective and preventative measures in place, there is also an additional obligation to put "further measures" in place. The only restriction on this secondary obligation is that it will not arise if the employer can demonstrate that this would be grossly disproportionate (and this would imply that the employer may indeed be required to take measures that are merely disproportionate without being grossly so) having regard to the unforeseeable and exceptional nature of the risk that a failure to put such a measure in place may lead to an accident at work or an injury to health[2].

As has been noted, this cuts across traditional standard of care analysis, in that many of the factors that would be relevant in assessing whether the defendant has acted reasonably in the circumstances (gravity of threatened harm, social utility of conduct,) are not to be factored into the equation. It becomes simply a balance between the cost of the preventative measure on the one hand and the likelihood or otherwise of an accident/injury on the other. And it is submitted that the tone of the definition suggests that it is only where the accident/injury is completely unlikely to accrue, so that the expenditure on preventing it would be a complete waste of money, that the employer need not take such preventative measures.

Finally, it would seem that as far as the reasonably practicable test is concerned, the onus (of proving that reasonably practicable steps have been taken) shifts to the defendant[3]. Thus in *Boyle v. Marathon Petroleum Ltd,*[4] O'Flaherty J. said that:

> "I have no doubt that the onus of proof does rest on the defendants to show that what they did was reasonably practicable. I am also of the opinion that this duty is more extensive than the common law duty which devolves on employers to exercise reasonable care in various respects as regards their employees. It is an obligation to take all practicable steps. That seems to me to involve more than that they should respond that they, as employers, did all that was reasonably to be expected of them in a particular situation. An employer might sometimes be able to say that what he did by way of exercising reasonable care was done in the 'agony of the moment', for example, but that might not be enough to discharge his statutory duty under the section in question."

As far as the hospital manager is concerned then, the 2005 Act may create a significant new responsibility in respect of the safety, health and welfare of anyone in the hospital. Equally, the essential focus for the employer involves the identification and remedying of foreseeable hazards. Hence it is perhaps unlikely that the 2005 Act would have application in the context of a situation where

---

2 See *Edwards v. National Coal Board* [1949] 1 K.B. 704.

3 Indeed this is implicit in the terms of s. 81 of the 2005 Act.

4 [1999] 2 I.R. 460.

a consultant surgeon (for instance) with an excellent reputation unexpectedly and uncharacteristically acted negligently. On the other hand it would have application where the hospital appointed someone to a position where there was some existing reason why it was unsafe to do so.

The manner in which the 2005 Act might apply to the hospital setting was exemplified in the somewhat unusual case of *Gwilliam v. West Hertfordshire Hospitals NHS Trust & Others*[5]. On July 5, 1997 the claimant, then aged 63, was injured when using an apparatus at a fund raising summer fair organised by the Mount Vernon Hospital in Northwood, Middlesex, part of the NHS Trust. The aim of the apparatus was to allow the participant to bounce from a trampoline and adhere by means of Velcro material to a wall known as a "splat wall". The claimant was injured because the apparatus had been negligently set up by the second defendant, Mr Cane, the proprietor of a business 'Club Entertainments' from whom the equipment had been hired. The first named defendants had in fact agreed to pay the second named defendant an extra £100 to provide staff for the splat wall in order to avail of his public liability insurance. However, it transpired that this insurance had elapsed four days before the event in question. The claimant sued the hospital claiming that it owed all persons entering the premises a duty to take reasonable care in appointing independent contractors which would extend to a duty to ensure that such persons were covered by public liability insurance.

The Court of Appeal found that in as much as the public were invited to take part in a dangerous or hazardous activity within the hospital premises which was organised by an independent contractor, the hospital owed a duty in respect of the appointment of such contractor, including a duty to ensure that he was properly insured. Equally such duty had, on the facts, been fulfilled in this case (in that the hospital had checked whether the contractor had insurance and had been misinformed).

The Occupiers' Liability Act 1995

The impact of the Occupiers' Liability Act on hospitals was considered by the High Court in *Sheehan v. Midwestern Health Board.*[6] The plaintiff had accompanied his wife to hospital after she sustained an injury to her lip. He alleged that a doctor has asked him to hold a paper or piece of gauze near his wife's lip as it was being sutured, and that, not being provided with a chair, he had fainted. The court rejected both his allegation that the doctor had asked him to assist with the surgical procedure (a contention which, it must be said, does appear unlikely) and also the suggestion that at law the hospital was under a duty to provide the plaintiff with a chair to sit on. What is surprising, however, is that the court regarded the issue as one of occupier's liability rather than medical negligence. The reason that this is surprising is that the Occupiers' Liability

---

5 [2003] Q.B. 443.

6 Unreported High Court, Murphy J., August 1, 2002.

Act only covers damage that arises as a result of the state of the premises, whereas this incident (at its height) involved a systemic failure on the part of the hospital in terms both of bad practice by the doctor in asking the plaintiff to assist with the procedure, and in not providing sufficient chairs so that visitors could have a seat.

Vicarious Liability of Hospitals and Health Boards

The traditional reason why a hospital might be liable for harm caused on its premises was on a vicarious liability basis. There is no doubt that an employer hospital can be vicariously liable for injures caused by the negligence of an employee. What is controversial, however, is the question of who exactly may be termed an employee of the hospital (and indeed whether vicarious liability can arise even where there is no employer-employee relationship). To answer this question a very brief analysis of the concept of vicarious liability is necessary.

Vicarious liability generally

Vicarious liability exists where the law holds a blameless person responsible for the misconduct of another, because of that person's supposed responsibility for the situation. With the industrial revolution and the impact of the world of commerce, an attempt was made to balance the two competing policy based aims of trying to protect a business from unjust litigation and trying to ensure that a plaintiff could find a financially responsible defendant. Included in this formula is a consideration of where there is insurance for such tortious conduct. Essentially, liability is being channelled from the poor employee to the rich employer, even where the employer does not owe a duty to the injured party but endures liability because of the employee's duty.

This traditional basis for vicarious liability was set out in *Reedie v. NW Railway Company,*[7] and focuses perhaps artificially on the notion that an employer, in selecting staff should be able to make good decisions, and certainly should not select negligent operatives. In other words, there was an attempt to draw a causal link between the employment/appointment process and the final harm caused. As has been noted by various commentators, this artificial line of reasoning has the fatal flaw that it seeks to impose liability purely on the basis of causation and without regard to notions of fault. Equally more recently, this "responsibility for appointment" logic has been used to ground a *direct* duty of care on the part of hospitals as regards ensuring a workable and safe hospital system.

Apart from anything else, however, this effort to find a principled basis for imposing vicarious liability in any case foundered to some extent on the

---

[7] (1894) 4 Exch. 244.

conflicting reality of the situation which was (and is) that vicarious liability is imposed because of economic reality and because of a policy which seeks to permit recovery on the part of an injured plaintiff where this would be appropriate. Thus Professor Williams pointed out that:

> "The master is liable because he has a purse worth opening. The master is frequently rich and he is usually insured - two arguments that might be used by any burglar if he ever troubled to justify his threats. The strange thing is to hear them put forward by judges of eminence...However distasteful the theory may be, we have to admit that vicarious liability owes its explanation if not its justification to the search for a solvent defendant."

In similar vein it may be suggested that vicarious liability exists purely to ensure that the socially beneficial concept of Loss Distribution can apply. After all if, for example, a hospital is sued successfully, then this will come out of its insurance company and ultimately the damages suffered by the plaintiff can be spread more thinly over the community generally.

The employment relationship

Despite this, the law has historically sought some principled basis for imposing vicarious liability which has traditionally been based on the employment relationship. Thus vicarious liability traditionally arose in the context of an employee/employer (or master/servant) relationship (contract of service), but not in a situation where a person engages an independent contractor to do some work for him(contract for services). Clearly, therefore, a pivotal question is whether, in any given situation, the relationship involved is the former or the latter – a question which also arises in the context of employment law and tax law (and which may receive different answers depending on the area of law under discussion).

Because of the historical genesis of vicarious liability in a situation where the master's knowledge on all matters was deemed to be superior to his servant's to whom he could give detailed instruction, the traditional test for determining whether there was a master/servant relationship was known as the *control test*, i.e. was the employee subject to the control of the master not only in respect of what work to do but also how to do it (master/servant) or was he merely responsible to do the job but in the manner in which he saw fit (independent contractor).

This test, however, could clearly not survive in the contemporary society where those performing even the least specialised tasks may legitimately be seen as having more expertise than their employers. As a result, the application of the control test has altered radically. The question is no longer whether the employer had the capacity to monitor the worker's behaviour but whether ultimate authority over the worker resided in the employer so that the former was subject to instruction from the latter. Moreover, a more flexible analysis of the situation is possible: for example, the contracts between the parties will be analysed and questions asked such as; had the employer a power of dismissal over the employee, how much work did the latter do for the former, what tax or social welfare payments was the "employer" paying on behalf of the "employee" etc. Thus for example, the master/servant relationship has been held to apply to a situation where a son was occasionally requested to drive his invalid parent in the latter's car. Furthermore, in an Irish case called *Phelan v. Coillte Teoranta Ireland,*[8] an employer/employee relationship was deemed to exist between the defendant state agency and a welder/fitter who carried out work for them, even though the latter was entitled to no holiday or pension rights, and the defendant paid no PRSI or tax for him. The court applied a control test, but were prepared to look at the reality of the welder's job (99% of his time was spent working for the Defendant), and recognised that different levels of control might apply to different jobs.

Interestingly, in the *Coillte* case, the court said that control was only a pivotal factor in establishing liability in cases *where the employer's right to direct the worker as to how he shall perform his task is the norm.* On the other hand, the court expressly referred to cases of *a specialist having a professional qualification such as a surgeon or physician on the staff of a hospital* and said that in such circumstances, control would not be a determinative factor. As we shall see, this proposition was reaffirmed by the High Court as recently as June 2007. As will also be noted, whatever the basis for such a conclusion, such professional staff have long been seen as being employed by the hospital.

For the sake of completeness it may be argued that the "control test" as a means for establishing the employer/employee relationship has now been replaced by an "organisation test", originally mooted by Lord Denning in the case *Stevenson v. MacDonald*[9] in 1952. Lord Denning argued that in a contract *of* service, i.e. a master/servant relationship,

> "A man is employed as part of the business and his work is done as an integral part of the business: whereas, under a contract for services, his work, although done for the business is not integrated into it but is only accessory to it."

Linked with this we have an "integration test". In other words, provided someone was integrated into an undertaking, he or she could be seen as an employee thereof, even in the absence of any sense of control.

From the vicarious liability standpoint, the courts will, on a case by case basis and with general policy considerations to the forefront, ask whether a particular person is acting like an employee or as an entrepreneur. Is she for

---

8 [1993] 1 I.R. 18.

9 [1952] 1 T.L.R. 101.

instance taking independent risks associated with private business, or is she essentially operating under the "employer's" umbrella. So in *Hall (Inspector of Taxes) v. Lorimer,*[10] the fact that an individual who worked almost exclusively for a company still himself bore the risks of bad debts or insolvency in the case of his clients, was extremely good evidence that there was not an employee/employer relationship present.[11]

The employment relationship within the hospital setting

One of the key points which emerges from the case law in this area, is that the courts in both Ireland and England are prepared to make exceptions to the normal rules of vicarious liability where hospitals are concerned. Originally in the UK, hospitals, which were regarded as charitable institutions which policy indicated should be protected from ungrateful litigants, were not vicariously liable for the negligence of their doctors and nurses. Stemming from the case *Hillyer v. Governors of St. Bartholomew's Hospital,*[12] this derived from a strict application of the control test. It was argued that, in the exercise of their professional judgement, doctors were dealing with matters beyond the competence or ability of the "hospital" *per se*. Hence the control test fell, hence there was no master/servant relationship, hence there was no vicarious liability. The responsibility of the hospital was limited to the selection of competent staff and the proper administration of hospital business. This logic, according to Lord Denning in *Cassidy v. Minister for Health,*[13] was based on a desire to "...relieve the charitable hospitals from liability which they could not afford".

With a realisation both that, by virtue of modern economic conditions virtually all tasks performed in a hospital were now beyond the control of the hospital authority and also that the vision of hospitals as impecunious charitable institutions was not strictly accurate, came a move away from the logic in *Hillyer*. In *Gold v. Essex County Council,*[14] the Court of Appeal, refusing to make a distinction between administrative duties and professional duties held that a hospital was vicariously liable for the negligence of a radiographer. Lord Greene M.R. argued that the duty of a hospital was not merely to provide a patient with equipment, but also to treat him or her therewith. This duty could not be avoided simply be employing someone to use the equipment. Lord Greene specifically left open the question of whether a hospital would be liable for the negligence of a doctor, although Lord Goddard suggested that a hospital would be vicariously liable for permanently employed doctors but not for visiting surgeons, physicians and consultants.

---

10 (1994) 1 All E.R. 250.

11 From an Irish perspective generally see *Denny & Sons v. Minister for Social Welfare* [1998] 1 I.R. 34 and Forde, *Employment Law* 2nd ed., (Round Hall 2001), pp.21 *et seq*.

12 [1909[2 K.B. 820.

13 [1951] 2 K.B. 348.

14 [1942] 2 K.B. 293.

This viewpoint appeared to be followed in a number of cases. Thus for example in *Collins v. Hertfordshire County Council*[15] a hospital was held vicariously liable for a full time junior house surgeon, but not for a part time equivalent. The modern rule, however, was set out in the UK in *Cassidy v. Ministry of Health* and in Ireland in *O'Donovan v. Cork County Council*,[16] to the effect that a hospital is vicariously liable for the negligence of *all* staff under a permanent contract of service to the hospital. This includes doctors, nurses etc. Thus in two Irish cases, *Mooney v. Terrett*[17] and *Morgan v. Galway Board of Health,*[18] a hospital and a nursing home respectively were held to be vicariously liable for the negligence of its nursing staff.

More importantly, at the time in the UK there was significant suggestion that the rules of vicarious liability had a broader principled application than had previously been thought, or more precisely, that vicarious liability could arise well outside of a "control" situation. In *Cassidy,* Lord Denning said that,

> "In my opinion, authorities who run a hospital be they local authorities, government boards or any other corporation are in law under the selfsame duty as the humblest doctor; wherever they accept a patient for treatment, they must use reasonable care and skill to cure him of his ailment. The hospital authorities cannot of course do it by themselves; they have no ears to listen through the stethoscope and no hands to hold the surgeon's knife. They must do it by the staff they employ and if their staff are negligent in giving the treatment they are just as liable for that negligence as is anyone else who employs others to do his duties for him."

The court in *Cassidy* was split over the question of whether this logic would apply to private consultants not specifically employed by the hospital, a question which remains unsettled. Two judges said that this was equivalent to a patient privately arranging treatment by a specific doctor. Lord Denning, however, said that in such circumstances, the hospital owed a non-delegable duty of care to the patient which could not be transferred to the visiting consultant.

The current approach, as set out in *Roe v. Minister for Health,*[19] is that, in line with the evolving general principles in respect of vicarious liability, the Courts are prepared to look flexibly and in some detail at the facts of each case to see what the precise nature of the business relationship in that case actually is. Thus, radiographers, resident house surgeons, pharmacists, doctors, nurses, anaesthetists, resident medical officers and assistant medical officers have all been found, in the particular circumstances of the cases, to be employees of

[15] [1947] 1 K.B. 598.

[16] [1967] I.R. 173.

[17] [1939] Ir. Jur. Rep 56.

[18] [1943] I.R. 255.

[19] [1954] 2 Q.B. 66.

their respective hospitals. Moreover, the courts appear not to be concerned with the distinction between part time and full time staff.

The courts have, in their assessment of the relevant facts been keen to look at the nature of the undertaking provided by the hospital. Furthermore, it would seem that they have taken on board the "organisation" test in determining who exactly is employed by the hospital. In other words, if a worker can be classified as being part of the hospital organisation, then he will be deemed to be an employee thereof.

As far as the Irish law in this area is concerned, a recent and methodical treatment of this issue was provided by Kelly J. in *Byrne v. Ryan*[20] a case which concerned the question of whether a hospital could be vicariously liable for negligence on the part of a consultant doctor on its staff in his treatment of a *public* patient. Equally the issue of the relationship between consultants and hospitals is sufficiently complex that it requires some measure of introduction.

Vicarious liability of hospitals for the negligence of consultants

It is not certain whether either exclusively or partially private consultants may legitimately be regarded as employees of a hospital. In *Razzel v. Snowball,*[21] Lord Denning had no doubt on the subject saying that, since the introduction of the National Health Service in Britain, the term *consultant* didn't denote a doctor/patient relationship, but rather it denoted a place on the hierarchy of the hospital staff. As he put it,

> "He is a senior member of the staff, but nevertheless just as much a member of the staff as the House Surgeon".

Lord Denning appeared, however, to be referring to a consultant who is engaged in a public practice within a hospital, or more probably, a consultant *when* he is so engaged. As we shall see, a significant distinction may exist in law for the purposes of vicarious liability between situations where a consultant is working for the hospital and situations where s/he is engaged in private practice.

This was the question which the High Court (Kelly J.) was required to address in *Byrne v. Ryan.* The facts of the case are relatively complex and should thus be stated in some detail.

The plaintiff who, by the time of the relevant events, had had five children was referred by her doctor to the Coombe Hospital under the care of a consultant (Dr Charles Murray) for sterilisation by way of tubal ligation. Dr Murray (who by the time of the hearing had retired) was an extremely experienced and highly qualified consultant gynaecologist and carried out the sterilisation procedure on the plaintiff. He estimated that by the year 2000 he would have carried out "in the high hundreds and probably in the thousands" of tubal ligation procedures,

---

20 [2007] IEHC 207 (June 20, 2007).

21 [1954] 1 W.L.R. 1382.

and whereas he would on rare occasions be concerned as to their success, in such circumstances he would require that further investigatory and remedial procedures be adopted. In the plaintiff's case, however, he had had (at the time) no doubt but that the procedure in question had been successful. This was despite the fact that, by reason, *inter alia,* of the fact that the plaintiff had previously suffered an ectopic pregnancy, the procedure (which was carried out laparoscopically) had required some preparatory work to remove adhesions from the anterior abdominal wall. Nonetheless, Dr Murray testified that he had dissected them off with instruments that he was using in order that he could see what he was doing and had then "just clipped the tubes". His report of the procedure at the time, was to the effect that it had been "straightforward" in the sense that there had been no complications.

In fact, for whatever reason (and Kelly J. concluded that it must have been because of the negligence of the consultant) the tubes had not been clipped, but rather the clip was placed on some tissue below the tubes. Thus the plaintiff went through two more pregnancies, and subsequently sued the hospital for negligence. Having concluded: (a) that the hospital organisation had been negligent in failing to inform the plaintiff when it became aware that the procedure had failed, and (b) that Dr Murray had acted negligently on *Dunne* principles, Kelly J. proceeded to deal with the question of whether, nonetheless, the hospital would be deemed to be vicariously liable for the negligence of Dr Murray who was, of course, a consultant.

Unsurprisingly, the most appropriate starting point for assessing whether the hospital was vicariously liable for such negligence was Dr Murray's contract. In this respect he was employed under what is known as the "consultant's common contract" by the terms of which he was required to work an aggregate of 33 "notional hours" at the hospital per week. He was also permitted to conduct private practice in accordance with the terms of a memorandum of agreement appended to the contract. On this basis, the defendants made two arguments as to why vicarious liability should not apply namely:

> "(1) This was a contract for services and not a contract of service, but in any event,
> (2) The relevant factor as far as vicarious liability was concerned was not the nature of the contract but rather the level of control which the alleged employer had over the alleged employee (and indeed, in the case of a hospital consultant such "control" was determinative of the vicarious liability issue whether or not the consultant was an employee of the hospital. In this case, there was no such control and hence, by definition, there was no vicarious liability."

In this respect, it is worth noting that in another recent decision (*Keaney v.*

Sullivan[22]) Finlay Geoghegan J. had appeared to endorse the "control" test as far as vicarious liability is concerned, saying that:

> "The plaintiff has not established any basis for a reasonable cause of action for a claim that one person could be considered as vicariously liable for alleged wrongs in the professional or business dealings of another person simply by reason of the fact that the two persons (albeit sharing a common profession) practised from the same premises.
>
> The law will in certain circumstances recognise that one person may be liable for the wrongs of another even where no formal legal relationship exists. However, the relevant test is whether the defendant has sufficient control over the acts of the other to be held liable for his wrongs. See McMahon & Binchy: *The Law of Torts* (3rd edition) pp. 1092-1094. The plaintiff in the statement of claim has not pleaded any facts in relation to the alleged association between the first defendant and Ormsby Rhodes which could support a claim that Ormsby Rhodes had any control over the actions of the first defendant in respect of his alleged dealings with the plaintiff and alleged wrongs committed."

In *Byrne v. Ryan*, however, Kelly J. appeared to take a considerably more expansive view of the application of vicarious liability rules – certainly in the case of hospitals. Indeed in concluding that the control test was not of universal application, Kelly J. suggested that "…hospital cases are to a considerable extent *sui generis*". As far as hospitals were concerned, Kelly J. adopted the approaches taken by Denning L.J. in *Cassidy v. Minister of Health* and Morris L.J. in *Roe v. Minister of Health* (decisions which he accepted were ahead of their time but which he felt, nonetheless, summed up the current position in both Ireland and the UK) such that what was relevant in the case of a person working in a hospital was not control but whether s/he was part of the organisation. Moreover this approached derived from the presumed attitude of the patient who comes to a hospital seeking healthcare and who is unaware of and unconcerned with the precise nature of the relationship between the organisation and the person treating him or her. Thus in a very important passage, Kelly J. concluded that:

> "The plaintiff was referred not to a particular surgeon but to the Coombe Hospital. She had no say in the choice of who would carry out her sterilisation. It was done by Dr Murray. He was part of the "organisation" or permanent staff of the hospital. The performance of the operation was part of a service provided by the hospital to the plaintiff. Dr. Murray was the person in the hospital's organisation via whom that service was provided.
>
> In these circumstances it matters not whether Dr. Murray was

[22] [2007] IEHC 8.

> employed under a contract of service or a contract for services. In my view having regard to the principles enunciated in both *Cassidy* and *Roe's* case the hospital here is liable for any want of care on the part of Dr. Murray."

The decision in *Byrne v. Ryan* then provides clarity on the question of whether a hospital can be vicariously liable for the negligence of a consultant engaged in *public* practice. The question remains however, as to whether such vicarious liability will arise in respect of consultants engaged in *private* practice yet who are working within the hospital setting.

Vicarious liability and private treatment

In general, where a doctor or consultant is engaged in his or her private practice, he or she will not be deemed to be employed by the hospital in which he or she is carrying out such practice. Thus in *Bolton v. Blackrock Clinic*,[23] Geoghegan J. commented that, "...as the plaintiff was a private patient of the doctors in a private hospital, the question of vicarious liability may not arise". From the rule in *Rogers v. Night Riders*,[24] the principle appears to be that unless the hospital has held the doctor out to the patient as being an employee, it won't be liable for his or her negligence. This may, however, depend on the interpretation of the contract between the hospital and the patient. Is the hospital in any particular case acting as a provider of health care, or is it merely a type of medical hotel, renting the patient a bed? It will be argued later that if it is the former, then the hospital will have implicitly undertaken a non delegable duty not only to provide facilities, but also to provide an adequate standard of health care. In *Roe v. Ministry for Health*, Morris L.J. said that such duty would arise not on the basis of fees paid but on the basis, essentially, of the legitimate expectations of the patient – and in *Byrne v. Ryan* Kelly J. seemed to endorse this logic. On the other hand, it is clear that if a doctor is privately and directly engaged by a patient and the hospital is merely a venue where he or she may be treated, then the hospital will not be liable for his or her negligence.

Further miscellaneous categories of employee

Finally, it is worth noting that there are other categories of persons who work in hospitals who may or may not be deemed to be hospital employees for vicarious liability purposes. These would include independently or temporarily employed radiographers or anaesthetists and agency nurses. In the UK, a lot of these questions have been answered by the fact that NHS insurance has been conceded by the courts as being sufficiently wide to cover all sorts of workers, including for example agency nurses even though, in reality they are for vicarious liability

---

[23] Unreported, High Court, December 20, 1994.

[24] [1983] R.T.A. 324. C.A.

purposes employees of the agency and not the hospital. These questions remain, however, unanswered in Ireland. Furthermore, if a consultant engaged in private employment has nurses working for him or her in, for example, theatre then the general rule in the UK is that they remain the employees of the hospital. On the other hand, they will not be deemed to be negligent if they correctly follow negligent instruction from the consultant. Moreover, it seems unlikely that a locum doctor is an employee, but will, more probably be regarded as an independent contractor. Finally, if, in the UK a hospital is under the financial control of a health board, then that Health Authority is the correct defendant in respect of any liability for the staff of that hospital.

Acting "in the course of employment"

One final point in respect of vicarious liability remains. A general rule is that the vicarious liability of an employer is limited to the torts of an employee *acting in the course of his or her employment.* There is of course an argument that a person employed within a hospital is employed to act reasonably, and hence whenever he or she commits a tort or, more obviously still, a crime, the action is outside the course of employment and hence vicarious liability should not arise. Obviously if such a proposition were to be accepted it would mean that the entire concept of vicarious liability would be illusory in nature. Nonetheless the question of precisely *when* a person is acting in the course of his or her employment remains somewhat uncertain.

In England the theoretical position is that a person is acting in the course of employment (and vicarious liability therefore arises) where the conduct of the employee was so closely connected with the nature and circumstances of the employment, and/or the risk of the breach was one so reasonably incidental to it, that it would be fair and just and reasonable to hold the employer vicariously liable for it.[25] This is, however, a question of fact to be answered on a case by case basis.[26] On this basis, for example, authorities in charge of children's homes have been held liable for sexual assaults perpetrated by employees thereof,[27] as has a nightclub where a bouncer (who had been trained to act aggressively) who had been hit by someone he ejected from the defendants' club, returned to his flat, found a knife and stabbed the claimant.[28] Similarly the employers of a policeman were held vicariously liable where he assaulted someone while off duty having told the victim that he was a police officer.[29] Perhaps even more controversially,

---

25 *Majrowski v. Guy's and St Thomas's NHS Trust*, [2005] Q.B. 848.

26 *Dubai Aluminium Co Ltd v. Salaam* [2003] 2 A.C. 366.

27 *Lister v. Helsey Hall Ltd* [2002] 1 A.C. 215, *Barnard v. Attorney General of Jamaica* [2005] I.R.K.R. para 23 and *Bazley v. Curry* [1999] 174 D.L.R. 4th. A less expansive approach to this question is perhaps manifest in the decision in *Godden v. Kent and Medway Strategic Health Authority* [2004] E.W.H.C. 1629 (Queen's Bench, July 8, 2004).

28 *Mattis v. Pollock* [2003] 1 W.L.R. 2158.

29 *Weir v. Chief Constable of Merseyside Police* [2003] I.C.R. 708.

on this basis the Privy Council found a security company vicariously liable for the action of one of its employees in shooting dead (from two paces) a man who was trying to gain entry to a football stadium.[30] On the other hand, vicarious liability has not been found, for example, where a policeman who offered to escort an inebriated female to a police station actually took her to his house and raped her as she slept,[31] or where a policeman while off duty simply and randomly shot someone with his service revolver.[32]

The approach of the Irish courts on this issue is somewhat uncertain. In the Northern Irish case *McCready v. Securicor*,[33] the plaintiff and a colleague were playing with large trolleys. The colleague pushed the plaintiff, who was on top of such a trolley, into a vault and then, as a prank, tried to slam the vault door shut on the plaintiff. Unhappily, in doing so, he seriously injured the plaintiff's hand. The plaintiff sued the company claiming that the colleague was negligent in his action and that the company was vicariously liable for this negligence. The court of appeal rejected this argument saying that the negligence did not arise in the course of the man's employment. Equally this is an obvious case with an obvious result.

Far less clear cut is the scenario that arose in *Delahunty v. South Eastern Health Board*.[34] Here, a young boy who had visited (but was not resident in) an industrial school managed by the defendants was sexually assaulted by a housemaster working within the school. The defendants were deemed *not* to be vicariously liable for the actions of the housemaster on the basis that there was not a sufficient connection between the functions of the housemaster in question and the assault on the plaintiff for it to be regarded as within the scope of his employment.[35] This approach is, however, arguably at variance with much of the English case-law in the area where an expansive approach has been taken (albeit on a case by case basis) to the question of whether and when it can be said that a person who commits a crime does so in the course of his or her employment. It is perhaps significant that in *L O'K v. LH and Others*[36] (a case whose appeal to the Supreme Court is being heard at the time of writing) Mr Justice de Valera adopted the approach taken in *Delahunty v. South Eastern Health Board*, but also seemed implicitly to endorse the view taken by the English Courts in *Lister v. Helsey Hall Ltd.*

The question of whether there is a sufficiently close connection between the action and the employment to deem that act to be done "in the course of employment" is a question of fact in each case, but it has been argued that a

---

30 *Brown v. Robinson* [2004] U.K.P.C. 56 (December 14, 2004).

31 *N v. Chief Constable of Merseyside Police* [2006] E.W.H.C. 3041.

32 *AG of British Virgin Islands v. Hartwell* [2004] 1 W.L.R. 1273.

33 [1991] N.I. 229.

34 [2003] 4 I.R. 361.

35 For the Canadian position on this see *Bazley v. Curry* (1999) 174 D.L.R. (4th) 45 and *Jacobi v. Griffiths* (1999) 174 D.L.R. (4th) 71.

36 [2006] IEHC 13.

surgeon who performs an operation outside the scope of his known experience is not acting in the course of employment. It is unlikely, however, that the courts would accept this argument. Similarly, *in the course of employment* is not restricted to the provision of medical treatment. In one case, for example, a hospital was held liable when owing to their negligence, a patient fell out of bed. Moreover, it is quite clear that a hospital can be vicariously liable in cases where an employee suffers harm by way of stress or bullying[37].

Moynihan v. Moynihan[38]

The *Moynihan* case should be briefly mentioned as an instance (albeit, it is submitted, a short lived one) where the concept of vicarious liability was widely and somewhat randomly extended. It may be taken that the reason for such extension was based on policy and on a desire that the injuries of an infant plaintiff be met, in financial terms, by the relevant insurance company. Nonetheless, on a principled level, it does appear to create the possibility of far greater vicarious liability within Ireland.

The facts are simple. The infant plaintiff went, along with her parents, to her paternal grandmother's house for tea one day. After the meal, the plaintiff's father left the house and the plaintiff's mother went from the breakfast room where the plaintiff was to the kitchen and started to wash the dishes. The plaintiff's grandmother started to dry the dishes. The plaintiff's aunt made a pot of tea. She then put a brightly coloured tea cosy in the pot and brought it into the breakfast room. The telephone rang and she rushed to answer it. At this point then, the plaintiff was left in the breakfast room alone with a full teapot clothed in a bright tea cosy. She covered herself in boiling hot tea and was seriously injured.

For insurance purposes the idea was to sue the grandmother for negligence. The court held that in fact the grandmother was vicariously liable for the negligence of her adult daughter (the plaintiffs aunt) who should not have left the child and teapot alone together. The argument against this of course is that the aunt was not employed by the grandmother. The court however, reverted to what was essentially a control test and said that as the person in control of the situation of hospitality being provided in her own home, the grandmother was vicariously liable for the negligence of the aunt in the performance of an unrewarded service provided in the course of the provision of such hospitality. The court was helped in its conclusions in this regard by the fact that the grandmother had no servant and hence the household tasks were delegated to both her adult daughters. Moreover, it characterised the relationship between aunt and grandmother in this case not as a mother/daughter relationship but as one between a head of a household and someone to whom she had delegated responsibility.

---

37 *Green v. DB Group Services (UK) Limited* [2006] E.W.H.C. 1898 and *Clark v. Chief Constable of Essex Police* [2006] E.W.H.C. 2290.

38 [1975] I.R. 192.

If this case was taken as defining the proper ambit of vicarious liability in Irish law, then clearly the ramifications are enormous for hospitals. On this basis, a hospital would be vicariously liable for anyone who provides a service within the hospital, which otherwise the hospital would have to provide. In other words, it would be vicariously liable for anyone who worked within its four walls.

There are however, several arguments against this conclusion. First, the more recent case of *Duffy v. Rooney and Dunne's Stores*,[39] seemed to downplay the total impact of *Moynihan*. In this case, a young girl was seriously burnt in her grandfather's house when her coat caught fire after the fireguard had been removed from the fire by the plaintiff's aunt. The High Court distinguished *Moynihan* saying that not only must the person providing the hospitality be in control of the situation, but also the doer of the act must be in *de facto* service of the person providing hospitality. Secondly, it is suggested that a distinction may be made between the banal kind of service provided by the aunt for the grandmother and the service provided by a member of the hospital staff and that the *Moynihan* case is easily distinguished on this basis. Neither of these arguments adequately explain why the *Moynihan* logic could not apply to the hospital situation. Far more significant, however, is the fact that *Moynihan* was arguably a very bad decision, which completely altered the traditional rules n respect of vicarious liability without offering any good reason why it did so. The guiding factor behind *Moynihan* was policy and it could easily be seen as bad policy to allow a similarly wide understanding of vicarious liability to apply in the hospital context.

Delay in proceedings and vicarious liability

It is well known that in recent times and under the influence of ECHR developments, the Irish courts have expressed concern with the notion of delays in prosecuting cases and have exercised their jurisdiction to strike out proceedings where excessive delay gives rise to a risk of prejudice. It is thus notable that in *O'Dwyer v. McDonnell*,[40] Quirke J. in the High Court made the point that such risk of prejudice was exacerbated where the claim was one for vicarious liability.

Direct Liability of Hospitals

Vicarious liability is, as has been mentioned, the more traditional basis for imposing liability on a hospital for negligence which occurs within it. A more recent and more far reaching development, however, is the increasingly frequent judicial acceptance of the possibility that in fact a hospital might owe a direct and non-delegable duty to its patients. By definition, this refers to situations

[39] Unreported, High Court, June 23, 1997.
[40] [2006] IEHC 281.

where it is the hospital itself which is deemed to be in breach of *its* duty to the patient rather than incurring liability for the fact that its employees are in breach of *their* duties. Moreover, and somewhat obviously, this ties in with the earlier reference to the statutory obligations of hospitals under health and safety legislation.

Organisational/systemic negligence

The first context in which a hospital might incur direct liability arising out of injuries to a patient is fairly uncontroversial namely where, owing to what may be termed direct systemic or organisational negligence on the part of the hospital, the plaintiff suffers damage. This may exist, for example,

- Where the tort of an individual doctor has been sanctioned by the hospital authority.
- Where the hospital has negligently appointed an incompetent private contractor.
- Where it has employed an inadequate quantity of staff or too many inexperienced staff (according to caselaw there must be a level of staff, which having regard to the current professional standards is *reasonably sufficient for the foreseeable requirements of the* patient). Thus in one Irish case, *Kelly v. Board of Governors of St Lawrence's Hospital*,[41] a patient who was known to suffer from epilepsy and from violent seizures and who had been taken off his medicine, injured himself by throwing himself out of a toilet window. He had been allowed to go to the toilet unaccompanied, and it was claimed that in this respect and given his history, the hospital was negligent. The court agreed, finding the hospital negligent in not providing adequate staff to accompany the man to the toilet.
- Organisational negligence may also occur where the hospital has failed to provide against errors in the administration of drugs.
- Where it permits an inexperienced doctor to administer anaesthetics without proper supervision.
- Where the hospital has directly interfered with the manner in which the work was being performed and in so doing has caused damage.
- Where the hospital, having discovered that the work in question was being performed negligently, condones such negligence or fails to inform the patient thereof and to take remedial action. Thus in *Byrne v. Ryan*[42] Kelly J. imposed liability on the hospital in question (in circumstances where there had been a failed sterilisation of the plaintiff) not merely because of its vicarious liability in respect of the consultant who had carried out the procedure, but also because of the negligence

---

[41] [1989] I.L.R.M. 437.

[42] [2007] IEHC 207.

of the hospital in failing to inform the plaintiff (when she subsequently became pregnant with her second last child) that the operation had been a failure and in failing to organise a further tubal ligation. In such circumstances it appears that the plaintiff was under the impression (when she was informed that she was pregnant with her second last child) that she must have been pregnant *at the date of the sterilisation* and thus that the operation had been a success – a misapprehension of which she only became aware when she became pregnant with her final child.

- Where there is an absence of hospital policy in respect of best practice in a particular situation. Thus in *Kavanagh v. Murphy*[43] twins had been born prematurely at Wexford General Hospital and only one had been transferred to an acknowledged centre of excellence for neonates at Waterford General Hospital. The other remained in Wexford, was apparently poorly cared for and developed a condition of cerebral palsy. O'Donovan J. felt that there should have been a policy that all babies in the situation of these twins should have been transferred to Waterford and that the absence of such a policy was the part cause of the plaintiff's injuries, in that it permitted the first named defendant (the plaintiff's mother's GP) to make decisions which, otherwise he would not have been able to make.
- Furthermore, it would seem that a hospital might be negligent if it does not provide its staff with up to the minute training. Thus in the 1994 case *Firth v. South Eastern Health Board,*[44] the defendant was held liable for the fact that a ward attendant injured her back when assisting a staff nurse to lift an eleven stone patient. The lift techniques which were used in the case, namely the drag lift and the cradle lift had been banned by the *Royal College of Nursing* since 1981 and 1987 respectively. The court imposed liability on the defendant hospital on the grounds that it was negligent in not having *all* staff retrained in the latest developments in lifts. Barr J. commented that;

  > "A Health Authority has a clear duty to keep itself abreast of developments in nursing practices so as to ensure that procedures adopted in hospitals under their control do not involve the nursing staff in risks of injury which could and should be avoided".

The key factor in the above cases is that the hospital is itself directly in breach of a duty to the plaintiff. Thus, in *Vancouver General Hospital v. McDaniel,*[45] the plaintiff went into a hospital for the treatment of infectious diseases. She went in for the treatment of diphtheria, and when in the hospital, she managed

---

[43] Unreported, High Court, November 28, 2003.

[44] Unreported, High Court, July 27, 1994.

[45] (1934) 152 L.T. 56.

to contract smallpox. She claimed that the defendants were negligent in the fact that they had placed her near smallpox sufferers and had allowed her to be treated by nurses who were also treating smallpox patients. The court noted that the plaintiff was not alleging negligence against any member of hospital staff but rather against the hospital itself. Similarly, in *Bull v. Devon Area Health Authority*,[46] the health authority was held liable for the fact that the hospital emergency communication system had broken down thus hindering the presence of an expert at an obstetric emergency. On the other hand, the damage must be the fault of lack of organisation within the health authority itself. The fact that a hospital is lacking in necessary resources will not establish liability if it is a general lack of such resources which causes this. Again, in Britain the extensive nature of the NHS means that this will frequently be a question as to the full obligations of the Health Secretary in this regard.

A primary non-delegable duty of care?

As has been mentioned, the above are not hugely controversial cases. After all, they concern cases where the hospital has been at fault as regards its system and is held liable accordingly. Indeed these are precisely the type of situations that would now be covered by the safety & health legislation. Far more controversial is the second category where a hospital may attract direct liability, namely where the hospital is deemed to have a duty to its patients, and, whereas it is permitted to transfer the *performance* of that duty to an independent contractor, it is not permitted to transfer responsibility for such performance and hence liability in the event of negligence causing harm. In other words, if the independent contractor is negligent, it is the *hospital* whose duty is still held to be breached, nor is it a defence for the hospital to claim that it transferred the performance of the duty to another party. Equally there will necessarily be a link between these two categories of direct duty, in that if an independent contractor *does* act negligently, then an obvious response on the part of the injured party is that the appointment by the hospital of a contractor capable of such negligence is evidence of a systemic failure on the part of the hospital.

In the UK it would seem that there are two bases for a patient claiming that, in law, the hospital owes him or her a primary and non-delegable duty of care. The first is of limited application here. In the UK, under the National Health Service Act 1977, it appears that a health authority is under a statutory duty to treat patients which involves a degree of responsibility for the manner in which the doctors whom they appoint carry out such treatment. In fact, the NHS policy of accepting responsibility for all negligent NHS treatment in NHS hospitals irrespective of whether it was caused by a staff doctor or a consultant has rather rendered the legal controversy over when a hospital may be sued redundant.

The second justification for deeming hospitals to have a non-delegable duty of care to patients, and one which continues to be relevant in Ireland first came

---

[46] [1993] 4 Med. L.R. 117, C.A.

from Lord Denning in the *Cassidy* case, to which reference has already been made. Lord Denning was clearly very keen to find liability in this case and did not feel that a distinction should be made between contracts for service and contracts *of* service. His point was that the hospital authorities had accepted this plaintiff as a patient for treatment, and as such had a duty to treat him with reasonable care. The plaintiff had no say in the selection of the staff and did not know the terms on which they were employed. He did, however, know that he was being treated in the hospital by persons who were appointed by the hospital. Accordingly, the hospital authorities were answerable for the way in which he was treated and in as much as the hospital authorities did not treat the patient with due care and skill, the hospital itself was in breach of their duty to him. Again, this is akin to, but not the same as the traditional and accepted argument that hospitals are liable for the appointment of incompetent staff. Essentially, Lord Denning's argument comes down to the proposition that by virtue of the fact that the hospital appointed this staff, on whatever basis, it is responsible for their performance.

Lord Denning repeated this view in several cases, but its precise authority is difficult to gauge, not least because of the fact that in all the cases where he found a hospital liable on the non-delegable duty of care view, the majority of the court in which he was speaking did so on the basis that the negligent operatives were employees for whom the hospital was vicariously liable.

Nonetheless the proposition has remained alive and has been considered in subsequent cases. Thus in *Wilsher v. Essex AHA*[47] - a case in which a junior doctor mistakenly inserted a catheter into a vein to measure arterial blood levels - Mustill L.J. suggested that the defendant health authority might be *directly liable* for any adverse consequences of the episode, saying:

> "For example it might have been said that the defendants owed a duty to ensure that the special baby care unit functioned according to the standard reasonably expected of such a unit".

Similarly in the same case, Browne Wilkinson L.J. suggested that:

> "...a health authority which so conducts its hospital that it fails to provide doctors of sufficient skill and experience to give the treatment offered at the hospital may be directly liable in negligence to the patient".

A similar conclusion was reached by the Court of Appeal in *Bull v. Devon Health Authority*[48] (duty of hospital to woman admitted in labour to provide a reasonable standard of obstetric and paediatric care) and in *X (minors) v. Bedfordshire CC*[49]

---

47 [1987] 1 Q.B. 730.

48 [1993] 4 Med. L.R. 117.

49 [1995] 2 A.C. 633.

(hospital under direct duty of care to those admitted to its premises irrespective of whether or not the member of staff responsible for harm is himself under a duty to the patient). Equally these cases and others like them, whereas they contain grand statements of principle about primary duties of care all contain facts which, it is submitted, involve *systemic* failures on the part of the hospital, and where the harm caused was the result of such systemic failures.[50] Thus the typical approach is to say that the hospital:

> "…had a duty to bring about for [the claimant] the effective provision of services, either by providing them themselves or causing others to effect this on her behalf."[51]

Finally, in *X (minors) v. Bedfordshire County Council*,[52] Lord Browne Wilkinson said that a hospital was under a direct duty of care to those admitted as patients to the hospital and that the hospital would be liable for such a breach of duty, even where the doctor himself would be liable for a breach of *his* duty. The impact of this was limited, however, by the fact that the judge expressly declined to give a view as to the extent of the duty owed. Accordingly, the extent in the UK to which such a direct duty may be owed by virtue of judicial interpretation of hospital procedure is unclear, but as has been mentioned, the overall responsibility accepted by the NHS means that the issue has, for practical purposes, been rendered otiose.

Since this time, it is arguable that the English courts have tended away from the conclusion that hospitals and health boards owe a duty of care to patients simply by virtue of the fact that activity occurs in the broadest of senses, under their auspices. Thus for example in the recent case *D v. East Berkshire Community Health NHS Trust & Others*,[53] the House of Lords invoked considerations of policy as a justification for not imposing liability on healthcare authorities for alleged psychiatric harm suffered by parents as a result of unfounded allegations that they had abused their children. Admittedly the policy considerations in this case focused on the need to ensure that allegations of abuse could be investigated in a full manner without being chilled by a fear of litigation – in other words they related to the duty of care which was alleged to be owed in the case and not to the question of who owed the duty. Nonetheless, it is submitted that an inference may be drawn from the conclusions in this case that public policy in this area is in favour of reducing incidences of litigation against healthcare authorities. Similarly in *Godden v. Kent & Medway Strategic Health Authority*,[54] the High Court while it refused to strike out a claim against a local authority for *vicarious liability* arising out of the actions of a GP who (it was alleged) had

---

[50] See also *Robertson v. Nottingham Health Authority* [1997] 8 Med. L.R. 1.

[51] *M v. Calderdale & Kirklees Health Authority* [1998] Lloyd's Med. Rep. 157.

[52] [1995] 3 W.L.R. 152.

[53] [2005] 2 A.C. 373.

[54] [2004] E.W.H.C. 1629.

indecently assaulted 31 former patients, did strike out a claim that the authority in question owed a direct duty to patients in respect of the actions of GPs which had been breached in this case. And a similar approach is manifest in the context of the liability of *education* authorities in England in the decision of the Court of Appeal in *Carty v. Croydon London Borough Council.*[55]

An important and most comprehensive analysis of this issue was given by Bell J. in the High Court in *A v. Ministry of Defence.*[56] The facts of the case are somewhat complicated, but the essential question that was asked was whether the United Kingdom Ministry for defence owed a direct duty (or indeed incurred vicarious liability) in respect of a situation where a British service man or woman stationed in Germany (or his or her dependants) had been injured in a designated German provider hospital owing to the negligence of staff there. In other words, in such a situation, was it necessary to take an action in Germany against the hospital, or would the MOD be liable as the body who had designated the German hospital as a care provider for *its* employees and their dependents. The plaintiffs had argued that the nature of the duty owed by the MOD was non-delegable and hence whether as a result of vicarious liability or as a result of a primary duty, the MOD was liable to the plaintiff (who had been injured in such a hospital).

Bell J. considered the older English cases dealing with the vicarious liability of hospitals for the negligence of persons working therein. He concluded that if the approach of Lord Greene in *Gold v. Essex County Council* was followed then:

> "...the special relationship between a hospital authority and its patient, leaves the hospital with a personal non-delegable duty to use reasonable care and skill in the treatment (including advice) of the patient, not simply to provide an appropriate regime of care".

Equally he noted that Lord Greene's approach in this regard had not found universal favour in later cases, not least because a just result in many such cases could generally be reached by the less drastic step of imposing liability on hospitals on a vicarious basis. As far as Bell J. was concerned, the net result of the cases mentioned above was that a primary non-delegable duty of care on the part of hospitals or health boards *may* arise depending on the facts of the case and specifically on whether the hospital *by itself* accepted the patient for treatment or advice. In other words, the pivotal question is the same as (under the integrated or organisational test) applies in assessing whether vicarious liability is deemed to arise, namely did the hospital accept a patient for the purposes of the provision of care, or did the independent contractor (the consultant acting in

[55] [2005] E.W.C.A. Civ. 19 (January 27, 2005).
[56] [2003] P.I.Q.R. 607 (April 16, 2003).

his private capacity) accept the patient and simply use the hospital as a setting in which he could engage in such private treatment?

Australian courts have been rather more ready to accept the possibility of a hospital owing a direct duty of care to patients. There is, however, only one case in which the issue had to be decided - *Ellis v. Wallsend District Hospital,*[57] and in this case the New South Wales Court was divided on the issue. Here the patient was treated by a doctor who was deemed an *honorary medical officer* with privileges at the hospital. The patient approached the doctor herself, and the doctor arranged for her admission to the hospital. He also performed the surgery. Owing to his negligence, the patient was injured. The dissenting judge took the view that the honorary medical officer was part of the hospital organisation. As he put it,

> "What he did in his own room was his affair. But when he came into the hospital, he was part of the hospital. When working on its premises he was part of its integrated medical team."

On this basis, the judge concluded that the hospital was both vicariously and directly liable for *all* its staff, honorary or otherwise. Thus Kirby P. contended that:

> "Even if no vicarious liability could be established there is a new and settled basis for the liability of the hospital. It is its direct responsibility pursuant to a non-delegable duty in tort which it owes its patient."

The majority judges did not go this far. For them, the crucial distinction was between a hospital which exists merely as a provider of a facility used by a doctor in the course of a private arrangement with a patient and a hospital which exists as a place where those in need of treatment go to receive such treatment. In the former case, (which applied in the instant case), where what is essentially a private agreement is in operation, a hospital will not have a non-delegable duty of care to that patient. In the latter case, the hospital, by virtue of accepting the patient, undertakes a non-delegable duty of care to that patient to provide him or her with all necessary treatment and to ensure that that treatment is given with proper care.

The link between this logic and the argument of Lord Denning in the *Cassidy* case is one to which reference has already been made, i.e. that the question whether a hospital owes a duty to a patient appears to turn on the patients understanding of what the hospital is and possibly on the precise nature of the consultant's relationship with that hospital. Is it a place where s/he goes to receive treatment, or is it merely a provider of a bed where s/he can stay while his or her personal physician heals him? Is s/he paying both the hospital and

---

[57] (1989) 17 N.S.W.L.R. 553.

the doctor (and any other relevant staff) or merely the hospital? Moreover, it seems to flow logically from the reasoning in both *Ellis* and *Cassidy* that a hospital can be both at the same time, depending on the subjective view of the patient and the nature of his relationship with his consultant. Thus in the case of an Irish consultant who works eleven three hour sessions within a hospital of which nine are public and two are private, the Hospital on this logic would have a non-delegable duty of care for the nine sessions in which he or she works for his or her public patients but not for the two sessions spent on private patients. (The significance of this may be somewhat tempered in Ireland by reason of the fact that the state will pay the medical insurance of any doctor in respect of his or her public consultancy work).

Primary non-delegable duties in Ireland

There are a number of different contexts in which it has been suggested that Irish law might impose primary and non-delegable duties of care – for example in the context of employers' liability or where ultra-hazardous substances or activities are involved. Some relatively recent judicial consideration of the issue was given by the High Court in *Delahunty v. SE Health Board,*[58] a case in which the court held that the defendant (who owned an industrial school) did not owe a non-delegable duty of care to a visitor to the school in respect of the wrongful actions of one of its employees. Judge O'Higgins held that because of the fact that the plaintiff was a visitor to the school rather than a resident there, there was an insufficient protective relationship between the parties for a non-delegable duty of care to arise. Equally he implicitly left open the possibility that wherever a defendant had such control over the life of a plaintiff that a "protective" relationship could be deemed to exist, then a primary and non-delegable duty of care might arise. On the other hand, the approach of Kelly J. in *Byrne v. Ryan* appears considerably more supportive of the view that hospitals may have direct (and non-delegable) responsibility for everything occurring within the organisation

If however this *was* the rule, then when could hospitals and health boards be sued? Quite apart from vicarious liability, it would mean that a hospital would be directly liable for all work carried on within its walls which affects patients who regard the hospital as a place where they have come *and have been accepted* to receive medical treatment; in other words, all public health care, but the hospital will *not* be liable where a consultant is hired by a private patient who views the hospital merely as a venue where the consultant can do his or her work. On the other hand, if during the course of such private treatment another member of hospital staff, for example a nurse, is negligent, then we revert to the terminology of vicarious liability and the hospital will again be liable (although it may well be, depending on the precise facts of the case, that in such circumstances, the nurse would attract vicarious liability not for the

[58] [2003] 4 I.R. 361.

hospital but for the private consultant if she was working *for him or her* and in the course of his or her private practice.

Conclusion

As was mentioned at the beginning, the question of suing hospitals and health boards is really of comparatively little practical significance. The only area in which vicarious liability does not attract to a hospital may be that of a private or visiting consultant and in such case he or she is required by law to have insurance and hence, will be a good target for litigation. Nonetheless, it is a feature of a great deal of medical negligence litigation that there is more than one defendant and that the hospital in question will be joined in any such litigation. Ultimately, the extent to which the law will allow this to continue may be answered most accurately by policy considerations.

CHAPTER 5

Expert Evidence in Medical Negligence Litigation

LIZ HEFFERNAN

INTRODUCTION

Expert evidence represents a departure from the general rule that witnesses must limit their testimony to facts within their personal knowledge or perception and are permitted neither to express opinions nor to draw inferences from the facts which form the basis of their testimony. The underlying premise is that the functions of drawing inferences from stated facts and reaching conclusions on material issues are the exclusive preserve of the finder of fact, whether judge or jury.[1] Nevertheless, common law courts have a long history of reaching out to other disciplines and admitting as means of proof the opinions of persons who are acknowledged experts in scientific, technical or other fields.[2] The formal justification for the admission of such opinion evidence is twofold: first, the disputed facts touch upon a matter beyond ordinary human experience and, second, the witness possesses specialised knowledge that will assist the finder of fact in resolving the dispute.[3] Such experts are drawn from all walks of life

---

1 *AG (Ruddy) v. Kenny* (1960) 94 I.L.T.R. 185 at 190. Opinion evidence has also been rejected as a species of hearsay. *Wright v. Doe d'Tatham* (1838) 5 C. & F. 670. It is admissible in a miscellany of situations in which the line between fact and opinion is sufficiently blurred that it is difficult to discern whether the witness is testifying as to the former or the latter. A ragbag of statutory provisions also permits the admission of opinion evidence in certain specific circumstances. *See generally* McGrath, *Evidence* (Thomson Round Hall, 2005), paras. 6.45-52; Howard, "Opinion and Expert Evidence" in Howard, ed., *Phipson on Evidence,* 15th ed. (Sweet & Maxwell, London, 2000), paras. 37.01-09.

2 On the law of expert evidence *see generally* McGrath, *op. cit.,* chap.6; Fennell, *Law of Evidence in Ireland,* 2nd ed., (LexisNexis, Dublin, 2003), chap.6; Healy, *Irish Laws of Evidence* (Thomson Round Hall, Dublin, 2004), chap.12; Kellher, "Expert Evidence in Ireland" (1996) 14 I.L.T.R. 42 and O'Flaherty, "The Expert Witness and the Courts" (1997) 3 M.L.J.I. 3; Heffernan, "Gauging the Reliability of Scientific Evidence in Tort" (2006) 6 J.S.I.J. 140.

3 *Folks v. Chadd* (1782) 3 Doug. K.B. 157 and *A.G.(Ruddy) v. Kenny* (1960) 94 I.L.T.R. 185.

and in the context of medical negligence actions include doctors, psychiatrists and actuaries.[4]

In recent years, expert evidence has flourished to the point where, paradoxically, it stands shoulder to shoulder with the rule against opinion evidence.[5] Nowhere is this phenomenon more prevalent than in medical negligence litigation where the ubiquity of the expert witness is matched by the influence he or she exerts over the resolution of the proceedings and the very culture of the courtroom. For its own part, medical negligence litigation, by virtue of its complexity and contestability, has become the paradigm for expert witness practice and the evidentiary testing ground for doctrinal and procedural challenges that impact on all manner of civil litigation. The law of expert evidence and the law of medical negligence, it seems, are inextricably intertwined.

Expert evidence may be a common, accepted feature of medical negligence litigation but the status and function of the expert witness is by no means straightforward. On the contrary, the law is beset with contradictions that explain underlying tensions in medical negligence practice. First, as noted, there is a discernible disconnect between the theory, which holds that expert evidence is exceptional, and the practice, which demonstrates that it is routine. A second source of tension is the contradiction between the independence of the expert witness, encapsulated in the legal tenet that he or she owes an overriding duty to the court, and the practical reality that the expert is retained by a party and, unlike an ordinary or lay witness, is generally remunerated for his or her services. Third, the need on the part of the judge for expert knowledge serves as the rationale for the admission of expert evidence yet, paradoxically, the law requires the judge to assess the probity of that evidence and, not infrequently, to decide which of two conflicting expert opinions is the more credible. Fourth, the relationship between the disciplines of law and medicine and the manner in which that relationship unfolds in the specific context of litigation has generated vibrant, contentious discourse. Fifth, whereas the four sources of tension noted above might apply to any legal proceeding involving a proffer of expert scientific evidence, there is an additional complicating factor common in proceedings for professional negligence in general and proceedings for medical negligence in particular. Invariably, the doctor who treated the plaintiff will be called to testify; indeed, typically, the plaintiff will have been treated by several doctors

---

4 These are some of the "experts" that appear on the non-exhaustive list contained in O.39, r.45(1) of the Rules of the Superior Courts.

5 As early as 1960, Mr. Justice Lavery observed: "This is the age of experts qualified to give opinions in every field of human knowledge – whether science, medical or other, in accountancy, finance, handwriting and technical matters in every aspect of manufacturing process and so on. I would certainly not wish to minimise the value of such evidence, but a sense of proportion should not be lost. There are innumerable incidents of everyday life upon which an ordinary person can express a useful opinion and one which ought to be admitted." *AG (Ruddy) v. Kenny* (1960) 94 I.L.T.R. 185 at 189.

during the material time-period and the court will be entitled to hear evidence from each of them.[6] This type of witness will generally straddle the law's divide between a fact or occurrence witness, on the one hand, and an expert witness, on the other. The witness will certainly be questioned about the facts relating to the plaintiff's medical treatment; but he or she may also be required to testify as to his or her opinion on the medical complaint at issue. Sixth, the adversarial nature of our trial process and the influence it may exert on the independence of expert scientific opinion is a matter of ongoing controversy.

Given these conundra, and the significant cost associated with expert evidence, it is not surprising that the heightened profile of the expert witness has been the subject of controversy. In other common law jurisdictions, critics have long complained that experts dominate trials, mislead judges and juries, exacerbate contention between parties, and needlessly increase the cost of litigation.[7] Whether these criticisms resonate here in Ireland is an open question but it is clear that the role of the expert witness, a veritable mainstay of medical negligence litigation, is under ever closer scrutiny.

Admissibility

Expert evidence no less than any other form of evidence must cross the threshold of admissibility. Consistent with the general rule against opinion evidence, the law requires that a party must justify recourse to expert evidence by demonstrating a genuine need on the part of the court for expert knowledge in relation to a matter at issue. In medical negligence litigation, this basic need is invariably conceded but disputes may arise regarding the nature and extent of the expert evidence required in a particular case.[8]

The onus on a party to demonstrate that expert evidence is essential to the proper resolution of the proceedings is the embodiment of the evidentiary touchstone of relevance. Before allowing a witness to testify or admitting testimony in documentary form, a court must be satisfied that the evidence is

---

6 See *H v. St. Vincent's Hospital,* unreported, High Court, December 20, 2006, in which Hanna J. criticised the defendant's failure to call a doctor whose note was disputed.

7 See e.g. Friedman, "Expert Testimony, Its Abuse and Reformation" (1910) 19 Yale L.J. 247 at p.247 ("Almost from the beginning of the use of expert testimony in our courts a conflict has been waged over its real probative value in settling vexed and close questions of fact."); Perrin, "Expert Witnesses: Back to the Future" (1995) 29 U. Richmond L. Rev. 1389 at 1389 ("Expert witnesses are at once detested and treasured. … Experts are seen as mercenaries, prostitutes, or hired guns, witnesses devoid of principle who sell their opinions to the highest bidder. Experts are not impartial professionals who explain difficult concepts to the trier of fact. Rather, experts become advocates for the side who hired them.")

8 If one party objects to another party adducing expert evidence, the latter must demonstrate that it is a necessity and, independent of the parties, the trial judge must be satisfied that the proffered opinion relates to a subject calling for expertise.

relevant to a matter at issue in the case. The requirement reflects the policy concern that the finder of fact (a judge in proceedings for medical negligence) should not be unduly influenced by any witness. As Lord President Cooper famously quipped in *Davie v. Edinburgh Magistrates:* "the parties have invoked the decision of a judicial tribunal and not an oracular pronouncement by an expert."[9] The danger that the court will be bamboozled by the high-sounding rhetoric of an esteemed expert is thought to be especially acute where the opinion relates to a scientific or medical matter.[10]

A second admissibility requirement relates to the status of the witness as an expert. Before admitting expert evidence, the court must be satisfied that the witness is suitably qualified in the field in question. The witness having been called and having taken the oath, the customary practice is for counsel to open examination-in-chief with a series of preliminary questions pertaining to the witness's qualifications and expertise.[11] Where a party challenges the credentials of another party's witness, the trial judge must determine whether the witness is qualified, by virtue of training or experience, to testify in relation to the disputed matter.

The term "expert witness" is broadly construed. Section 2 of the Civil Liability and Courts Act 2004 defines expert evidence as "evidence of fact or opinion given by a person who would not be competent to give such evidence unless he or she had a special skill or expertise." As Murphy J. explained in *Galvin v. Murray*:

> "In general terms, an expert may be defined as a person whose qualifications or expertise give an added authority to opinions or statements given or made by him within the area of his expertise."[12]

The law imposes no stock requirements in terms of qualifications or experience. In theory, the expert need neither have acquired a professional qualification nor undergone specialised education or training.[13] In practice, however, contemporary society places a premium on formal qualifications and the fact that a witness's expertise has been recognised by respected institutions or entities greatly enhances his standing as an expert.

---

9 [1953] S.C. 34 at 40. *See also AG (Ruddy) v. Kenny, loc. cit.*

10 *R v. Turner* [1975] Q.B. 834; *People (DPP) v. Keogh* [1992] I.L.R.M. 481. From a practical standpoint, irrelevant evidence, whether lay or expert, suffers the additional taint of being superfluous and a needless drain on the time and resources of the parties and the court.

11 Healy, *op. cit.,* p.361.

12 [2001] 1 I.R. 331.

13 *R v. Silverlock* [1894] 2 Q.B. 766 (solicitor qualified as a handwriting expert); *Southern Health Board v. CH* [1996] 1 I.R. 219, [1996] 2 I.L.R.M. 142 (senior social worker qualified to testify in relation to child sexual abuse); O'Flaherty, *op. cit.,* p.3: "[T]he admissibility of opinion evidence is not confined to those with university degrees or, indeed, expert qualifications."

Questions about the admissibility of expert evidence *per se* rarely arise in proceedings for medical negligence as opposed to other species of civil litigation and when they do they tend to be more sophisticated than the previous paragraphs would suggest. The need for some form of expert opinion (the first admissibility hurdle) is obvious and invariably conceded. But precisely what kind of expertise from within the broad and highly specialised field of medicine is required in a particular case? Similarly, having regard to the second admissibility hurdle, witnesses in medical negligence litigation are invariably "experts" in the sense that they tend to be highly qualified in terms of educational and professional achievement. The question may not be whether the witness is qualified in his or her stated medical field but rather whether his or her expertise relates directly to the issue or issues raised in the litigation. A person may be highly qualified and experienced in a particular branch of the medical profession but lack the necessary degree of specialisation to testify on the matter at issue; conversely, his or her spcialty may be too narrow to support an alternative position, standing alone. The matter can be particularly complicated in cases involving technical medical issues because the limits of the witness's expertise may emerge only through the *denouement* of the proceedings. For lawyers, the selection of an expert is pivotal and should involve careful consideration of the proficiency of the witness in the particular context of the litigation. A guiding principle is to instruct an expert of the same specialty as the doctor whose treatment is at issue in the proceedings.[14] It is customary to instruct more than one expert, depending upon the need for a range of specialties or for independent opinions in relation to different aspects of negligence (e.g. breach of duty as opposed to causation).[15] A balance must be struck, however; too many experts or too great an emphasis on specialisation may counterproductively complicate the issues and will certainly increase the length and cost of the proceedings.

The Duties of the Expert Witness

In *The Ikarian Reefer*, Cresswell J. provided a classic statement of the duties and responsibilities of an expert witness in civil litigation:

"1. Expert evidence presented to the Court should be, and should be seen to be, the independent product of the expert uninfluenced as to form or content by the exigencies of litigation (*Whitehouse v. Jordan* [1981] 1 W.L.R. 246 at p.256, *per* Lord Wilberforce).

2. An expert witness should provide independent assistance to the Court by way of objective unbiased opinion in relation to matters within his expertise (*see Polivitte Ltd v. Commercial Union Assurance Co. Plc.* [1987] 1 Lloyd's Rep. 379 at p.386 *per* Mr. Justice Garland and *Re J.*

[14] See Chap.6, *infra*.

[15] *Id.*

[1990] F.C.R. 193 *per* Mr. Justice Cazalet). An expert witness in the High Court should never assume the role of an advocate.
3. An expert witness should state the facts or assumption upon which his opinion is based. He should not omit to consider material facts which could detract from his concluded opinion (*Re J. sup.*).
4. An expert witness should make it clear when a particular question or issue falls outside his expertise.
5. If an expert's opinion is not properly researched because he considers that insufficient data is available, then this must be stated with an indication that the opinion is no more than a provisional one (*Re J. sup.*). In cases where an expert witness who has prepared a report could not assert that the report contained the truth, the whole truth and nothing but the truth without some qualification, that qualification should be stated in the report (*Derby & co. and Others v. Weldon and Others, The Times*, November 9, 1990 *per* Lord Justice Staughton).
6. If, after exchange of reports, an expert witness changes his view on a material matter having read the other side's expert's report or for any other reason, such change of view should be communicated (through legal representatives) to the other side without delay and when appropriate to the Court.
7. Where expert evidence refers to photographs, plans, calculations, analyses, measurements, survey reports or other similar documents, these must be provided to the opposite party at the same time as the exchange of reports (see 15.5 of the Guide to Commercial Court Practice)."[16]

Mr Justice O'Flaherty, speaking extra judicially, has echoed the sentiments of Cresswell J. in more informal terms:

> "What then are the essentials for the reception of expert testimony? What discipline should the expert bring to his particular expertise when he comes to give evidence? By what commandments must be abide?
>
> *First*: the person must be properly qualified in the field in which he says he is qualified. To put it colloquially: he must know his stuff or, if he cannot give an immediate answer, he should say so and point the way to where the answer is to be found. …
>
> *Second*: the expert should always be a minister or servant of justice rather than act as the hireling of one side or the other. If he can advance his side fairly and properly, well let it be so. If not he should say so. He, like the judge, must make a judgment too, in his case a personal subjective

[16] *National Justice Compania Naviera S.A. v. Prudential Assurance Co. Ltd (The Ikarian Reefer)* [1993] 2 Lloyd's Rep. 68 at 81-82.

> one, whether it is on the reliability of his experiments, the disposition of the experiments or whatever. …
>
> *Third*: he should have the confidence to discuss in advance of the trial with the lawyers on the other side of the case his findings, if asked. This most likely will benefit all at the subsequent exposition of the evidence in the course of the trial and may help to speed it up.
>
> *Fourth*: he should cultivate the gift of being able to explain his conclusions in terms that will be understood by lay people whether they are judges or jurors, or both. …
>
> *Fifth*: he should be meticulous in his record keeping. …
>
> *Sixth*: he should never take a chance in pretending to expertise that he has not got. If he does not know the answer to a question, he should say so, or if he needs time to check something or other no one will think less of him for asking for that opportunity.
>
> *Seventh*: he must always be patient and never lose his temper no matter how stupid or absurd the questions that he is asked may appear to him to be."[17]

Expert Support for Grounds to Pursue a Claim

In medical negligence proceedings, experts are typically enlisted at the very outset of the process before legal proceedings have been formally initiated.[18] As Barr J. explained in *Reidy v. National Maternity Hospital,* a plaintiff must have reasonable medical grounds to justify the commencement of a lawsuit:

> "[It] is irresponsible and an abuse of the process of the Court to lodge a professional medical negligence action against institutions such as hospitals and professional personnel without first ascertaining that there are reasonable grounds for so doing. Initiation and prosecution of an action in negligence on behalf of the plaintiff against the hospital necessarily requires appropriate expert evidence to support it."[19]

The need for "some credible evidence to support the plaintiff's case" was

---

[17] *Loc. cit.* It should be noted that just as the expert witness has duties, he also enjoys certain privileges and immunities in relation to his testimony. For example, an expert witness is immune from suit in respect of his oral testimony and any documents produced in the course of a hearing. *E. O'K. v. D.K.* [2001] 1 I.R. 636.

[18] For a comprehensive discussion of the commencement of personal injuries proceedings *see* Delany and McGrath, *Civil Procedure in the Superior Courts,* 2nd ed. (Thompson Round Hall, 2005), chap.25.

[19] Unreported, High Court, July 31, 1997. *See also Connolly v. Casey* [2001] 1 I.R. 345; *Sugg v. O'Keefe,* unreported, Supreme Court, October14, 2005; *Quinn v. Mid Western Health Board* [2005] 4 I.R. 1.

subsequently recognised by the Supreme Court in *Cooke v. Cronin*.[20] Denham J. stated:

> "To issue proceedings alleging professional negligence puts an individual in a situation where for professional or practice reasons to have the case proceed in open court may be perceived and feared to that professional as being detrimental to his professional reputation and practice. This fear should not be utilised by unprofessional conduct."[21]

This sentiment was echoed by Geoghegan J. in *Sugg v. O'Keefe* in relation to the dismissal of a medical negligence action:

> "This action would have been regarded by all courts as in fact an abuse of the process of the courts and at the very least as unsustainable once there was not some backup obtained in advance of a [motion to strike] from a medical expert that supported the plaintiff's claim."[22]

This reality turns virtually on its head the traditional premise in relation to the admissibility of expert evidence, namely, that an onus rests on the party tendering an expert witness to demonstrate the need for his or her testimony in the given case. Now the law not only concedes that need in proceedings for medical negligence but, in addition, requires the plaintiff to secure a medical report supporting his or her case before proceedings are instituted.[23] The force of judicial rhetoric on this point coupled with the two-year limitations period imposed by section 7 of the Civil Liability and Courts Act 2004 highlight the need for lawyers to act promptly in determining the issues calling for expert opinion, the number and kind of experts required, and the identity of potential experts whether located in Ireland or, more usually, abroad.

Expert Reports

In former times, the expert witness was a black swan, a rare bird treated with a degree of deference by judges and lawyers alike. Experts are now routine participants in litigation and their function has been woven into the adversarial fabric of the courtroom.[24] The procedures governing the presentation of expert opinion are designed to facilitate its admission and, at the same time, limit and control its role in legal proceedings. The basic principles of fairness and

---

20 Unreported, July 14, 1999 (*per* Lynch J.).

21 *Id.*

22 Unreported, October 14, 2005.

23 See Chap.6, *infra.*

24 *See generally* Ormrod, "Scientific Evidence in Court" [1968] Crim. L.R. 241; Kenny, "The Expert in Court" (1983) 99 L.Q.R. 197.

reciprocity that underpin the disclosure of evidence apply with particular force in relation to experts. Where one side presents expert evidence, the other side is entitled to respond by testing that evidence and by presenting its own expert opinion.

The formal presentation of expert evidence unfolds in two stages. Having been enlisted by a party to prospective legal proceedings, the expert will compile a written report; where the case subsequently goes to trial, the expert will generally be called to testify.

Although orality remains the guiding principle for ordinary witnesses, expert evidence is initially furnished in documentary form and, at least in civil proceedings, there is an emerging trend in the common law world in favour of admitting it in that guise at trial.[25] Expert reports are exchanged during discovery[26] and typically have an important bearing on settlement negotiations.[27] The law in this area has undergone considerable change in recent years with the introduction of a series of measures designed to expedite and streamline personal injuries litigation and reduce the length and cost of proceedings, for example by extending pre-trial disclosure and minimising the element of surprise at trial.[28] The evidentiary consequences include some diminution in the privilege parties traditionally enjoyed from disclosing their preparations for trial.[29]

SI 391 of 1998 governs the disclosure of expert reports in personal injuries actions including actions for medical negligence.[30] Its provisions were inserted into Order 39 of the Rules of the Superior Courts as rules 45 to 51.

Rule 46(1) provides:

> "The plaintiff in an action shall furnish to the other party or parties or their respective solicitors (as the case may be) a schedule listing all reports from expert witnesses intended to be called within one month of the service of the notice of trial in respect of the action or within such further time as may be agreed by the parties or permitted by the Court.
>
> Within seven days of receipt of the plaintiff's schedule, the defendant or any other party or parties shall furnish to the plaintiff or any other party

---

25 *See e.g.* s.19 of the Civil Liability and Courts Act 2004; Practice Direction of September 8, 1993; English Civil Procedure Rules, pt 35, and accompanying practice direction.

26 *See* Rules of the Superior Courts (No.6) (Disclosure of Reports and Statements) 1998 (S.I. No.391 of 1998 (adding a new pt VI to O.39)); Delany and McGrath, *op. cit.*, paras 25.44 - 25.79.

27 *Id.*, paras 25.36 - 25.43.

28 *See* Courts and Courts Officers Act 1995; S.I. No.391 of 1998; Civil Liability and Courts Act 2004. The Personal Injuries Assessment Board Act 2003 does not apply to medical negligence litigation.

29 On legal professional privilege *see generally* McGrath, *op. cit.*, chap.10; Healy, *op. cit.*, chap.13.II; Fennell, *op. cit.*, chap.8.

30 Rules of the Superior Courts (No.6) (Disclosure of Reports and Statements) 1998, S.I. No.391 of 1998.

or parties a schedule listing all reports from expert witnesses intended to be called. Within seven days of the receipt of the schedule of the defendant or other party or parties, the parties shall exchange copies of the reports listed in the relevant schedule."

The concept of an "expert report" is broadly defined for purposes of disclosure. Rule 45(1)(e) states:

> "'report' means a report or reports or statement from accountants, actuaries, architects, dentists, doctors, occupational therapists, psychologists, psychiatrists, scientists, or any other expert whatsoever intended to be called to give evidence in relation to an issue in an action and containing the substance of the evidence to be adduced and shall also include any maps, drawings, photographs, graphs, charts, calculations or other like matter referred to in any such report."[31]

A few points may be raised in relation to the scope of the rules.

Experts

The net is cast wide over the potential range of witnesses to whom the rules apply. In addition to the species of expert listed in rule 45(1)(e) (to whom the rules might be said to routinely apply), it extends to "any other expert whatsoever." Section 2 of the Civil Liability and Courts Act 2004 defines expert evidence as "evidence of fact or opinion given by a person who would not be competent to give such evidence unless he or she had a special skill or expertise." The wording of rule 45(1)(e) hints at a liberal conception of expertise embracing not only skills and experience traditionally recognised but also scientific or medical knowledge of a novel or unconventional kind.

On a literal reading, rule 45(1)(e) is also broad in so far as it applies to any intended witness who is an expert regardless of the nature of his or her intended evidence. For example, so read it covers a treating doctor who may be called primarily for his or her factual account of relevant events (and who may even be a named party to the proceedings). This reading is consistent with section 2 of the 2004 Act which refers to "evidence of fact or opinion." Nevertheless, the courts will not allow disclosure to take privilege hostage and thereby excessively inhibit the parties in their preparation for trial. For example, in *O'Sullivan v. Kieran,* O'Neill J. refused to order disclosure from the defendant doctor of

---

[31] It continues: "Any copy report (including a copy report in the form of a letter), copy statement or copy letter however made, recorded or retained from any such expert mentioned above intended to be called to give evidence in relation to an issue or action and containing the substance of the evidence to be adduced, the original of which has been concealed, destroyed, lost, mislaid or is not otherwise readily available, shall also be deemed to be a report for the purposes of this rule."

a letter he had written to his indemnifiers on the basis that disclosure would undermine the important confidence that existed in communications between the defendant and his lawyers and indemnifiers.[32]

The obligation to disclose is limited in the sense that it applies to any expert witness "intended to be called to give evidence in relation to an issue in the action." Where a party enlists the services of an expert in an exclusively advisory capacity and does not intend to call the expert to give evidence, his or her report is privileged from disclosure.[33] Care must be taken in relation to witnesses who provide expert advice to a party in the capacity of employee. In *Galvin v. Murray,* the Supreme Court held that the defendant County Council could not resist disclosing the reports of their expert employee engineers on the basis that the reports contained observations that an independent expert might not have provided and which the defendant did not wish to disclose. As Murphy J. explained:

> "[I]t seems to me that the two engineers are beyond doubt experts and, accordingly, if the second defendant is determined to call them as witnesses to give evidence of a technical nature included in the reports, that those documents would fall squarely within the disclosure rules. … The fact that an engineer is employed by one or other of the parties may affect his independence with a consequent reduction in the weight to be attached to his evidence but it could not deprive him of his status as an expert."[34]

Thus, the decision of the party to call the expert to give evidence triggers the application of the rules; assuming the expert is so called, his or her relationship with the party does not alter the obligation to disclose. Finally, it should be noted that the decision to call an expert to give evidence is not written in stone. In *Kincaid v. Aer Lingus Teoranta,* the Supreme Court held that, prior to exchanging reports, a party may change its mind with respect to calling a particular expert witness and withdraw his or her name from its schedule of witness reports.[35]

Expert reports

A second issue concerns the material that must be disclosed. The rule refers to a report or statement from the witness in relation to an issue in the action and containing "the substance of the evidence to be adduced." The intention, it seems, was to require the parties to disclose not just the expert's description of the relevant facts or circumstances but also the substance of the opinion which

---

32 Unreported, High Court, February 11, 2004.

33 *Galvin v. Murray* [2001] 1 I.R. 331 (expert employee); *Fyffes plc. v. DCC* [2005] 1 I.L.R.M. 357 (disclosure of advisory expert report to a third party).

34 [2001] 1 I.R. 331.

35 [2003] 2 I.R. 314.

constitutes the very justification for calling the expert to testify.[36] The depth and breadth of the obligation to disclose is underscored by the reference in rule 45(1)(e) to the need to include "any maps, drawings, photographs, graphs, charts, calculations or other like matter" to which the expert refers. It is further reinforced by section 45(3) of the Courts and Court Officers Act 1995 which lends the term "expert report" a broad construction.[37]

The meaning of the phrase "maps, drawings, photographs, graphs, charts, calculations or other like matters referred to in any such report" was considered in *Doherty v. North Western Health Board.* Following the exchange of expert reports, the defendant sought an order compelling the first third party to furnish certain documents which two expert medical witnesses had referred to in their respective reports. The documents included solicitor-client correspondence and the first third party resisted disclosure on the grounds that the documents were privileged. Finnegan P. rejected the defendant's submission that the documents came within the phrase "other like matter referred to in any such report."

> "The phrase 'other like matter referred to in any such report' must be construed *ejusdem generis* with the words preceding it. I am satisfied that the documents referred to by [the two expert witnesses] cannot be considered as a like matter to a map, drawing, photograph, graph, chart or calculation. There is accordingly no obligation to disclose the same or to exchange the same arising under Order 39 rule 46(1) the documents in question not coming within the definition of report."[38]

Again, this case serves as a reminder that the courts will give effect to the legislative intention to favour disclosure over privilege but only in so far as that intention is reflected in the rules.

The recent case of *Payne v. Shovlin*[39] has shed some additional light on the meaning of expert report for purposes of the obligation to disclose. The Supreme Court held that where an expert compiles two reports, a preliminary report and subsequently a final report, the first report is not necessarily exempt from disclosure. The party contended that it was not obliged to disclose the preliminary report because it did not contain the expert's final views or intended evidence in chief. Kearns J. stated:

> "The relevant test, it seems to me, is whether or not the 'substance' of the evidence to be given, or part of it, is contained in the first report even if the views in that first report are later altered or modified or even given subject to qualification in such first report."[40]

---

36 *Ollett v. Bristol Aerojet Ltd* [1979] 1 W.L.R. 1197 at 1197 (*per* Ackner J.).

37 Delany and McGrath, *op. cit.*, para.25.57.

38 Unreported, High Court, December 1, 2005.

39 [2006] 2 I.L.R.M. 1.

40 *Id.*, p.11.

Unfavourable information

There are divergent views as to whether the rules are designed solely to remove the element of surprise and therefore do not require a party to disclose information unfavourable to his or her case or whether they support disclosure *per se* and consequently extend to the bad as well as the good aspects of the expert's opinion. In *Galvin v. Murray,* Murphy J. took the former view: "Clearly, the disclosure rules are designed to forewarn other parties of expert evidence with which they may be confronted. The rules have no role to play in investigating strengths or weaknesses of an opponent's case."[41] This position was endorsed by Geoghegan J. in *Kincaid v. Aer Lingus Teoranta.*[42] Arguably it finds support in a literal, commonsense reading of the rules: on this reading, what is required to be disclosed is the substance of the evidence the expert *intends* to give in examination-in-chief and not any conceivable concession he or she might be forced to make on cross-examination.

The view that the rules are designed to support disclosure *per se* starts with the premise that a party decides to call an expert because he or she believes that, on balance, the expert's evidence will be more favourable than not; having made that decision, the party must live with it, and call the expert on the basis of all the evidence that he or she can give. Delany and McGrath find support for the latter interpretation elsewhere in the rules[43] and go on to observe:

> "Interpreted in this way, the disclosure rules serve to reinforce the duties and responsibilities owed by an expert to the court and can be viewed as, at least in part, an attempt to restore in some small measure the impartiality and independence of experts which was originally the hallmark and, indeed, to some extent, the justification for their evidence but which has become very much eroded in recent years. The knowledge that any report or statement by him has been disclosed should discourage attempts by an expert to tailor his evidence in court for the benefit of the party calling him, as he could well find himself being cross-examined on an inconsistent statement made by him in a previous report. …The practical effect is more likely to be that experts will simply become more careful in drafting their reports to omit anything that could be construed as damaging to the case of the party retaining them, reserving such comments for oral communication. …"[44]

---

41 [2001] 1 I.R. 331.

42 [2003] 2 I.R. 314.

43 Specifically, rule 50 which permits a party to apply for an order of exemption from disclosure in the interests of justice and which the authors argue would not be necessary if a party was obliged merely to disclose a "sanitised expert report." *Op. cit.,* para.25.63.

44 *Op. cit.,* para.25.64 (internal citations omitted).

In *Payne v. Shovlin,* Kearns J. quoted from the judgment Murphy J. in *Galvin v. Murray* (as above) and went on to observe:

> "No one could cavil or disagree with this proposition and it is common case between the parties before this court that the mischief of ambush and/or surprise is something to be avoided. However, the failure to produce an earlier report which contains a view different from that contained in the final report may produce exactly the kind of surprises about which Murphy J. and Geoghegan J. warned."[45]

Kearns J. rejected the suggestion that the objective of preventing surprises necessarily leads to a "will say" form of disclosure. Rather, the rules require "such production or disclosure of reports that will ensure that surprises do not occur, either in the course of examination-in-chief or in cross-examination of an expert witness." While this judgment may not set down a bright-line in relation to what must be disclosed for purposes of the rules, it goes further than previous cases in elucidating the amorphous phrase "the substance of the evidence to be adduced." More generally, it suggests a judicial leaning towards a more robust interpretation of a party's disclosure obligations.

Disclosure

Rule 46 set down a timetable for the exchange of expert reports and the names and addresses of all witnesses intended to be called.[46] It provides that within seven days of the receipt by the plaintiff of the schedule of the defendant or other party or parties, "the parties shall exchange copies of the reports in the relevant schedule."[47] In *Kincaid v. Aer Lingus Teoranta,* Geoghegan J. suggested that exchange should be contemporaneous so as to guard against mischief of abuse of the procedure.[48]

The obligation to disclose is a continuing one and applies to any additional expert reports or statements received by a party after the initial exchange. [49] Conversely, a party may withdraw any previously disclosed report by confirming that he or she no longer intends to call the expert as a witness.[50] The act of

---

45 [2006] 2 I.L.R.M. 1 at 12.

46 R.46. Service of expert reports may be effected by letter in writing enclosing the report and sent by ordinary pre-paid post.

47 R.46(1).

48 [2003] 2 I.R. 314. R.46(3) states "where a party or his or her solicitor certifies in writing that no report exists which requires to be exchanged pursuant to subrule 1, any other party shall, on the expiry of the time fixed, agreed or permitted (as the case may be) deliver any report within the meaning of the section to all other parties to the proceedings.

49 R.46(4).

50 R.46(6).

withdrawal is deemed to reactivate any privilege which originally existed in relation to the report.[51]

The rules provide that directions of the court may be sought in relation to any alleged default in compliance with the obligation to disclose.[52] The court may deal with an instance of non-compliance in a number of ways, such as adjourning the action to permit compliance or prohibiting the errant party from adducing the evidence in question.[53] A party may also apply to the court for an order that in the interests of justice a particular report or statement should not be disclosed.[54]

Expert Testimony

Where the case goes to trial, the expert may be called to testify by the party that enlisted his or her services and, whether or not so called, may be subject to cross-examination by any other party. The trend towards limiting the appearance of witnesses at trial is reflected in section 19 of the Civil Liability and Courts Act 2004 which provides that evidence as to any matter in a personal injuries action shall be given by affidavit where the court so directs.[55] The right to cross-examine the witness remains intact, however, with the practical consequence that expert evidence will likely be given by affidavit only in exceptional circumstances.

The desirability of admitting medical evidence in documentary form, thereby obviating the need for *viva voce* evidence, was reflected in a practice direction dated September 8, 1993 some five years prior to the adoption of S.I. No. 391 of 1998. It urges counsel to consider whether the attendance of medical experts at trial is necessary and, where appropriate, to request that the court admit expert reports in evidence without recourse to oral testimony.[56] The practice direction also provides that where medical experts take the stand, their reports should be made available to the court, admitted in evidence, and form the basis for the examination of the witness.[57] As regards oral testimony, given the adversarial nature of the trial process, the testifying expert can anticipate a tough grilling from cross-examining counsel in relation to his or her qualifications, expertise and substantive conclusions, together with critical rebuttal evidence from the experts retained by the other parties.

---

51 *Id.*

52 R.47.

53 R.48.

54 R.50.

55 Subs.(1).

56 On the dangers of judicial reliance on documentary expert evidence without the benefit of expert oral testimony, *see Curran v. Finn,* unreported, Supreme Court, May 20, 1999.

57 Delany and McGrath, *op. cit.,* para.25.86.

The Expert's Opinion

As we have seen, the expert witness enjoys a somewhat exalted status in the trial process by virtue of his or her role in assisting the jury on a matter outside ordinary human experience. Although the expert must take the oath and deliver his or her testimony in a manner not unlike the ordinary or lay witness, the substance of his evidence and the manner in which it is delivered are otherwise governed by special rules and practices. Witnesses must generally limit their testimony to facts within their personal knowledge or perception thereby allowing the finder of face to carry out the essential function of drawing the necessary inferences from the stated facts. The expert witness, in contrast, assists the finder of fact in drawing those very inferences and, by virtue of this dependency, enjoys wide latitude in relation to the scope of his or her testimony.

Expert opinion embodies the application of the expert's training and experience to the facts of the case. In compiling his or her report and delivering his or her evidence, the expert may rely on facts both within and outside his or her personal knowledge. The expert may testify as to matters of opinion and may incorporate secondary material, such as documents, videotapes or the views of other experts, that would otherwise fall foul of the rule against hearsay.[58] Indeed, typically much of the relevant factual information on which the expert relies has been gleaned second-hand. Any such facts must be proved at some point in the proceedings by other independent evidence,[59] a technical obstacle that is side-stepped in examination-in-chief through the expedient of counsel asking the witness to couch his or her expert opinion in hypothetical terms. The opinion is elicited in the form of responses to a series of hypothetical questions which assume facts that have yet to be proved by the party presenting the expert testimony. The expert's opinion is thus intrinsically linked to the promised proof of the facts on which the hypothesis is based.[60]

The expert is permitted to draw inferences from facts and, indeed, the value of expert opinion lies in the inferential light it shines on matters which have left the court in the dark. However, the insight offered by the expert frequently eschews any firm distinction between fact and inference. By virtue of his or her skill and training, the expert may be equipped not only to draw inferences from observed fact but also to perceive facts that would escape the lay witness.[61] Attempts to identify the precise point at which the expert departs from the realm of fact into that of opinion are consequently somewhat futile and it may be more helpful simply to observe that courts generally adopt a flexible attitude to the testimony of experts on matters within their field of expertise. In particular,

---

[58] On the rule against hearsay, *see* McGrath, *op. cit.,* chap.5; Healy, *op. cit.,* chap.9 and Fennell, *op. cit,* chap.9.

[59] *R.T. v. V.P.* [1990] 1 I.R. 545 at 551; *R. v. Somers* [1963] 1 W.L.R. 1306.

[60] *Conley v. Strain* [1988] I.R. 628.

[61] Howard, *op. cit.,* para.37.10.

experts may marshal a wide range of material in support of their opinions, including the views of their peers.[62]

The Expert is Methodology

The basis for the expert opinion – item no.3 on Cresswell J.'s list of the duties of the expert – has been a source of controversy in the Irish courts. During examination-in-chief, the expert is typically asked to explain both the facts and the criteria or standards on which his or her opinion is based. The premise behind this line of questioning is that the court should be appraised not only of the expert's conclusions but also of the *method* by which those conclusions were reached. Armed with this information, the court is then in a position to test the accuracy of the expert's conclusions and to exercise its own independent judgment on the ultimate issue in dispute.[63] In *quasi* inquisitorial proceedings, such as those relating to the welfare of children, judges have a duty to ensure that expert witnesses adequately explain the methodologies that underpin their conclusions.[64] A less interventionist judicial stance is generally adopted in the strictly adversarial context of proceedings in tort. However, it may be argued that the complexity of medical evidence provides a compelling practical rationale for raising the bar on expert testimony. The key to judicial comprehension of expert medical opinion must surely lie in the clear, logical and adequate explication of the predicate scientific methodology. And just as the expert bears must explain the basis for his or her conclusions, so counsel bears a corresponding responsibility to ask questions of the witness that will facilitate the proper presentation of the evidence.

The Scope and Weight of Expert Opinion

The relationship between the expert witness and the judge, as finder of fact, is one of the more complex aspects of testimonial trial practice. It is the function of the judge to determine the course of events to which the legal proceedings give rise and whereas he or she may be guided by the expert's opinion in relation to those events, the task of finding the dispositive facts remains his or hers alone. Whether the expert is merely guiding the judge or has strayed into the realm of impermissible direction may be difficult to discern.

The traditional response to this dilemma is encapsulated in the so-called "ultimate issue" rule whereby the witness is free to draw inferences from facts but is precluded from expressing an opinion on the ultimate issues in the case.

---

62 *Foyle and Bann Fisheries Ltd v. A.G.* (1949) 83 I.L.T.R. 29.

63 *Davie v. Edinburgh Magistrates* [1953] S.C 34.

64 *State (D. & D.) v. Groarke* [1990] 1 I.R. 305, [1990 I.L.R.M. 130; *Southern Health Board v. C.H.* [1996] 2 I.L.R.M. 142; *Re N*, unreported, Court of Appeal, March 14, 1996.

The case law on point has been neither clear nor consistent,[65] however, and the precise scope of the rule has long been uncertain.[66] Courts have tended to treat the contexts of expert and non-expert opinion interchangeably and, in justifying the exclusion of expert opinion, have routinely merged the ultimate issue rule with the broad requirement that the opinion pertain to a matter on which expertise is necessary. At its zenith, the rule clearly undercut the admission of expert evidence and was objectionable in theory since the very presence of the expert in the proceedings signals the inability of the finder of fact to resolve the disputed matter. In practice, it required the courts to engage in the Herculean task of identifying those facts and inferences that related exclusively to the ultimate issues in a case and it led to an unwieldy and inconsistent body of case law. For these reasons, the ultimate issue rule has largely been abandoned in contemporary practice civil trial practice.[67] The contrary premise, namely that an expert may opine on an ultimate issue, does not always hold true, however, and may depend upon the field of expertise and the evidentiary backdrop against which the expert opinion unfolds.[68]

A related source of tension in the relationship between the expert and the court is the weight or probative value of expert evidence. Whereas the need for expert opinion and the scope of that opinion are factors bearing on admissibility, this further issue assumes that the evidence in question has been properly admitted. The outstanding question is the degree of latitude that the judge enjoys in assessing the probative value of expert opinion. Typically, the judge must weigh the opinion of two or more experts and, furthermore, grapple with disagreements among the experts over substance and methodology.

The judge must give any admissible expert opinion due consideration and weigh it along with all the other evidence in deciding the case; but he or she is not bound to adopt any part of it and is free to choose between conflicting expert opinions.[69] In *Egan v. Midland Health Board,* for example, Johnson J. observed:

---

[65] See e.g. *D.P.P. v. A. and B.C. Chewing Gum Ltd.* [1968] 1 Q.B. 159 and *Anderson v. Neville* [1971] 3 All E.R. 1152 (psychiatric evidence on obscenity); *R. v. Chard* (1971) 56 Cr. App. R. 268 and *R. v. Toner* (1991) 93 Cr. App. R. 382 (psychiatric evidence on intention to kill).

[66] See Jackson, "The Ultimate Issue Rule: One Rule Too Many" [1984] Crim. L. R. 75.

[67] See e.g. *R. v. Stockwell* (1993) 97 Cr. App. R. 260; *F(Orse C) v. C* [1991] 2 I.R. 330. In England the rule was formally removed for civil proceedings by s.3 of the Civil Evidence Act 1972.

[68] McGrath, *op. cit.,* para.6.14.

[69] *Winston v. O'Leary,* unreported, High Court, December 19, 2006. In *Fitzpatrick v. White,* unreported, High Court, June 3, 2005, White J. dismissed the plaintiff's claim for damages for negligence in respect of an operation to improve the cosmetic appearance of the plaintiff's eye. Both parties had tendered expert evidence. However, White J. concluded that the plaintiff was not a credible witness and that the plaintiff's expert evidence fell short of establishing negligence.

> "In regard to the disagreement between the parties two experts of great eminence and experience were called, each of whose curriculum vitae is such as to demonstrate that they are each leaders in the field of orthopaedic surgery and in particular the field of hip replacement."

With regard to all the evidence, Johnson J. concluded that the defendant's account of what took place was "on the balance of probabilities much more likely to have occurred."[70] Similarly, in *Shuit v. Moylette,* considering evidence from five consultants, White J. concluded that "there are two *bona fide* schools of thought on the issue as to whether the first named defendant acted appropriately in the circumstances presented to him" and, ultimately, dismissed the plaintiff's claim. As noted *infra,* expert evidentiary conflicts of this kind are often resolved by recourse to the burden of proof.

There is scant practical guidance in the case law on the factors that inform the weighing of expert opinion – such as the expert's qualifications, methodology, demeanour, persuasiveness, or the logic of his or her conclusions – nor the relative weight that is accorded such factors. Because the courts do not approach expert evidence in an agreed, systematic fashion, its impact on proceedings may be unpredictable and uncertain.[71] Written judgments often do not reveal the evidentiary preferences of judges; moreover, the import of expert opinion may vary from one context to the next.

Concerns about undue expert influence are aggravated in jurisdictions such as the United States where civil actions, including medical negligence actions, are frequently resolved by jury trial. Conventional wisdom suggests that juries are more likely to be swayed by the eminence or high sounding rhetoric of an expert witness.[72] That objection may have less force today although it does not negate the reality that juries lack the routine experience of trial judges in receiving and assessing expert evidence. The absence of juries in Irish medical negligence proceedings arguably alleviates some of these concerns about the weight of expert evidence but it does not extinguish them altogether.[73]

The Reliability of Expert Evidence

The reliability of expert evidence has generated surprisingly little discourse in our case law and jurisprudence and such discussion as exists tends to be cautious and

---

[70] Unreported, High Court, July 7, 2006.

[71] See discussion *infra* on the reliability of expert evidence and the American *Daubert* test.

[72] See e.g. Imwinkelried, "'Junk Science' in the Courtroom: Will the Changes in the American Law of Expert Testimony Influence the Irish Courts?" (2004) 26 D.U.L.J. 83.

[73] The landmark *Dunne v. National Maternity Hospital* [1989] I.R. 91 was decided in the era of civil jury trials. See O'Flaherty, "The William Dunne Baby Case: Is There Another Way?" (1989) 7 I.L.T. 193.

indirect. In tort actions, the issue surfaces if at all under the rubric of the weight of the evidence. Conflicts among experts are commonplace, indeed expected, and the law leaves it up to the judge, as finder of fact, to decide which opinion he or she should follow. Provided that the judge's evidentiary assessment is reasonable, his or her ultimate decision will generally be upheld on appeal.

Although Irish law contains no explicit rule on point, several mechanisms implicitly address the reliability of expert evidence to a greater or lesser extent. First, as noted, the law has traditionally placed great store on judicial scrutiny of expert qualifications as a safeguard against the unreliability of expert opinion. Second, the adversarial trial process and the testing of evidence through examination and cross-examination is seen as an essential bulwark against unreliable evidence. Third, great faith is placed in the common sense of the judge as finder of fact, particularly in the face of complicated and conflicting expert opinion. As Finlay C.J. stated in *Best v. Wellcome Foundation Ltd:*

> "I am satisfied that it is not possible either for a judge of trial or for an appellate court to take upon itself the role of a determining scientific authority resolving disputes between distinguished scientists in any particular line of technical expertise. The function which a court can and must perform in the trial of a case in order to achieve a just result is to apply common sense and a careful understanding of the logic and likelihood of events to conflicting opinions and conflicting theories concerning a matter of this kind."[74]

Finally, the resolution of cases involving conflicting medical evidence frequently turns on the burden of proof.

Concerns over the reliability of expert evidence tend to be heightened in the context of scientific or medical expertise.[75] There is thought to be a greater danger that the finder of fact will be overawed by the scientist, blinded by the science itself, or simply predisposed to the notion that science is objective and reliable. When asked to choose between diametrically opposing conclusions offered by eminent medical experts, the finder of fact may possibly be swayed by form and appearance rather than substance. Nor is the challenge of unravelling expert scientific or medical testimony a matter for the finder of fact alone; lawyers must grapple both with the science and the persona of the expert in order to elicit the expert's opinion through examination-in-chief or, conversely, undermine it through cross-examination.

---

[74] [1993] 3 I.R. 421, applied in *Quinn v. Mid Western Health Board* [2005] 4 I.R. 1. *See also H v. St. Vincent's Hospital Trustees Ltd,* unreported, High Court, December 20, 2006.

[75] See generally Jasanoff, *Science at the Bar: Law, Science and Technology in America* (Harvard University Press, Cambridge, Mass., 1995); Freeman and Reece, eds., *Science in Court* (Ashgate, Dartmouth, Aldershot, 1998); Huber, *Galileo's Revenge: Junk Science in the Courtroom* (Basic Books, New York, 1991); Foster and Huber, *Judging Science* (MIT Press, Cambridge, Mass., 1999).

The prevailing test for medical negligence, set down in *Dunne v. National Maternity Hospital*,[76] may exacerbate these tendencies. The so-called *Dunne* principles provide that in order to prove negligence in diagnosis or treatment a plaintiff must demonstrate that the medical practitioner has been guilty of such failure as no medical practitioner of equal specialist or general status and skill would be guilty of if acting with ordinary care. If the allegation is that he or she deviated from a general and approved practice, the plaintiff must show that the course was one which no medical practitioner of like specialisation and skill would have followed had he or she been exercising ordinary care. If the medical practitioner followed customary practice and the allegation is that the practice was flawed, the plaintiff must establish that there were inherent defects in the practice that ought to have been obvious to anyone giving the matter consideration.[77] Under this standard of care, the conventional wisdom of the medical profession is the evidentiary centre of gravity and is usually reflected in the defendant's expert medical testimony.[78] Thus, some writers have observed that the standard may be excessively deferential to doctors[79] and that it may ascribe to plaintiffs the enormous task of displacing traditional medical thinking.[80]

A further concern associated with scientific evidence is the need to distinguish between good science and bad or so-called "junk" science. Against the contested and evolving backdrop of the world of science, disputes over theory, methodology and empirical research are not uncommon. How can the courts best ensure that a proffered expert opinion constitutes reliable science as opposed to junk science? The issue has galvanised reform in other jurisdictions and is ripe for consideration here.[81]

---

76 [1989] I.R. 91.

77 *Id.*, p.109. The Supreme Court also stated that the function of the finder of fact (then jury, now judge) is to decide whether the course of treatment followed complied with the careful conduct of a medical practitioner of like specialisation and skill (and not to decide whether one of two alternative forms of treatment is better than the other).

78 Healy, *op. cit.*, p.363 describes the position thus: "The practical implication of the professional standard model of liability … is often that the plaintiff fails to prove his case where the defendant produces credible expert opinion to support the course he took in the given circumstances: in the light of traditional medical negligence principles, the courts are disinclined to find negligence where there appears to be an honest difference of opinion between doctors, so long as each view appears to represent an approved or respectable strand of medical thought. It is thus usually the case that the *defendant's* expert medical testimony is pivotal to the action" (internal citations omitted).

79 See e.g. Byrne, "An Overview of Recent Decisions in the Tort of Medical Negligence" (2005) 11 M.L.J.I. 30; Comyn, "Medical Negligence" (1987) 5 I.L.T. 139.

80 See e.g. Binchy, "The Impact of the New Act on Tort Law" in C. Craven and W. Binchy, eds., *Civil Liability and Courts Act 2004: Implications for Personal Injuries Litigation* (First Law, Dublin, 2005), 44 at 58-59.

81 On the possible application of American reforms in the Irish courts, *see* Imwinkelried, *loc. cit.* and Heffernan, *loc. cit.*

In the United States, for example, Federal Rule of Evidence 702 requires a trial judge to make a pre-trial, admissibility determination that proposed expert evidence is not only relevant but also reliable. As Blackmun J. explained in the landmark *Daubert v. Merrell Dow Pharmaceuticals, Inc.*:

> "[I]n order to qualify as 'scientific knowledge,' an inference or assertion must be derived by scientific method. Proposed testimony must be supported by an appropriate validation – i.e., 'good grounds,' based on what is known. In short, the requirement that an expert's testimony pertain to 'scientific knowledge' establishes a standard of evidentiary reliability."[82]

Emphasising that the trial judge's inquiry is a flexible one, Blackmun J. offered, by way of guidance, the following non-exhaustive list of factors which a trial judge might take into account in determining admissibility:

(1) Whether the theory or technique can be tested;
(2) whether the theory or technique has been tested;
(3) whether the theory or technique has been subjected to peer review and publication;
(4) whether the theory or technique has a known or potential rate of error; and
(5) whether the theory or technique has been generally accepted within the community.[83]

The law assigns no equivalent, formal gate-keeping function to Irish trial judges. Notwithstanding some of the developments discussed above, the system continues to emphasise trial over pre-trial procedures. The reliability of expert evidence is tackled *ad hoc* as a matter of weight rather than admissibility.[84] Arguably there are benefits to this approach: it provides judges with a degree of flexibility because issues relating to expert evidence can be left over for resolution on the merits, and it may avoid some of the contention and cost associated with expert practice in the United States. There is a downside to a *laissez faire* regime, however: it may be less transparent, consistent and predictable; it may encourage lax standards in the admission of expert evidence; and rather than resolve contentious issues, it may merely postpone them, ultimately increasing the complexity and cost of the proceedings.

---

[82] 509 U.S. 579 at 590, 113 S.Ct. 2786, 125 L.Ed.2d 469 (1993).

[83] *Id.*, pp.593-94. Prior to *Daubert,* general acceptance (the fifth factor) had been the sole indicator or reliability under the governing authority, *Frye v. United States,* 293 F.1013 (D.C. cir. 1923).

[84] *See also News Datacom Ltd v. Lyons* [1994] 1 I.L.R.M. 450 (refusing an interlocutory injunction on the basis that the plaintiffs had not offered any scientific basis for their claim of copyright infringement).

The Burden of Proof

The task of the judge in making findings based on medical evidence is expedited by the burden of proof which in medical negligence proceedings rests with the plaintiff.[85] The apposite inquiry is not whether the evidence of one side is to be preferred over that of the other in the abstract but rather whether the plaintiff has adduced sufficient evidence to establish negligence on the balance of probabilities.[86] A consequence of the onus of proof resting on the plaintiff is that questions regarding the sufficiency and reliability of the evidence may hover disproportionately over plaintiff's experts. In making their findings, judges rarely go so far as to find that the plaintiff's evidence is unreliable in the conventional sense of the term; often, it is enough simply to find that the plaintiff's evidence is not substantial enough to be relied upon.

In *Quinn v. Mid Western Health Board,* for example, the plaintiff instituted proceedings against a consultant obstetrician at the Regional Hospital Limerick alleging that the defendant had negligently failed to conduct timely ultrasound and other scans on the plaintiff's mother which would have prevented the serious injuries the plaintiff sustained at birth. In reviewing the evidence, including the evidence of several eminent experts, O'Sullivan J. acknowledged that there were significant difficulties with the propositions put forward by both sides in the case. He continued:

> "I am left, therefore, with two mutually inconsistent bodies of evidence neither of which wholly and satisfactorily resolves the issues in the case. It is not for me … to set myself up as a determining authority in regard to these specialist issues, nor do I attempt to do so. I am unable to conclude, that is, that on the balance of probabilities that had the plaintiff been delivered by the 35th week of gestation she would have been spared all or a significant part of her injuries. In that event I must dismiss her claim."[87]

Keogh v. Dowling involved a dispute of fact between experts over an alleged undetected shoulder dystocia suffered by the infant plaintiff. Having summarised the conflicting evidence, Johnson J. observed that he found the defence witnesses

---

[85] There may be some limited instances in which the plaintiff can rely on *res ipsa loquitur.* But see Chap.6, *infra* (observing that *res ipsa loquitur* has rarely been successfully applied in medical negligence situations). *See, e.g., Quinn v. South Eastern Health Board,* unreported, High Court, March 22, 2002 (Ó Caoimh J.), in which the plaintiff submitted that the evidence in the case suggested that the injuries she manifest in the wake of an appendicectomy were not a result to be anticipated in the normal course of events, especially in the case of a child. The procedural effect of the presumption of negligence is not entirely clear. See Chap.6, *infra.*

[86] *Dempsey v. Moen,* unreported, High Court, November 5, 2005.

[87] [2005] 4 I.R. 1.

"very impressive" and the authorities produced by one of the defence witnesses particularly helpful. The statistics cited were in favour of the defendant but, "quite apart from that" Johnson J. concluded that the plaintiff had "failed to discharge the onus of establishing that on the balance of probabilities in this case there was shoulder dystocia which was undetected and untreated."[88]

In *Shuit v. Moylette,* the plaintiff sought damages against a consultant obstetrician/gynaecologist for pain and suffering and loss arising out of an unnecessary hysterectomy. In dismissing the plaintiff's claim, White J. stated:

> "In light of my findings in relation to the integrity, and bona fides, of the expert witnesses called by the respective parties herein, the plaintiff has failed to satisfy me that no obstetrician of like skill, acting with ordinary care, would have performed the surgery carried our by the first named defendant, rather I am satisfied that a number of reputable obstetricians would have done as the first named defendant did."[89]

The Expert Witness and the Adversarial Trial Process

The references by Cresswell J. and O'Flaherty J., above, to the expert's duty to the court reflect the traditional doctrinal assumption that an expert's opinion is neutral and unbiased both in substance and appearance. This is consistent with conventional judicial rhetoric which downplays the adversarial character of expert evidence. The reality is that the expert, unlike an ordinary witness, participates in the proceedings in his professional capacity; he or she is retained by one of the parties and is generally paid for his or her services. In addition to providing factual data, he or she performs an advisory function, identifying the strengths and weaknesses of the party's case, and laying the groundwork for a possible settlement. The relationship is implicitly partisan and, for example, even where the expert is unable to provide evidence favourable to the party, he or she is ethically bound to refrain from making his or her services available to any other party to the same litigation. In Taylor's classic assessment:

> "[Experts] do not, indeed, wilfully misrepresent what they think but their judgments become so warped by their regarding the subject in one point of view, that even when conscientiously disposed they are incapable of forming independent opinion."[90]

This may be something of an overstatement but it is a truism that an expert

---

[88] Unreported, High Court, October 11, 2005.

[89] Unreported, High Court, March 2, 2006.

[90] Taylor, *Treatise on the Law of Evidence as Administered in England and Ireland* (Croom-Johnson and Bridgman, eds.) 12th ed., (Sweet & Maxwell, London, 1931), p.59.

witness is identified exclusively with one or other side in legal proceedings and that his or her opinion is expected to support that party's position.

The subjectivity of expert evidence is a logical incident of the adversarial trial process which some writers associate generally with the failings of science and medicine in the courtroom. Alldridge, for example, has argued that the "[t]he most conspicuous dangers of adversarial expertise at trial are that a partisan choice of witnesses will produce experts who are unrepresentative of the range of possible experts, and that the fact that they are being paid will further induce bias."[91] Arguably, these dangers are exacerbated by the system's overriding emphasis on testimony in open court, a process that is costly and resource-intensive and that may reward advocacy at the expense of scientific knowledge.[92] A few caveats may be entered, however, from an Irish perspective. It is worth recalling that in a small jurisdiction such as our own, the regularity with which a limited community of experts may appear in the courts may have a tempering effect on the "hired gun" phenomenon.[93] In addition, some reformist steps have been taken to curb the rigors of adversarialism. As we have seen, changes to the Rules of the Superior Courts introduced in 1998 have made a modest dent in the orality of proceedings by placing greater emphasis on documentary expert evidence[94] and, more recently, the Oireachtas has made provision for the use of court appointed experts in personal injuries actions.[95]

Independent Experts

The Civil Liability and Courts Act 2004[96] permits a court to appoint an expert witness in a personal injuries action.[97] Section 20 of the Act provides as follows:

---

91 Alldridge, "Scientific Expertise and Comparative Criminal Procedure" (1999) 3 E. & P 141 at 149. In a similar vein, Healy, *op. cit.,* p.364, has observed that "[t]he tendency of experts to be partisan, whether or not consciously, is stoked by the gladiatorial or adversarial nature of the common law trial".

92 *Id.* The traditional response to criticisms of this kind is to highlight the strengths of adversarialism and the shortcomings of inquisitorial systems of justice. Criticism and counter-criticism in this vein may be overstated and lend itself to crude caricature. In truth, each system is a creature of its own culture and neither may have a monopoly of wisdom on issues of evidentiary probity.

93 Given the tendency of parties to enlist the services of medical experts from abroad, this observation may have greater force in areas of tort litigation other than medical negligence.

94 S.I. No.391 of 1998.

95 S.20 of the Civil Liability and Courts Act 2004.

96 No. 31 of 2004.

97 See *Chap.3, infra*; Nolan, "The Civil Liability and Courts Act 2004 (Part II)" (2005) Bar Rev. 38 at 41; See Chap.6, *infra.*

"(1) In a personal injuries action, the court may appoint such approved persons as it considers appropriate to carry out investigations into, and give expert evidence in relation to, such matters as the court directs.

(2) A party in a personal injuries action shall cooperate with a person appointed under this section and shall, in particular, provide the person with:

(a)(i) any report or other document prepared by the party, or

(ii) any report or other document prepared on behalf of the party concerned, for the purposes of or in contemplation of the personal injuries action,

and

(b) any document or information used or referred to for the purpose of preparing the report.

(3) The costs incurred in the appointment of, and carrying out of an investigation by, a person appointed under this section shall be paid by such party to the personal injuries action concerned as the court hearing the action shall direct.

(4) A party in a personal injuries action shall be entitled to cross-examine a person appointed under this section in relation to any matter that he or she was appointed to investigate and give expert evidence on.

(5) The President of the High Court in consultation with the President of the Circuit Court and the President of the District Court shall approve such persons as he or she considers appropriate for the purposes of this section, and a person so approved is in this section referred to as an 'approved person'."

In terms of reform, section 20 is a more limited measure than the changes to the rules embodied in S.I. No.391 of 1998 in the sense that it is permissive rather than mandatory but it embodies a more radical departure from standard adversarial practice. A more controversial development, it holds no similar guarantees in terms of judicial economy and cost efficiency.

The Minister explained the intention behind the provision in the following terms:

> "In many personal injuries actions, conflicting evidence from experts must be decided by the court. Section 19 allows a court to appoint approved persons to investigate and give expert evidence on any issue the court may direct. The section also provides that any party to a personal injuries action shall co-operate with an approved person. An 'approved person' is a person approved by the President of the High Court, in consultation with the Presidents of the Circuit and District Courts, for the purposes of the section. The intention behind this provision is that an expert, independent of any expert witness retained by the parties, could be appointed to assist the court. To take a medical example, a court might decide to appoint its

> own medical assessor, who will testify and be liable to cross examination, but will give an objective view to the court having listened to the medical experts on either side."[98]

Although the Act has entered into force, it will be some time yet before the first of the personal injuries proceedings to which it applies come on stream. From this speculative standpoint, it is difficult to see how the provision will realise the stated legislative objective in practice.

One view is that it represents a half-hearted attempt to emulate the corresponding English provision adopted as part of the case management reforms which followed in the wake of Lord Woolf's review of the civil justice system.[99] Lord Woolf had identified expert evidence as a source of unnecessary cost in civil proceedings and had expressed disquiet over the lack of impartiality of expert witnesses.

The new English rules[100] distinguish between testifying experts and advising experts. The former are retained to prepare and give evidence and in such capacity are bound by an overriding duty to the court. In relation to their evidence, the rules require advance disclosure and condition the amount of expert evidence that may be given and the form that it may take. Advising experts, as the term suggests, are retained by a party for the sole purpose of advising that party. They are paid by the party, they owe no duty to the court, and their advice is privileged against disclosure. Rule 35.7 enables a court to direct that the expert evidence in a case be given by a single joint expert. The parties may agree on the identity of the expert and, indeed, are encouraged to do so, subject to the approval of the court. In the absence of such agreement, the court may appoint the expert independently or from a list drawn up by the parties. Although there is nothing to prevent a party from retaining its own expert, over and above the single joint expert, intuitively the party is unlikely to recover his or her costs relating to the expert or to have the expert's evidence admitted. Each party wishing to submit expert evidence may instruct the single joint expert and may have access to the instructions of any other party and to any conference with the expert. Unless the court otherwise directs, the parties are jointly and severally liable for expert's fees and expenses.[101] The wisdom and propriety of appointing a single joint expert turns upon a number of factors including the nature and complexity of the proceedings, the likely cost efficiency, and the need to establishing a level playing field between the parties.[102] Interestingly, single joint experts are far

---

98 Seanad Debates, March 11, col.1808, see Chap.3, *infra.*

99 *Access to Justice, Final Report* (HMSO, 1996).

100 Civil Procedure Rules, pt 35, and Practice Direction. The rules pertaining to experts are summarised by A. Keane, *Modern Law of Evidence,* 6th ed. (Oxford University Press, Oxford, 2005), pp.572-580.

101 R.35.8.

102 Keane, *loc. cit.,* p.574 (citing *Oxley v. Penwarden* [2001] Lloyd's Rep. Med. 347; *Peet v.*

less common in cases of medical negligence involving different schools of medical thought.[103]

Section 20 of the 2004 Act enables the court to appoint not a single joint expert but rather an independent expert or an "approved person" in the language of the section. It clearly allows for the possibility that such an approved person will serve in a manner akin to the English single joint expert to the exclusion of party or adversarial experts. However, the section does not preclude the possibility that an approved person will contribute to the proceedings in addition to (rather than *in lieu* of) the parties' respective experts. This seems to be what the Minister had in mind when he stated: "The intention behind this provision is that an expert, independent of any expert witness retained by the parties, could be appointed to assist the court."[104] Moreover, in establishing a duty on the parties to co-operate with an approved person, the section refers to the disclosure of "reports or documents prepared for the purposes of or in contemplation of the personal injuries action" which would normally embrace expert reports. Thus, depending upon the number of parties tendering expert evidence, there will be at least three testifying experts in the proceedings in the English sense of the term. The effect of casting an additional expert opinion into the adversarial mix is difficult to predict. In some cases, a third, independent expert may assist the court in resolving a sharp division between two experts but, in others, he or she may merely compound the dilemma by increasing the complexity and confusion. Although there is nothing in the section obliging the court to accept the conclusions of the approved person, the pressure to do so will likely be greater under this inquisitorial model.

Professor Binchy has raised a further cogent concern, namely, that the use of an approved person may operate to the detriment of plaintiffs who are seeking to advance a theory that contradicts orthodox practice.[105] The ability of plaintiffs to challenge conventional wisdom in relation to scientific controversies may be compromised if the approved person represents a traditional or established position within the profession. In tandem with the relatively recent establishment of the Personal Injuries Assessment Board,[106] section 20 might arguably be perceived as a further initiative aimed at curbing the excesses of personal injuries litigation.

Certain practical issues surrounding the operation of section 20 remain. The trial court will appoint an approved person in a particular case but for the purposes of the section, the President of the High Court will approve a person, in consultation with the President of the Circuit Court and the President of the District Court. No further guidance is offered, for example, as to whether the

---

Mid Kent Healthcare Trust [2002] 1 W.L.R. 210 and *ES v. Chesterfield & North Derbushire Royal Hospital NHS Trust* (2003) E.W.C.A. Civ. 1284).

103 *Id.*

104 *Loc. cit.*

105 See Chap.2, *supra.*

106 Personal Injuries Assessment Board Act 2003.

President will approve standing panels of experts for purposes of the section or whether the system of approval will operate on an *ad hoc* basis. Issues might also arise relating to potential conflicts of interest. For example, would appointment as an approved person necessarily preclude an expert from being retained by private parties in separate proceedings? Further questions are raised by the statutory duty placed on the parties to co-operate with the approved person. Section 20(2) requires a party to furnish the approved person with any report or other document prepared by or on behalf of the party in connection with the litigation. How will this provision operate logistically and can it be reconciled with the doctrine of legal professional privilege?[107] Finally, some thought should be given to the impact which this provision will have on costs. Section 20 states that the costs of an approved person shall be allocated by the court presumably on the same basis as any other costs. Even if it were the intention of the court to service the proceedings with just one expert in the form of an approved person, this would not obviate the need for the parties to retain their own experts at a minimum in an advisory capacity. Unlike the corresponding English provision, section 20 makes no attempt to exclude party experts from the realm of recoverable costs. Thus, the appointment of an approved person will likely increase rather than decrease the cost of expert evidence in the proceedings.

In summary, section 20 embodies an attempt to incorporate an inquisitorial element into the heart of adversarial personal injuries litigation. It remains to be seen whether judges will seek to avail of the services of approved persons. Given the somewhat half-hearted nature of the reform and the lack of clarity surrounding its terms, one may hazard a guess that the impact of the provision will be relatively limited in practice.

---

[107] See Chap.6, *infra*.

CHAPTER 6

Medical Negligence Litigation Challenges for the Plaintiff's Lawyers

MICHAEL BOYLAN

The purpose of this chapter is to give a broad overview and some guidance to practitioners acting for plaintiffs in relation to common challenges and issues that arise in prosecuting medical negligence actions. It is beyond the scope of this chapter to deal in depth with the principles of law relating to medical negligence, which are covered by other contributors.

GETTING STARTED/ASSIMILATING ESSENTIAL FACTUAL INFORMATION

Probably the greatest difficulty for a plaintiff to overcome to be successful in an action for medical negligence is to ascertain all the crucial facts relevant to liability concerning the treatment complained of. Often the patient will be in total ignorance as to what has occurred to result in the unexpected adverse outcome to treatment. The crucial evidence that will often determine whether or not a cause of action may lie is in the possession of the potential defendant doctor or hospital. The onus of proof rests with the plaintiff and thus it is essential that all possible efforts are made to reverse this information deficit prior to commencing action. The following are some suggested steps that may be useful to take to overcome the evidential deficit.

Medical records - check list

Obviously it is an essential step to obtain all the relevant treatment records and to check their contents against the client's version of events. Also, when the records are received it is important to check carefully that all of the usual types of records are contained in the chart provided. The following is usually in every hospital chart:

(a) A&E Records/triage records.
(b) Doctor's clinical notes.
(c) Nursing notes/cardex.

(d) Blood pressure, heart and temperature chart.
(e) Fluid Intake/Output chart.
(f) Drug administration records.
(g) Surgeon's operative notes.
(h) Anaesthetist's records.
(i) Recovery room records.
(j) Pathology/lab test results.
(k) X-Ray/Ultrasound/MRI scan films and reports.
(l) Discharge summary.
(m) Consultant's reports/correspondence/letters to other treating doctors/ hospitals.

Hospital complaints procedures

Every hospital in the State now has a hospital complaints procedure. The effectiveness of these procedures is patchy; some complaints procedures are much more robust, vigorous and effective. The effectiveness of the hospital complaints procedure depends very largely on the ethos or culture operating within the particular hospital. Furthermore the effectiveness of the complaints procedure is largely dependant upon the willingness of the medical staff attached to the hospital to cooperate with the hospital administrators in dealing with the patient's complaint. Medical consultants are now showing a greater willingness to engage in the process and to devote the necessary time to deal with patient complaints. However, it is unfortunately still the case that, if medical consultants decide not to engage fully with the hospital administrators in dealing with a patient's complaint, the hospital authorities are effectively powerless to compel the relevant medical consultants to provide the necessary factual information to deal with the complaint.

If there is an effective complaints procedure within the hospital it can be an invaluable source of additional factual information and can unearth a huge amount of additional information for the patient, which is not contained within the chart or apparent from reading the hospital chart. This additional factual information can have a significant impact on whether or not the treatment complained of could be regarded as substandard.

Practitioners should always consider availing of this route before commencing to write a letter of claim. Generally once a letter of claim is written by a lawyer the flow of factual information ceases and opportunities to gather crucial facts become much more limited.

Inquest into hospital deaths

If the patient has been unfortunate enough to die following the medical treatment being enquired into and you are representing the interests of the family, the inquest is a potential source of extremely valuable factual information. Up until recent legislative changes, the coroner was severely restricted in the scope of the enquiry that he or she could conduct into a hospital death by reason of the Supreme Court decision in *Eastern Health Board v. Farrell,*[1] which interpreted section 26 of the Coroners Act 1962. Until December 2005, effectively an inquest into a hospital death could only call two medical practitioners one of whom necessarily had to be the pathologist performing the autopsy. In an era where hospital based medicine can involve a multidisciplinary approach to treatment with several different Consultants being involved in patient care, being permitted only to call two medical practitioners was most unsatisfactory and severely undermined the usefulness of the coroner's inquest.

However, since the passing of the Coroners (Amendment) Act 2005,[2] there is now no limit on the number of medical practitioners who the coroner can decide to call as witnesses at an inquest into a hospital death. This is undoubtedly going to mean that the coroners' inquest will be a much more effective venue to ascertain vital information surrounding the death of patients and can be a very valuable source of crucial information which might not otherwise be available. While it will be appreciated that it is not permissible in the coroner's inquest to ask witnesses any questions that may imply fault or blame on the part of any doctor or individual nevertheless vital factual information can be unearthed by skilful cross-examination of medical witnesses. This could be an essential preliminary hearing that will or could be of significant assistance to the practitioner in the event that civil proceedings are subsequently initiated.

It is submitted that hospital based deaths come within the ambit of Article 2 of the European Convention on Human Rights and oblige the State to hold a proper enquiry into the cause of death in a State hospital. The coroner's inquest system in the UK has been held in the UK courts[3] to allow the State to comply with its obligations pursuant to Article 2 of the European Convention of Human Rights. It is thus likely that if the matter were tested in this country that the same result would follow and that the coroner's inquest would satisfy the State's obligations under Article 2. However, to be Article 2 compliant it is arguable that the parties at the Inquest should have equality of arms and that in particular the family of the deceased should be enabled to participate fully in the inquest for it to be an effective enquiry. It has been held in the UK that to be Article 2 compliant that the family should be provided with effective legal aid to instruct lawyers and experts so that they can participate fully in the coroners' inquest into a hospital death.[4]

---

1 *Eastern Health Board v. Farrell, Coroner for the City of Dublin & Ors.* [2001] IESC 96.

2 S.1 repeals s.26.2 of the Coroners Act 1962 which had limited medical witnesses to two; only one of which had to be the pathologist who performed the autopsy, at inquests.

3 *R (Middleton) v. West Somerset Coroner* [2004] U.K.H.L. 10 at 47: "In the absence of full criminal proceedings, and unless otherwise notified, a coroner should assume that his inquest is the means by which the state will discharge its procedural investigative obligation under Article 2.."

4 As a result of the decision of *The Queen on the Application of Mohammed Farooq Khan*

No case has been taken yet in this country but in the writer's view there are sound grounds for believing that the courts may adopt a similar approach to the UK Courts if the State is to comply with it's obligations pursuant to Article 2 in circumstances where the next of kin would not otherwise have the financial means to obtain proper legal advice/representation.

Hospital protocols and guidelines

In modern hospital practice with large hospitals and 24 hour care regimes, changing shifts etc., it has been almost universal practice for hospitals to develop guidelines or protocols for dealing with common clinical problems/injuries, e.g. limb fractures, head injuries, surgical emergencies, the management of labour etc. To endeavour to achieve a consistent and good standard of care for the treatment of common medical conditions senior clinical staff develop guidelines or protocols to be followed routinely in the treatment of patients and to be used particularly by the more junior staff as guidelines when senior colleagues may not be available. These guidelines and protocols are in effect setting out what is the hospital's general and approved practice for the treatment of the patient in particular clinical circumstances.

Hospitals will have these guidelines for most common diseases/injuries. It is therefore essential that as soon as possible the practitioner for the plaintiff should seek the voluntary discovery/disclosure of these guidelines/protocols. They might be of enormous value in establishing early whether or not the patient may have a valid cause of action. If for example the treatment on the occasion in question clearly departs from the hospital's own guidelines this is *prima facia* evidence that the patient has a valid claim and indeed arguably puts the onus on the hospital to defend its departure from its own guidelines/protocol. Thus it is always advisable to seek these protocols and guidelines at the earliest possible time.

Briefing medical experts

This is a crucial decision for the lawyer. It is invariably necessary to seek expert opinions from abroad, usually the UK or Northern Ireland if you are acting for a plaintiff. Try and choose an expert who is currently in practice, recently retired or at least was practising at the time when the treatment complained of

---

v. The Secretary of State for Health [2003] E.W.C.A. Civ. 1129, the Community Legal Services (Financial) (Amendment No.2) Regulations 2003 (S.I. No.2838 of 2003), have been made, conferring power on the Legal Services Commission to ask the Secretary of State to disapply the financial limits for eligibility and contribution in relation to an application for funding of legal representation at an inquest into the death of a member of the immediate family of the client. Note that these regulations do not confer any *rights* on anyone. Instead, they permit *government officials* to make decisions in *individual cases,* the result of which may lawfully be to permit funding to be made available to a person, so that the UK is not in breach of Art.2 of the ECHR.

occurred. Obviously ensure that the expert you instruct is of the same speciality and experience as the doctor or surgeon whose treatment is being enquired into. Often it will be necessary to instruct more then one medical expert. For example, it may be necessary to instruct one expert to deal with the issue of breach of duty and another to deal with the issue of causation.

There is a UK based organisation called Avma (Action against Medical Accidents – www.avma.org.uk) whom you can subscribe to annually and who hold a large database of several thousand UK based medical experts with experience in medical legal/clinical medical negligence actions and who are available to provide expert advice. This organisation is a registered charity established to work for and promote patient's rights but who also run a lawyers resource service and any lawyer interested in the field of medical negligence litigation would be well advised to join as a member to gain access to this invaluable resource service and expert database.

Are There Reasonable Grounds to Pursue a Claim?

As to the requirement to have supportive evidence, a number of decisions have emphasised that there must be sound evidential grounds before medical negligence proceedings are commenced. The matter has been considered in a number of cases *vis-à-vis Reidy v. The National Maternity Hospital*[5], *Connolly v. Casey*[6] and *Cooke v. Cronin.*[7]

Barr J., in *Reidy v. The National Maternity Hospital*, stated:

> "...it is irresponsible and an abuse of the process of the Court to lodge a professional medical negligence action against institutions such as hospitals and professional personnel without first ascertaining that there are reasonable grounds for so doing. Initiation and prosecution of an action in negligence on behalf of the plaintiff against the hospital necessarily requires appropriate expert evidence to support it".[8]

In *Connolly v. Casey*, Kelly J. expressed support for this statement of the law and stated:

> "I have no difficulty endorsing the views of Barr J. that the commencement of proceedings alleging professional negligence is irresponsible and an abuse of the process of the Court unless the persons advising such proceedings have reasonable grounds for so doing".[9]

---

5 [1997] IEHC 143.
6 [2000] 1 I.R. 345.
7 [1999] IESC 54.
8 [1997] IEHC 143 at [24].
9 *Op. cit.*

In the appeal, in *Connolly v. Casey*, Denham J. stated:

> "It is important in professional negligence cases to act reasonably, proceedings must have an appropriate basis, Counsel have a duty of care".[10]

In the Supreme Court judgment of *Cooke v. Cronin*, Denham J. endorsed the statements of Barr J. in *Reidy* and Kelly J. in *Connolly* referred to above and stated:

> "While bearing in mind the important right of access to the Courts I am satisfied that these statements of law are correct. To issue proceedings alleging professional negligence puts an individual in a situation where for professional or practice reasons to have the case proceed in open Court may be perceived and feared to that professional as being detrimental to his professional reputation and practice. This fear should not be utilised by unprofessional conduct."[11]

In the same case, in his judgment, Lynch J. stated:

> "In all cases of alleged negligence on the part of a qualified professional person in carrying out his professional duties there should be some credible evidence to support the plaintiffs case before such an action is commenced".[12]

Again in the *Cooke* case, Keane J. stated:

> "I agree with the observations of Denham J. and Lynch J. as to the serious responsibility which rests on both branches of the legal profession in the institution and conduct of proceedings for negligence against professional persons. It is most regrettable that those standards were not met in the present case."[13]

From all of the foregoing it can be seen that the courts will be extremely hostile towards plaintiffs and their legal advisers who bring unsustainable professional negligence actions. It is therefore essential that before proceedings are instituted the plaintiff's legal advisers have a supportive medical expert report. The one possible exception to the foregoing could be when a potential claim is about to become statute barred.

---

[10] [2000] 1 I.R. 345 at 15.

[11] [1999] IESC 54 at 10.

[12] *Ibid.*, at [32].

[13] *Ibid.*, at [18].

Causation

It is essential that at the outset the plaintiff lawyer not only considers whether there has been a breach of duty of care but also considers the issue of causation. It must be remembered that the plaintiff must show that the doctors' or hospitals' breach of duty of care caused an injury to the plaintiff in the legal sense. It is beyond the scope of this chapter to discuss the extremely complex law relating to legal causation particularly as it pertains to medical negligence actions. Ray and Desmond Ryan address this issue in detail in Chapter 2. Suffice to say that in most medical negligence actions causation issues are every bit as controversial as issues relating to the duty of care. In most cases the patient has come into see their doctor with some underlying disease/pathology and in many cases the argument centres around whether the alleged substandard treatment complained of caused any significant harm. Often the defence case is that the patient's residual complaints are attributable to the underlying pathology or injury that brought the patient to the doctor/hospital in the first place rather then being caused by substandard treatment.

Before proceeding with an action you should have, at a minimum, expert evidence that on the balance of probabilities the treatment alleged to be substandard materially contributed to the patient's injury. Indeed it could be argued that the plaintiff ought to be able to establish on the balance of probabilities that but for the breach of duty the injury would have been avoided.[14]

For the most recent Supreme Court judgment dealing with this issue see *Quinn (a minor) v. Midwestern Health Board & Anor.*[15] In that case, Kearns J. considered the law relating to causation as it pertained to medical negligence actions and although his comments were *in obiter*, nevertheless, it is quite clear that the court was very reluctant to depart from the traditional rules relating to causation and was reluctant to adopt a more flexible approach to the issue.

Onus of proof

This will almost always rest with the plaintiff as *res ipsa loquitur* has rarely been applied successfully in medical negligence situations.

In *Quinn*, the importance of the plaintiff having to discharge the onus of proof on all issues was emphasised. The learned trial judge, O'Sullivan J., found himself quite unable to resolve the extremely complex scientific conflict on the cause of the injuries, which had developed between the very eminent medical experts on both sides of the litigation. He felt unable to decide between the respective experts as to which of the complex evidence was the most reliable. As a result he simply could not make a decision on which evidence to prefer and therefore dismissed the plaintiff's claim on the basis that she had not

---

[14] See detailed analysis in White, *Medical Negligence Actions*, (Oak Tree Press, 1996), chap.11, pp.238-284.

[15] [2005] IESC 19.

discharged the onus of proof. This occurred notwithstanding that breach of duty was admitted on day seventeen of the trial. The Supreme Court upheld the trial judge's entitlement to adopt such an approach in an exceptional case.

Loss of chance

In the case of *Gregg v. Scott*[16], the House of Lords in recent times by a 3-2 majority rejected, on policy grounds, the entitlement of a plaintiff to recover damages for injuries which would probably have occurred even with proper care although it is proven that the negligence further increased the likelihood of those injuries occurring or reduced the chances of a cure.

Less then three months before the Law Lords delivered their judgment, the Irish Supreme Court had delivered judgment in the case of *Philp v. Ryan*[17] and indeed Lord Hoffman in his speech in *Gregg v. Scott* referred to the judgment of the Irish Court. The Irish Supreme Court took a different view on the entitlement to recover for loss of chance and Fennelly J. in the course of his speech stated:

> "I should say that it seems to me to be contrary to instinct and logic that a plaintiff should not be entitled to be compensated for the fact that due to the negligent diagnosis of his medical condition he has been deprived of appropriate medical advice and the consequent opportunity to avail of treatment which *might* (emphasis added) improve his condition, I can identify no contrary principle of law or justice. It is common place that allowance is made in awards and in settlements for the risk that an injured plaintiff may in the future develop arthritis in an injured joint. The risk may be high or low – 15% risk is often mentioned – but damages are paid. I cannot agree that this is in any different from what is sought in the present case. It does not matter that the damage suffered by the plaintiff consists of the loss of an opportunity to avail of treatment. It might with equal logic be described as an increased risk of shorter life expectancy. It seems to me as illogical to award damages for a probable future injury as if it were a certainty, as to withhold them where the risk is low on the basis it will not happen at all."[18]

In the later case of *Quinn*, referred to above, which was heard by the Supreme Court some six months after *Philp v. Ryan*, Kearns J., having quoted from the opinion of Lord Hoffman in *Gregg v. Scott* stated:

> "It may be noted in passant, that this decision of the House of Lords is also the most recent authority in support of the proposition that actionable

---

16 [2005] U.K.H.L. 2.

17 [2004] IESC 105.

18 [2004] IESC 105.

claims for loss of chance do not lie. A useful resume of the relevant policy considerations suggesting why this is the preferred approach appear in the judgment of Baroness Hale of Richmond at paras 2.12 – 2.26 given that the decision of Peart J. in *Philp v. Ryan* unreported High Court March 11th 2004 was referred to in the judgment of Lord Hoffman it is perhaps appropriate to comment that that judgment containing as it does an excellent analysis of the facts on which that particular case turns does not purport to address the underlying legal principles".[19]

In fact, the reference in Lord Hoffman's speech was to the Supreme Court judgment of Fennelly J., rather than to the judgment of Peart J. in the High Court. It would therefore seem that Kearns J. when delivering his judgment in Quinn may possibly not have been aware of Fennelly J.s judgment dealing with loss of chance in *Philp v Ryan.*

It is clear that the comments by Kearns J., were *obiter* and Fennelly J. was delivering the unanimous decision of the Supreme Court in approving recovery of loss of chance in Irish law. This makes Irish law consistent with Australian Law, (see *Ruffo v. Hosking*[20]) and a majority of the Federal Supreme courts in the United States. I suspect our Supreme Court will revisit this matter perhaps with a full Court of five on a future occasion, particularly in light of the decision of the House of Lords in *Gregg v. Scott*. It will be very interesting to see if the court adopts a restrictive policy approach, per *Glencar*[21] or *Fletcher,*[22] or adopts a policy neutral approach as per the judgment of Finlay J. in *Dunne.*[23]

It will be noted that in *Dunne* the court balanced equally and gave equal weight, to the competing interests of doctors having to be protected from the frequent threat of unsustainable legal actions and a patient's right to protection by the courts not adopting a permissive or lax legal standard of care in the interest of patient's health and well being. It is difficult to envisage a policy justification for a blanket denial of an entitlement to recover any damages in all circumstances, particularly where the proven negligence of the medical attendant has completely destroyed what may have been reasonable prospects of a cure. To deny an entitlement to damages in all circumstances, in the words of one American judge; *"would be a blanket release from liability for doctors and hospitals anytime there was less than a fifty per cent chance of survival, regardless of how flagrant the negligence".*[24]

---

19 [2005] IESC 19.

20 [2004] N.S.W.C.A. 391.

21 *Glencar Exploration PLC v. Mayo County Council* [2001] IESC 64.

22 *Fletcher v. The Commissioners of Public Works in Ireland* [2003] IESC 13.

23 *Dunne v. National Maternity Hospital*, [1989] I.R. 1, [1989] I.L.R.M. 735.

24 *Herskovits v. Group Health Co-Operative of Puget Sound* (1983) 664 P. 2d 474, 477, *per* Dore J., in the Supreme Court of Washington *en banc*.

The Statute of Limitations

In many medical negligence cases the Statute of Limitations will pose problems for practitioners. Firstly practitioners should be aware that as a result of recent changes in the Civil Liability and Courts Act 2004, the time limit for bringing proceedings has been reduced from three years to two years from the date of accrual of the cause of action[25]. The new two year statutory limitation period affecting medical negligence actions came into effect in respect of claims accruing after March 31, 2005. There were special limitation provisions enacted to cover causes of action accruing before the Act became operative.

Further confusion will be caused to practitioners as a result of the introduction of the Personal Injuries Assessment Board Act 2003. Under that Act the period of limitation is frozen for most types of personal injury actions, from a time beginning on the date of receipt of an application by PIAB and ending 6 months after the date that PIAB issues an authorisation or waiver in respect of the claim.[26]

However, it is vital that all practitioners note that under the PIAB Act 2003, section 3, medical negligence actions are specifically excluded from the scope of the PIAB. Thus medical negligence actions will have a two-year period of limitation with no possibility of a temporary cessation of the time limit running while a PIAB assessment takes place.

The combined effects of sections 3 and 50 of the PIAB 2003 Act, will, in many personal injury cases, be to effectively add approximately 12 to 18 months to the statutory time limit. However, as medical negligence cases are excluded from the scope of the PIAB, they now have a period of limitation considerably shorter than for the more straight forward type of personal injury claims. This is illogical as medical negligence claims are likely to be more complex and difficult to investigate then the more straight forward type of claim.

These factors, combined with a natural reluctance on the part of patients to sue their doctors which often results in victims of medical error consulting lawyers very late in the day, will undoubtedly cause many plaintiffs great difficulties.

It is therefore essential that the plaintiff's legal representatives investigate the medical accident with all possible speed, so as to be in a position to issue a personal injury summons, if possible, within two years from the date of the treatment complained of. This will avoid any potential difficulties with the Statute of Limitations. It will be appreciated that in many cases, even where a patient consults their lawyer very shortly after the treatment complained of, it will be difficult to be in a position to serve a personal injury summons within two years. In most cases, it will be a race against time to comply with this deadline, bearing in mind, the necessity to obtain medical records from various

---

25 Civil Liability and Courts Act 2004, s.7.

26 Personal Injuries Assessment Board Act 2003, s.50.

sources, brief various medical experts on breach of duty and causation matters, obtain medical reports on condition and prognosis, obtain particulars of special damage, instruct counsel, etc.

In many cases plaintiffs will seek to rely on the "*date of knowledge*" saver contained in section 2 of the Statute of Limitations (Amendment) Act 1991.

There have been three recent Supreme Court decisions dealing specifically with the above section and the problems caused by it and how it ought to be interpreted; these are *Gough v. Neary,*[27] *Cunningham v. Neary*[28] and *Fortune v. McLoughlin.*[29]

In a key passage of the *Gough* judgment, Geoghegan J. stated:

> "while it may not be necessary for the purposes of starting the statute to run to know enough detail to draft a statement of claim, a plaintiff in my opinion must know enough facts as would be capable of at least upon elaboration of establishing a cause of action even if the plaintiff has no idea that those facts of which he had knowledge do in fact constitute a cause of action as that particular knowledge is irrelevant under the act. But the adequacy of the knowledge must be related to the context and in this case the plaintiff who was a person of limited education was entitled to assume that the hysterectomy was carried out by Dr Neary to save her life at the time of childbirth because that is what she was told by him. Mere knowledge that a hysterectomy was carried out therefore is irrelevant. Nor do the pieces of additional information that she did have from the doctor provide her with any relevant knowledge. It was only when she discovered that the operation was unnecessary that the period started to run. Of course constructive knowledge under the Act that the operation was unnecessary would suffice. But this plaintiff in my view had neither actual nor constructive notice when the ordinary period "that the injury was attributable in whole or in part to the act or omission which is alleged to constitute negligence".[30]

Geoghegan J. cited with approval the English case of *Spargo v. North Essex District Health Authority*[31] and the judgment of Brooke L.J. where he formulates certain principles to be derived from all of the relevant case law. The relevant portion of the judgment of Brooke L.J. from *Spargo* which was cited with approval in the *Gough* case is as follows:[32]

> (1) The knowledge required to satisfy section 4(1)(b) is a broad knowledge

[27] [2003] IESC 39.
[28] [2004] IESC 43.
[29] [2004] IESC 34.
[30] Gough, *loc. cit.*
[31] [1997] P.I.Q.R. 235.
[32] *Op. cit.*

of the essence of the cause of the relevant act or omission to which injury is attributable

(2) Attributable in this context means capable of being attributed to in the sense of being a real possibility

(3) A plaintiff has the requisite knowledge when she knows enough to make it reasonable for her to begin to investigate whether or not she has a case against the defendant. Another way of putting this is to say that she will have such knowledge if she so firmly believes that her condition is capable of being attributed to an act or omission, which she can identify (in broad terms) that she goes to a solicitor to seek advice about making a claim for compensation.

(4) On the other hand she will not have the requisite knowledge if she thinks she knows the acts or omissions she should investigate but in fact is barking up the wrong tree or if her knowledge of what the defendant did or did not do is so vague or general that she can not fairly be expected to know what she should investigate or if her state of mind is such that she thinks her condition is capable of being attributed to the act or omission alleged to constitute negligence but she is not sure about this and would need to check with an expert before she could be properly said to have known that it was.

In the case of *Fortune*, the *Gough* principles were cited with approval by the Supreme Court. However, in the *Fortune* case the claim was held not to be statute barred as even though the unfortunate plaintiff who suffered brain damage during the course of giving birth to her first child as a result of eclamptic fits which were negligently inflicted did not have constructive knowledge for the purposes of section 2 of the 1991 Act that her injuries were attributable to the treatment given by the plaintiff rather the unfortunate plaintiff believed that they were simply one of the hazards of childbirth She had suffered cognitive impairment as a result of the eclamptic fits and having been told by a nurse that eclampsia can occur in the course of delivery of a first child accepted her injury as having been naturally caused.

In the *Cunningham* case the court on the other hand found the claim to be statute barred and in effect held that the statute had begun to run from at least the moment the plaintiff wrote a letter of complaint to the Medical Council notwithstanding that at that point in time she did not have a supportive medical expert report indicating that the defendant doctor had been negligent. The rationale of the Court's decision was that once the plaintiff had decided to make the complaint to the Medical Council she had the requisite knowledge (constructive knowledge) pursuant to section 2 of the 1991 Act and at that time it was reasonable for the plaintiff to seek medical and other expert advice therefore time had begun to run from that moment. The Supreme Court rejected the argument that time only began to run from the date that the plaintiff received supportive expert reports.

In light of all of the above cases, it will be appreciated that it is often very difficult to determine precisely when the statute has begun to run and it would be very unwise for a practitioner to assume that the date of knowledge can always be postponed until such time as a supportive expert report has been sought and received. As a general rule it would be good practice to assume that the statute of limitations may begin to run from the time of the treatment ultimately complained of. It would be preferable if proceedings can be issued within a two year time period from date of treatment complained of rather then run the risk of subsequent complicated arguments about the date of knowledge.

It is to be anticipated that in future with reduced time limits there is likely to be more controversy regarding the issue of the statute, with more trials of preliminary issues, uncertainty, consequential delays in the pace of the proceedings and increased cost. If this is what occurs it would be ironic as it would be the opposite of what the legislature intended.

Issuing Proceedings without an Expert Report to Prevent a Claim Becoming Statute Barred

In light of the Supreme Court decision in the *Cunningham* case, the plaintiff's lawyer is faced with a serious professional dilemma if he receives instructions shortly before he believes that the statute of limitations is about to expire. As we have seen previously in the cases of *Cooke v. Cronin*, *Reidy v. The National Maternity Hospital* and *Connolly v. Casey*, the courts have roundly condemned legal practitioners for commencing medical negligence litigation without first of all obtaining a supportive expert report. On the other hand the court in *Cunningham* clearly held that time can begin to run against a plaintiff even in the absence of being in possession of a supportive medical expert report. Can the plaintiff's legal advisers simply now ignore the strictures of the Supreme Court in the *Cooke* case and assume that they must issue proceedings to preserve their client's statutory rights even though they have not yet obtained a supportive expert report? Would the Court criticise such tactics and characterise them as professional misconduct or abuse of the process of court as suggested by the Supreme Court in the *Cooke* case? In any event, the statutory pleading requirements set out in section 10 of the Civil Liability and Courts Act 2004 which demand detailed particulars of the negligence to be set out in the personal injury summons now appear to pose a major practical difficulty barring the plaintiff from issuing proceedings without the benefit of an expert report. It will now be very difficult for a plaintiff to issue proceedings to prevent the statute from running without being in possession of an expert report unless they decide to avail of new Order 1A ,II, rule 6 of the Rules of Superior Courts.

When a claim is about to become time barred the plaintiff's lawyers choice is between on the one hand, awaiting receipt of a supportive medical expert report so as to avoid any accusation of an abuse of the process of court and to ensure accuracy of pleading and on the other hand launching proceedings without such a report as a protective measure to preserve a clients rights. Which option should the plaintiff's lawyer take? This is certainly a dilemma. Obviously neither the plaintiff's solicitor or counsel instructed by them can be party to an abuse of the process of court; on the other hand, both clearly owe a legal professional duty to the client and are obliged to take steps to preserve the clients legitimate rights of access to the court. Surely the lesser of two evils must be to serve the clients interests first of all and to issue the proceedings to preserve the clients constitutional right of access to justice. Surely in such circumstances the courts will have to be sympathetic and accept a plaintiff lawyers' bona fides. The Rules of Court surely are there to serve the constitution and justice and not to impede it. The practical option might be to issue proceedings as a protective step and not to serve the proceedings until such time as the claim has been properly investigated and supportive expert opinion obtained. Why otherwise would the Superior Courts' Rules Committee have incorporated a proviso that seemed to envisage such a scenario into the new statutory instrument relating to pleadings albeit one that is not apparently contemplated by section 10 of the 2004 Act itself?

New Rule – Order 1A. II. Commencement of proceedings, rule 6

The Rules Committee have adopted a new Order 1A which clearly appears to contemplate plaintiff's issuing Personal Injury Summons without all of the requisite information demanded by section 10 inserted in the summons and by later providing the missing information by way of amendment. Order 1A. II, rule 6 of the Rules of the Superior Courts (Personal Injuries) 2005 reads as follows:

> "Where a plaintiff alleges that he was unable at the time at which a Personal Injury Summons was issued to include in the Personal Injuries Summons any information required by this order to be specified in the Personal Injuries Summons, he shall include in the Personal Injuries Summons a statement of the reasons why it is claimed that any such information could not be provided at the time of issue of the summons. The plaintiff shall, at the time the Personal Injuries Summons is served or as soon as may be thereafter (whether by amendment or otherwise) provide such of the information required by this order as was not included in the Personal Injuries Summons". [33]

---

[33] S.I. No.248 of 2005, Rules of the Superior Courts (Personal Injuries) 2005, O.1, A.II, r.6.

Impact of Civil Liability and Courts Act 2004 on Medical Negligence Actions

This Act made major changes to civil procedure. While the Act was primarily designed to deal with other types of personal injury litigation it has made major significant procedural changes, which affect medical negligence actions and can pose significant difficulties for legal practitioners. There may be significant cost penalties imposed for non-compliance with the changes introduced by the act. It is clear from section 2 of the Act and the manner in which a personal injuries action is defined therein that the provisions of the Act would apply to any medical negligence action.

Letter of claim

Section 8 (1) of the 2004 Act provides

> "where a plaintiff in a personal injuries action fails without reasonable cause to serve a notice in writing on the alleged wrongdoer before the expiration of 2 months from the date of the cause of action or as soon as practical thereafter stating the nature of the wrong alleged to have been committed the Court hearing the action may draw such inferences from the failure as appear proper and where the interests of justice so require make no order as to the plaintiffs costs or deduct that amount as it considers appropriate from those costs that would otherwise have been payable"

Section 8(2) of the 2004 Act defines;

> "The date of the cause of action means the date of accrual of the cause of action or the date of knowledge whichever occurs later".

The foregoing requirement to effectively send letters of claim within two months of the treatment complained of will in most cases of medical negligence be impossible to comply with. Thus, in most cases of alleged medical negligence, the plaintiff will be seeking to rely on section 8 (2). As in most cases it will be impossible to define the nature of the wrong being alleged against the medical practitioner within 2 months of the treatment being complained of.

The potentially draconian cost penalties that might be imposed for failure to send a letter of claim within the said two-month period may in fact have the opposite effect of the stated purpose of the Act which was to discourage frivolous or unmeritorious claims. Surely it cannot be in the public interest to impose such potentially draconian cost penalties on plaintiffs so as to compel them to write letters of claim to their hospital or doctor within 2 months of treatment so as to avoid potential cost penalties in the event that litigation is necessary down the line. Surely it would have been preferable if within the saver "without reasonable cause" it was expressly recognised that awaiting expert advice would constitute a reasonable cause for non compliance with the two month period.

The personal injury summons

Section 10 of the 2004 Act provides that the personal injury actions should be commenced by a personal injury summons. A personal injury summons should specify, *inter alia*, full particulars of the acts of the defendant constituting the wrong claimed and the circumstances relating to the commission of the wrong.

In the event of the plaintiff failing to comply with the provisions of Section 10, the court if it considers it in the interest of justice dismiss the plaintiff's action and/or further a failure may impact on costs and a court can draw such inferences as it deems fit.

Obviously in light of the requirements imposed by section 10, before issuing a personal injury summons, a supportive medical expert report must have first of all been obtained by the plaintiff.

Mediation

Sections 15 and 16 of the 2004 Act deal with parties obligations to mediate and apply to all personal injury actions including of course medical negligence actions. On the request of any party to a medical negligence action the court may at any time, before the trial of the action and if it considers that the holding of a mediation conference would assist in reaching a settlement, direct that the parties meet up to discuss an attempt to settle the action at such a conference.

If the court directs, the party must comply and thus a party may be compelled to attend a mediation conference even against its will. This will undoubtedly cause the party compelled into mediation to be resentful which is likely to reduce the prospect of successful medication. The costs incurred in holding such a conference can be directed against either party. A report is prepared by the chairman of the conference and is submitted to the court hearing the action but the trial judge will not be made aware of what may have been conceded by either party at mediation, merely that it has or has not occurred and whether it has been successful or not . The net effects of these provisions mean, in fact, that a party who does not meaningfully engage in the mediation process risks being penalised as to costs whenever the final order is being made.

To the writers knowledge a mediation conference has yet to be held in relation to any medical negligence action and it remains to be seen how effective such conferences might be in the context of medical negligence litigation. It is submitted that this is a tactic that might be utilised by any party and particularly the plaintiff in a very technical complex medical negligence action where all of the facts and issues remain unclear or in doubt even after obtaining the medical records, expert reports, discovery etc. It may be a worthwhile option to consider, particularly if the outcome of the litigation is very uncertain from the plaintiff's point of view and if the trial is likely to be prolonged.

On the other hand even where the plaintiff has an apparently strong case in negligence against the defendant doctor or hospital but refuses to engage in a mediation conference in a meaningful way they may find that even if they are successful in the action there is a heavy penalty as to costs. The reason being that a failure to properly engage in a non-consensual mediation process may result in even the successful party in the legal action being penalised in respect of all costs incurred after the court has directed mediation.

Formal offers

Section 17 of the 2004 Act became operative in respect of medical negligence actions commenced after March 31, 2005. As and from that date any action commenced requires the plaintiff to serve a notice in writing of an offer of terms of settlement on the defendant. Likewise the defendant is required to serve a notice in writing on the plaintiff of an offer of terms of settlement or stating that they are not prepared to pay any sum of money to the plaintiff in settlement. Copies of the offers of settlement must be lodged in Court after 14 days of service of notice of trial. After the judge has determined the issues at the trial and when considering making an order as to payment of costs he must have regard to the terms of the formal offer.

It is difficult to see precisely how this will operate in practice but it does seem to be more favourable to defendants then to plaintiffs. What is the extra penalty that can be imposed on an unsuccessful defendant who makes an unrealistically low settlement offer? If he loses the action an order for costs will be made against him regardless of the size of the award and thus there will be no additional sanction against an unsuccessful defendant who makes an unrealistically low settlement offer. On the other hand if the plaintiff for whatever reason pitches his settlement offer at higher than the ultimate award made at trial they are on risk for costs. This could have the effect of artificially suppressing or coercing plaintiffs into pitching their settlement offers at less then the true value of the claim.

Experts appointed by the court

Section 20 of the 2004 Act gives the court power to appoint persons to act as expert witnesses and to prepare expert reports and give expert evidence to the court. This is a radical new departure in Irish jurisprudence, as up to the present time, the parties have been left more or less completely unfettered in their right to choose the nature and number of expert witnesses that they intend to call. The section apparently permits the court appointed expert to have unlimited access to all expert reports prepared by either party or any document prepared for or on behalf of a party and any document or information used or referred to for the purposes of preparing the report in question. This would seem to permit a Court-appointed expert to have unlimited, unfettered access to all relevant documentation to include, *inter alia*, documentation covered by legal professional privilege. This would have potentially far reaching ramifications, as it could conceivably result in a situation where the expert could demand access to information that the trial judge would not be entitled to consider e.g. reports from expert witnesses not intended to be called at the trial, clients' statements to their solicitors, solicitors' notes/memos etc. In such circumstances there must be a doubt over the constitutionality of the section, unless it is interpreted more narrowly than its language may suggest.

Unfortunately there are no provisions in the Act itself or in any statutory instrument or rules of court giving any guidance as to the practices and procedures to be following by such a court-appointed expert. For example, is any party at liberty to challenge the appointment of such an expert by querying their expertise, experience or qualifications? What about potential conflicts of interest? Precisely who will nominate the expert or, if there is to be a panel of experts, who will nominate the panel of experts?

The role of an expert witness in medical negligence actions is of pivotal importance and if courts are going to appoint expert witnesses to report to the court obviously such an appointment is of potentially crucial importance. It is to be hoped that detailed consideration will be given to such a radically new development and that if it is to be adopted in medical negligence litigation there should be very careful consideration of the rules of practice and procedure to be followed. Otherwise there is a risk of injustice being caused by the lack of adequate safeguards to challenge the opinion of the court appointed expert.

For example in extreme cases what is to be done when the court-appointed expert has preconceived, dogmatic, biased, conservative, radical or eccentric views, which are not representative of mainstream medical opinion/views? Is there not a danger that such views will be given undue weight by the court in the mistaken belief that they are more reliable than the medical experts chosen by the parties?

It may also prove difficult for plaintiffs to repose complete confidence in Irish based experts particularly in a specialty with a small number of practising consultants where the cost and availability of malpractice indemnity cover is a cause of great concern to the specialty involved.

Rules relating to Disclosure of Expert Reports

The rules relating to disclosure of expert reports in personal injury actions and in particular medical negligence actions which have been introduced in recent years have caused certain difficulties in their interpretation. The impetus for the introduction of the rules was the widespread dissatisfaction caused by surprises being thrown up during trial. They were an attempt to end "*trial by ambush*". The first attempt at reform was introduced by the Rules of the Superior

Courts (No. 7) 1997,[34] but that instrument was repealed entirely and replaced by the current regime contained in the Rules of the Superior Courts (No. 6) (Disclosure of Reports and Statements), 1998.[35] The key difference between the two statutory instruments was in the definition of what constituted a report, with the 1997 statutory instrument containing a much broader definition of what would constitute a report.

The 1998 Rules redefined "report" by including as part of the definition that it be "in relation to an issue in the action and containing the substance of the evidence to be adduced".

Rule 46 (1) of S.I. No.391 of 1998 then provided:

> "the plaintiff in an action shall furnish to the other party or parties or their respective solicitors (as the case may be) a schedule listing all reports from expert witnesses intended to be called within one month of the service of the notice of trial in respect of the action or within such further time as may be agreed by the parties or permitted by the Court".

In *Payne v. Shovlin & Ors*[36], the Supreme Court considered the issue of exactly what constituted a "report" and what reports had to be disclosed pursuant to the 1998 Rules. At issue was the plaintiff's contention that a preliminary draft report which did not contain the expert's final views ought not to be disclosable and that the rules merely required disclosure of the expert's final report. It was submitted by the plaintiff that the 1998 statutory instrument, by introducing the phrase "*reports containing the substance of the evidence to be adduced*," should be understood as meaning that the obligation of disclosure should be confined to the report or reports which contain the intended evidence in chief of the expert witness in question and this was the obvious implication and inference to be drawn from the repeal of the more extensive obligations contained in the 1997 rules.

The defendants on the other hand maintained and submitted that the wording of rule 46(1) of the 1998 Rules was quite specific in stating that "all" reports of expert witnesses must be listed in the schedule to be furnished and nothing in the 1998 definition of "report" suggested that it was intended by the Rules Committee to convert or confine the obligation to disclose to something in the nature of a "will say" obligation which in effect was what the plaintiffs were contending for.

The Supreme Court per Kearns J. gave judgment and directed that both the preliminary report of the plaintiff's expert and his final report were obliged to be disclosed to the defendants. In the course of the judgment Kearns J. stated:

---

[34] S.I. No.348 of 1997.

[35] S.I. No.391 of 1998.

[36] [2006] IESC 5 (February 9, 2006).

"While no direct evidence was offered to this Court to explain why the Rules Committee elected to replace the 1997 rules with a new definition of 'report' in S.I. 391 of 1998 I have no difficulty in accepting what the Court was told in that regard by the plaintiff's counsel namely that the requirements and obligations created by the 1997 rules posed huge practical difficulties for practitioners because of the scope of what was required to be disclosed, I would also accept Mr McCullough's submission that the altered wording of the 1998 rules which redefines a 'report' as a document 'containing the substance of the evidence to be adduced should be seen as easing the obligations which existed under the previous regulations.'"[37]

As will be seen from the foregoing excerpt from the judgment the Court had no difficulty accepting that the 1998 rules required less disclosure and reduced the scope of what had to be disclosed from the 1997 rules. Unfortunately the Court did not give any explicit guidance as to precisely what communications from an expert or material produced by an expert would not come within the disclosure obligations. As all parties to the *Payne* case accepted that the Rules Committee had adopted the amending definition of "report" from the English Rules of Court, order 25, the court then reviewed the corresponding disclosure obligations in England and Wales.

Kearns J. stated:

"While it is correct to say that S.I. 391 of 1998 introduced an exception to the general privilege attaching to the communications made in contemplation or in furtherance of litigation it should be remembered that litigation privilege is in itself an exception to the general principle that all relevant information should be before the Court. The consequent need to construe this latter exception strictly has been recognised frequently by the Courts."[38]

Kearns J. then quoted from the decisions of the Supreme Court, *Smurfit Paribas v. AIB Export Finance*[39] and *Gallagher v. Stanley*,[40] before going on to state:

"Thus the exception to the privilege rule introduced by the 1998 rules may be seen in itself as an exception to an exception and one which has its purpose the furtherance of the principle that justice is best served where all relevant documentary evidence is available. That approach is underlined by the provisions of the Court and Courts Officers Act 1995

---

37 [2006] IESC 5.
38 *Ibid.*
39 [1990] 1 I.R. 469.
40 [1992] IR 267.

which empowered the Rules Committee to make the 1998 Rules limiting he ordinary rights of privilege."[41]

Kearns J. continued:

"That the failure to produce an earlier report providing it contains the substance or part of the substance of the evidence which at the time of its compilation was intended to give may lead to a situation where in the course of cross-examination it may emerge that the author expressed a different view for example in relation to causation in a medical negligence action at an earlier time and averted to same in a first report, how can the interests of expedition and efficiency be served if such information only emerges in cross examination it may well require that the trial be adjourned while further lines of enquiry are pursued in the light of the particular revelation, further it would always be possible that such additional enquiries might lead to the claim being dropped altogether. All of these costly and undesirable consequences are avoided by disclosure of all reports which contain any of the substance of the evidence intended to be led". [42]

On the question of whether or not the obligation to disclose the substance of an expert's evidence included matters which might arise not only in evidence in chief but also in cross examination unfortunately Kearns J. explicitly declined to rule on the point but stated the following:

"It does seem to be an arguable point although apparently not the subject of any legal authority in this country. Certainly when personal injuries actions were tried in this jurisdiction by judge and jury, judges were always careful to instruct a jury that in considering evidence adduced by an expert witness that the jury should have regard not merely to his direct evidence but also to his evidence and answers given in cross examination also. However, it is not necessary for the purposes of this ruling to offer a view on that issue and I expressly resile from so doing."[43]

Finally, the court did not make any ruling on whether commentaries by experts on the opponent's expert reports prepared to assist counsel in cross-examination of the other side's experts should be disclosed or not.

Unfortunately while the judgment does give us guidance on the issue of disclosure and certainly the broad thrust of the judgment would indicate that the court demands a broad and generous interpretation of a party's disclosure

---

41 [2006] IESC 5.

42 *Ibid.*

43 *Ibid.*

obligations, it does not explicitly define the meaning of the key phrase "*substance of the evidence to be adduced*" and specifically whether that phrase includes not only the direct evidence intended to be given by the expert but all of the evidence that might possibly emerge following cross examination of that expert. Furthermore although the court accepted that the replacement of the more onerous disclosure obligations under the 1997 Rules by the current regime under the 1998 Rules "*should be seen as easing the obligation which existed under the previous regulations*,"[44] it did not inform us as to precisely how the obligations have been eased and what categories of communications from an expert do not require disclosure.

Other documents referred to in an expert report, are they disclosable?

The question arises as to whether documents specifically referred to in an expert's report are required to be disclosed under the terms of the 1998 Rules or retain privilege. This very issue was dealt with in *Doherty (a minor) v. Davidson, The Medical Defence Union Ltd & MDU Services Ltd.*[45] In that case two expert reports were disclosed. These reports explicitly listed various documents to which the experts had regard for the purposes of preparing their respective reports. The defendant required that the documents set out in these two expert reports be disclosed pursuant to the parties' obligations under the 1998 Rules and in particular sought disclosure on that basis that the definition of report also included "any maps, drawings, photographs, graphs, charts, calculations or other like matter referred to in any such report".[46]

Disclosure of the documents was resisted on the ground that they were covered by privilege. It appears that many of the documents in question were solicitor client correspondence, solicitor's attendances and expert reports from other medical witnesses not intended to be called as witnesses at the trial. Finnegan J. ruled that the documents did not have to be disclosed and stated:

> "The defendant contends that the documents which I have listed above and in respect of which privilege is claimed come within the clause 'other like matter referred to in any such report.' I am satisfied that the defendant is incorrect; the phrase "other like matter referred to in any such report" must be construed *ejusdem generis* with the words preceding it. I am satisfied that the documents referred to by Professor Symonds and Dr McKenzie cannot be considered as a like matter to a map, drawing, photograph, graph, chart or calculation. There is accordingly no obligation to disclose the same or to exchange the same arising under order 39 rule 46 (1), the documents in question not coming within the definition of report. It may well be in the case of some of the documents that they require to

---

[44] *Ibid.*

[45] Unreported, High Court, Finnegan J., December 1, 2005.

[46] *Ibid.*

be discovered upon an order for discovery being made … Many of them it would appear are clearly privileged correspondence between the third party and his own insurers, statements taken by his solicitors from him and correspondence between the third party and his insurer. Others less clearly so".[47]

Exchange of reports

As will be observed from the requirements of the 1998 Rules, the obligation of the parties is to exchange copies of the reports listed in each party's' schedule. The purpose of the rules is not to oblige the plaintiff to furnish all of his or her reports to the defendant prior to receiving the defendant's reports which might otherwise enable the defendant to have his or her experts prepare their own reports with the full knowledge of what is contained in the plaintiff's expert opinions. As was noted by Geoghegan J. in *Kincaid v. Aer Lingus Teoranta*[48], the obligation under order 39, rule 46(1) is to "*exchange*" the scheduled reports and thus as is suggested by Geoghegan J. if each party's solicitor ensures that there is an actual contemporaneous exchange of such reports there is no danger that the procedure can be abused or mischief occur. Therefore in medical negligence actions it is always advisable that there should be a contemporaneous exchange of reports rather then a serial exchange.

Human Rights Considerations in Medical Negligence Claims – Possible Future Developments

The European Convention on Human Rights Act 2003 was commenced by ministerial order on December 31, 2003. At the time of writing it is extremely difficult to predict what implications, if any, the formal adoption of the European Convention on Human Rights into Irish law might have on medical negligence litigation. It is beyond the scope of this chapter to deal in any detail with the provisions and possible implications of the Convention. It is possible, however, to foresee that the Act may have an impact on medical negligence litigation. Section 2(1) of the 2003 Act provides:

> "In interpreting and applying any statutory provision or rule of law, a court shall so far as possible, subject to the rules of law relating to such an interpretation and application, do so in a matter compatible with the State's obligations under the Convention provisions."

It will be noted that the Oireachtas has chosen to use the words "so far as possible" rather then the lower standard which would have been implied by the

---

47 Unreported High Court, Finnegan J., December 1, 2005.

48 [2003] IESC 31.

use of the expression "so far as practicable." Thus the test and the obligations are quite stringent.

Section 3 of the Act imposes a substantive obligation on all organs of the State (which would obviously include the Health Service Executive) to act in conformity with the Convention, backed up by a remedial provision to a person who has suffered injury being entitled to claim damages for breach of the Convention provided no other remedy in damages is available to him or her.

However, the Convention has been adopted into our law with the specific proviso in the title to the Act making it clear that it is subject to our Constitution. In the event of irreconcilable conflict, it seems clear therefore, that the constitutional provision must prevail. The articles of the Convention that might be engaged in cases concerning the provision of health care are perhaps Articles 2, 3 and 8.

Article 2 - the right to life

The right to life in Article 2 has been consistently stressed by the European Court of Human Rights to be one of the most fundamental provisions of the Convention. It requires a Member State not only to refrain from taking life intentionally but also in combination with Article 1 to put in place a framework of laws, precautions, procedures and means of enforcement to safeguard the right to life to the greatest extent reasonably practicable. The scope of the State's positive obligations will depend on the factual circumstances so therefore a high level of protection will be likely required where the victim is in State custody, e.g. a prisoner requiring medical care or a patient involuntarily detained pursuant to the Mental Health Acts. In cases of hospital deaths or where the adequacy of medical treatment in the community is an issue the positive duties under Article 2 may simply require the State to make adequate regulations for the provision of health care and to ensure that there are proper criminal and/or civil remedies which the patient's family can access to establish liability against medical practitioners or hospitals. It must be emphasised that Article 2 is unlikely to be engaged where there has been simple negligence as a consequence of an error in clinical practice by a hospital or doctor.

In *Powell v. The UK*,[49] the European Court of Human Rights stated that:

> "where a contracting State has made adequate provision for securing high professional standards among health professionals and the protection of the lives of patients it cannot accept that matters such as error of judgment on the part of a health professional or negligent co-ordination among health professionals in the treatment of a particular patient are sufficient of themselves to call a contracting State to account from the

[49] APP 45305/1999, ECHR.

> stand point of its positive obligations under Article 2 of the Convention to protect life".[50]

In *Seimenska v. Poland,*[51] the Court held that:

> "the positive obligations the State has to protect life under Article 2 of the Convention includes the requirement for hospitals to have regulations for the protection of their patients' lives".[52]

Similarly in *Calvelli v. Italy,*[53] the Court reasoned as follows:

> "Those principles i.e. the principles giving rise to the obligation on the State to take appropriate steps to safeguard life apply in the public health sphere too. The aforementioned positive obligations therefore require States to make regulations compelling hospitals whether public or private to adopt appropriate measures for the protection of their patients lives".[54]

Other authors have taken the view that:

> "a successful complaint under Article 2 is highly unlikely in relation to the general standard of healthcare available, the financial arrangements for such care and the policies governing its organisation and delivery within the State. Under the doctrine of the margin of appreciation it is the place of National Courts to determine compliance with the Convention given their direct and continuous contact with the vital forces of the responsible State".[55]

In conclusion, therefore, it is submitted that the threshold for bringing a claim under Article 2 against a healthcare provider might be found where there is a systems failure, a lacuna or the complete absence of a system so as to threaten the adequate protection of life. For example:

- Where a bureaucratic administrative procedure pays no heed to the urgent clinical need for a potentially life saving medical device, which is relatively inexpensive.[56]
- The death of a profoundly disabled adult where the risk to life was real and obvious but reasonable precautions were not taken.

---

50 *Op. cit.*

51 APP 37602/97, ECHR.

52 *Ibid.*

53 Human Rights Case Digest, Vol.13, Nos 1-2, 2002, pp. 23-26(4).

54 *Op. cit.*

55 Lester and Pannick, *Human Rights Law and Practice*, 2nd ed., (Reed Elsevier UK, 1999), p.110.

56 *Britton v. Cardiff & Vale NHS Trust, Clinical Risk* Volume 11, No.3, May 2005, p.121.

- The death of an elderly patient in health board care following serious systemic neglect in a State-run nursing home.

There have been several medical negligence claims successfully brought in the UK invoking Article 2 arguments. All have been settled out of Court so there have been no judicial decisions on the point. One notable case[57] was taken by the daughter of her deceased father (aged 57) who had been suffering from a chronic medical condition and who was in urgent need of surgery to insert an artificial stent in his subclavian artery. The man died following a delay in providing the life saving surgery. The delay in providing the surgery arose principally as a result of bureaucratic/administrative systems delay in providing the surgical team with the artificial stent that was needed in the operation. The stent had to be procured by centrally controlled NHS managers subsequent to the local clinicians' completing the relevant written requisition forms. The system was not designed adequately so as to enable the device to be delivered to the hospital in cases of urgent medical need. As a result the hospital clinicians were unable to procure a suitable stent for use in the surgery for a period of 36 hours and unfortunately the patient died. Under the terms of the settlement the plaintiff, the deceased's daughter received stg£15,000 in damages approved of by the Court for breach of Article 2 of the Convention.

This case is noteworthy and a good example of how a cause of action founded on the Convention might in appropriate cases be a suitable alternative to an action based in common law for breach of duty of care. First, it is submitted that the courts are not constrained or restricted to awarding damages limited to the statutory amount available for mental distress/bereavement as prescribed in the Civil Liability Act 1961 as amended. The Court can in appropriate cases take into account the defendant's conduct and the nature of the Article 2 violation in assessing damages. Thus it might be possible to increase the level of damages in an appropriate case involving a particularly flagrant breach of Article 2 with particularly shocking results. It may be appropriate to consider such a form of action in circumstances where the plaintiff does not meet the criteria for a nervous shock action.

Secondly, it may be appropriate to invoke an Article 2 argument in a case where it is impossible to point the finger of blame at any particular individual clinician or hospital administrator.

Thirdly, it might be possible to avoid difficult causation issues and difficulties that may arise in satisfying the "but for" test of causation. However, there needs to be a sufficient causal connection between the violation found and the loss for which an applicant claims to be compensated. In appropriate cases the European Court of Human Rights will award a modest amount for loss of chance where it is persuaded that justice requires it to do so.

---

[57] *Ibid.*

Article 3 – Prohibition against torture/inhuman or degrading treatment

Article 3 ranks among the most important rights guaranteed by the Convention. The prohibition against torture and other forms of inhuman or degrading treatment is absolute, and is generally enforced by the European Court of Human Rights with rigour. Mistreatment must attain a minimum level of severity in order to fall within the scope of Article 3. The assessment of this minimum is relative and depends on factors including the duration of the treatment, its physical or mental effects, and the age, sex, vulnerability and state of health of the victim.[58]

An omission to provide for basic medical care to a mentally ill person may therefore amount to a breach of Article 3.[59] The State may be obliged to make reasonable adjustments to cater for the special needs of a disabled person if their treatment is not to be degrading.[60] The relationship between the claimant and the State is important. The *Keenan*[61] and *Price*[62] cases both concerned prisoners and it is clear that an enhanced level of protection is required under Article 3 in the case of the involuntarily detained. The more vulnerable and dependant on the State the claimant is, the greater the positive obligation is likely to be to ensure that their living conditions are humane. It is important to note in this context that the victim does not need to be able to complain coherently or at all about how they are being affected by the treatment (or even, possibly, have an awareness they are being ill-treated) if their living conditions constitute an affront to essential human dignity.[63]

Where the actions to be taken by the State would have significant resource implications, and therefore will involve social, economic or political considerations, the courts are likely to be much slower to find a breach of Article 3 as the obligations of the State can never be unlimited. As the Convention is a 'living instrument' to be interpreted in light of contemporary social conditions, views of what constitutes humane treatment are likely to evolve over time, so what is regarded as adequate now may in future become unacceptable.

Some suggested applications of Article 3 might be the following:

- Adopting a "blanket no lifting" policy, as a result of which a disabled person in a State nursing home is left sitting in bodily waste or on the lavatory for hours, unable to be moved (e.g., *A, B, X, Y v. East Sussex County Council*[64]).
- On discovering that an elderly person in residential care has been abused

[58] *Ireland v. United Kingdom* (1980) 2 E.H.R.R. 25, ECt HR at 162.

[59] *Keenan v. UK* (2001) 33 E.H.R.R. 913.

[60] *Price v. UK* (2002) 34 E.H.R.R. 1285.

[61] (2001) 33 E.H.R.R. 913.

[62] (2002) 34 E.H.R.R. 1285.

[63] *Keenan and A, B, X & Y v. East Sussex* [2003] E.W.H.C. 167

[64] *Ibid.*

by a fellow resident, failing to implement a transfer to ensure she no longer has to live with the abuser.

- Refusal of funding for a new or even existing treatment for a debilitating disease without proper appraisal of clinical need.

Article 8 – Right to respect for private and family life

Article 8 is one of the Articles lawyers are likely to have to consider in cases concerning the provision of care and medical treatment. Article 8 (1) provides that everyone has the right to respect for his private and family life, his home and his correspondence. Article 8 (2) sets out conditions, upon which the State may interfere with the enjoyment of these rights. Medical treatment administered to an individual without consent does not amount to interference if that individual cannot give informed consent.[65]

The Convention is a living instrument. This is a principle with special resonance for Article 8 cases, as the very subject matter it protects is constantly evolving. Arguments that may have failed 10 years ago may now succeed.[66] Indeed, this changing context may impose special obligations on the State to keep policy in such sensitive areas under active review.

Private life has been defined as the right to establish and develop relationships with other human beings. Private life is likely to encompass protection against compulsory medical intervention such as compulsory blood tests in paternity actions. In *X v. Austria*, the applicant complained that the obligation upon him to submit to a blood test in affiliation proceedings was in violation of Article 8. The Commission held that the medical intervention, even if it was of minor significance, must be considered as an interference with this right.

Article 8 (1) also imposes controls on how the State (and as a result of the Council of Europe's intervention, any individual) stores, processes and disseminates information about individuals. Access to and protection of personal information gathered by way of medical data and medical reports are also covered by this Article.[67]

The case of *Glass v. UK*[68] is authority for the proposition that there will be an Article 8 breach, if an NHS Trust administers treatment to a child in the face of parental opposition without first obtaining a declaration from the court, where there is the opportunity to do this. In the judgment in the *National Organ Group* litigation,[69] it was accepted that the retention and use of human tissue for the

65 *Herczegfalvy v. Austria* (1992) 15 E.H.R.R. 437, ECt HR. Nor, similarly, did the appointment of a guardian *ad litem* on the application of legal advisors of a person of full age: see *X v. United Kingdom* 14 DR 224 (1978) E Com HR.

66 See *Goodwin v. United Kingdom* (2002) 35 E.H.R.R. 447 at 72-75.

67 *Chare (nee Jullien) v. France* 71 DR 141 (1991), E Com HR.

68 (2004) 39 E.H.R.R. 15.

69 *National Organ Group Litigation (AB & Others v. Leeds Teaching Hospital NHS Trust* [2004] E.W.H.C. 644.

purposes of research following a post-mortem, without the family's knowledge or consent, was liable to engage Article 8 (1).

Much more problematic is the extent to which Convention rights under Articles 2, 3 & 8 enable a patient to require treatment to be continued where doctors judge that this is clinically inappropriate.

As has been mentioned, the European Court of Human Rights has also interpreted Article 8 to include a right to establish and develop relationships with other human beings. This includes a duty on the State to take appropriate measures to ensure the disabled can participate in the life of the community and have "access to essential economic and social activities and to an appropriate range of cultural activities".[70] This has obvious relevance to the rights of chronically ill and disabled people, their families and carers. Underpinning this is the concept of human dignity and the right of the disabled to have some life, over and above the mere performance of bodily functions.[71]

It is important to note that Article 8 is a qualified right and interference with it can be justified by the State under Article 8 (2) where lawful. This requires some weighting by the authorities of the respective interests of the individual and the State, although not always. The authorities are allowed a margin of appreciation in this balancing exercise, particularly in public welfare decisions and undoubtedly an "allocation of scarce resources" argument can be made.

Possible examples of situations where Article 8 may be engaged are as follows:

- Misdiagnosis of non-accidental injury causing the removal of a child into local authority care.[72]
- Adequacy of provision of day care to a learning disabled adult.
- Refusal or serious restriction on visitors attending a residential institution.

Conclusion

All of the above are raised as possible implications of the incorporation of the Convention into Irish Law and are very much in the realms of speculation. Much will depend upon the attitude of the judiciary and whether they adopt a radical judicially activist approach or a more conservative approach. Much will also depend on the political response from the State to medical negligence litigation incorporating allegations of breaches of fundamental human rights. In my own view there is much potential for the Act to have a considerable influence on the law relating to medical care.

---

70 *Botta v. Italy* [1198] 26 E.H.R.R. 241.

71 *A, B, X, Y v. East Sussex County Council* [2003] E.W.H.C. 167 (Admin).

72 *Ibid.*

Chapter 7

Informed Consent. Should there be a Reasonable Parent Test?

Estelle Feldman*

Introduction

The law is not settled as to the correct test to apply when considering the issue of informed consent. Is it the reasonable doctor or the reasonable or prudent patient? Nevertheless, it does appear that, increasingly, respecting the autonomy of the patient is a required factor in doctor/patient relationships. With regard to minors, is it possible to apply a reasonable or prudent child test? Certainly the courts appear willing to exercise judgement on a child's capability to reason in criminal cases, in negligence cases and, indeed, in adoption and custody cases. However, because of constitutional imperatives in relation to the parent's role in the family, there appears to be little if any room for a child's autonomy in medical treatment to be considered. For this reason it seems that in respect of medical treatment, a child of marital parents in a loving, warm and functional family is at a disadvantage when compared to a child who due to exceptional circumstances has been removed from the parent.

Informed Consent

The reasonable patient

The development of the current law relating to informed consent to medical treatment owes much to the United States Court of Appeals decision in *Canterbury v. Spence,*[1] which held that respect for the patient's right to self-

---

* **Author's note**: My interest in medical law has been nurtured, if not force-fed, by the editors, Ciaran Craven and William Binchy. A specific interest in the complicated and relatively uncharted sphere of medical law and children has been informed through the practical and legally challenging discussions initiated by the post-graduate paediatric nursing students of the National Children's Hospital, Tallaght. In particular, acknowledgement is due to Edel Coleman, Sharon Dawson, Sadie Kerr, Kelley Leonard, Suzanne McDonald, Nicola Murphy and Emma Nolan who were the first class to be examined by project (awarded well-deserved high first class honours) for my brief course in Law for Paediatric Nurses. Naturally, any errors and omissions are my sole responsibility.

[1] 464 F2d 772 (1972).

determination demands a standard set by law. The judgment elevated the autonomy of the patient as the proper focus for the court's attention as opposed to deference to standards of behaviour defined for doctors by doctors, and it noted that the patient's right of self-decision shapes the boundaries of the duty to reveal. In giving this judgment Robinson J. maintained that a patient must be possessed of enough information to enable him/her form an intelligent choice between alternative courses. "This is dependent on disclosure by a doctor of all the risks which could materially affect a patient's decision." Healy notes that in *Sidaway v. Bethlehem Royal Hospital*:[2]

> "Lord Scarman, dissenting, firmly aligned himself with *Canterbury v. Spence*, identifying, beyond its humanistic protection of self-determination, the practical benefits of enabling each patient "to consider and balance the medical advantages and risks alongside other relevant matters, such as, for example, his family business or social responsibilities of which the doctor may only be partially, if at all, informed.'"[3]

Irish case law with regard to the standards to be applied for consent issues, as described elsewhere, travels via *Daniels v. Heskin*,[4] *Dunne v. National Maternity Hospital*,[5] *Walsh v. Family Planning Services*,[6] and *Geoghegan v. Harris*.[7] "It is fair to say that no other Irish judge has examined the issue of informed consent to treatment in as thorough and philosophical manner as Kearns J. did in *Geoghegan v. Harris*."[8]

> "The application of the reasonable patient test seems more logical in respect of disclosure. This would establish the proposition that, as a general principle, the patient has the right to know and the practitioner a duty to advise of all material risks associated with a proposed form of treatment. The Court must ultimately decide what is material. 'Materiality' includes consideration of both: (a) the severity of the consequences, and (b) statistical frequency of the risk. That both are critical is obvious because a risk may have serious consequences and yet historically or predictably be so rare as not to be regarded as significant by many people. For example, a tourist might be deterred from visiting a country where there had been an earthquake causing loss of life, but if told the event

---

2 [1985] 1 A.C. 871.

3 Healy, J. "Failure of doctors to communicate risks to patients at the pre-treatment stage: a case of Negligence or Medical Negligence?: Part I" (1995) 13 I.L.T. 196 .

4 [1954] I.R. 73.

5 [1989] I.L.R.M. 735.

6 [1992] I.R. 486.

7 [2000] IEHC 129; [2000] 3 I.R. 536.

8 McMahon and Binchy, *Law of Torts*, 3rd ed., (Butterworths, Dublin, 2000), chap.14 "Professional Negligence" para.14.135.

> happened fifty years ago without repetition since, he might well wonder why his travel agent caused him unnecessary worry by mentioning it at all.
>
> The reasonable man, entitled as he must be to full information of material risks, does not have impossible expectations nor does he seek to impose impossible standards. He does not invoke only the wisdom of hindsight if things go wrong. He must be taken as needing medical practitioners to deliver on their medical expertise without excessive restraint or gross limitation on their ability to do so."[9]

Medical paternalism

Nevertheless, the courts continue to assess consent issues based in negligence rather than in rights. As Healy noted, albeit in 1995:

> "Judicial analysis by reasonable patient standards can afford to offer no guarantee that it will be appreciably less policy-saturated or appreciably more beneficial to plaintiff patients. The defence of therapeutic privilege, as drafted by Robinson J. in *Canterbury v. Spence,* covers much of the ground already mapped out by the medical negligence model as spheres of professional privilege, recognising discretion to withhold information where disclosure would, in the doctor's view, render the patient 'emotionally distraught … or complicate or hinder the treatment, or perhaps even pose psychological damage to the patient.'[10]
>
> Definitions of general and specific risks, specialised clinical judgment, therapeutic privilege, and materiality all remain to be ascertained, which the court cannot do in a vacuum. Perhaps more obviously than for any other profession, the court is reliant on elucidatory evidence of in-house medical theory and practice; and there is much scope in elucidation for medical paternalism, the mischief which the informed consent model avowed originally to remedy."[11]

If one recognises that there is still considerable paternalism in the relationship many health professionals maintain with their adult patients, how do they relate to the child patient? Moreover, it is not unreasonable to assume that the parent or legal guardian may already be "emotionally distraught" before ever seeing a doctor or a nurse. How then does one assess the reasonable patient in terms of children? Is there any room for child patient self-determination? This has been considered by both the House of Lords and the English Court of Appeal in a number of cases dealing with minors.

---

9 [2000] IEHC 129 at [98] and [99].

10 464 F2d 772 (1972) at 789.

11 Healy, "Failure of doctors to communicate risks to patients at the pre-treatment stage: a case of Negligence or Medical Negligence?: Part II" (1995) 13 I.L.T. 222 at 224.

The competent child and consent

Whereas the age of majority is 18, section 8(1) of the United Kingdom Family Law Reform Act 1969 provides that a child over sixteen can validly consent to medical treatment. With regard to those under 16, the seminal case on the competence or otherwise of a minor to consent to medical treatment is *Gillick v. West Norfolk and Wisbech Area Health Authority.*[12] A majority of the House of Lords held that doctors can, in certain circumstances, prescribe contraception for girls under sixteen without informing or seeking the consent of her parents. The House of Lords recognised the right of the minor to autonomy in this area holding that the fact that a girl was under the age of sixteen did not imply that she was incapable of consenting to such treatment and advice. The relevant factor was not the age of the individual but rather her ability to understand fully what was proposed. According to Lord Scarman "[i]t will be a question of fact whether a child seeking advice has sufficient understanding of what is involved to give a consent valid in law."[13]

The impact of the decision in *Gillick* is evidenced by the fact that the term "Gillick competent" has entered the lexicon of medical law. Indeed, one contemporaneous commentator argued that *Gillick* extends to other decisions that a child might wish to make:

> "For example, can a parent still prevent his 'competent' child from going on a school trip or attending sex education classes? Once a child is 'competent' in relation to a particular matter, the power to decide would seem to be the child's. A more sensible view might be some sort of concurrent involvement of parents and child. To view the role of parents as one of control up to the point of the child's 'competence' and thereafter as nothing more than advisory is unrealistic and (frankly) foolish."[14]

Creeping autonomy

The notion of "concurrent involvement" seems more in line with a child's growth towards self-determination. Lord Denning MR is credited with first describing what is, in a sense, creeping autonomy. In *Hewer v. Bryant,*[15] the Court of Appeal considered whether the Statute of Limitations barred litigation by a 22-year old plaintiff[16] who had been seriously injured while a minor and thus unable himself to take an action for damages. The question was whether the plaintiff was at the time when the cause of action accrued to him … "in the custody of a parent".

---

12 [1986] A.C. 112.

13 *Ibid.* at 186.

14 Grubb, "Contraceptive advice and medical treatment for children" (1986) Camb.L.J. 3 at 5.

15 [1970] 1 Q.B. 357.

16 At the time he commenced the action the age of majority was 21.

> "I would get rid of the rule in *In re Agar-Ellis*[17] and of the suggested exceptions to it. That case was decided in the year 1883. It reflects the attitude of a Victorian parent towards his children He expected unquestioning obedience to his commands. If a son disobeyed, his father would cut him off with a shilling. If a daughter had an illegitimate child, he would turn her out of the house. His power only ceased when the child became 21. I decline to accept a view so much out of date. The common law can, and should, keep pace with the times. It should declare, in conformity with the recent Report of the Committee on the Age of Majority [Cmnd. 3342, 1967], that *the legal right of a parent to the custody of a child ends at the 18th birthday: and even up till then, it is a dwindling right which the courts will hesitate to enforce against the wishes of the child, and the more so the older he is. It starts with a right of control and ends with little more than advice.*" (emphasis added)

The competent child and refusal

However, Tomkin and Hanafin note that a serious blow to the autonomy of minors in relation to medical treatment was suffered by the judgment of Lord Donaldson MR in *In re R (a minor) (Wardship: Consent to Treatment)*.[18] He stated that the failure or refusal of the "*Gillick* competent child to consent is a very important factor in the doctor's decision, whether or not to treat, but does not prevent the necessary consent being obtained from another competent source."[19] A parent or someone acting *in loco parentis* is the other competent source.[20]

Lord Donaldson reiterated this view in *In Re W (a Minor) (Medical Treatment: Court's Jurisdiction)*.[21] He held that while a Gillick competent minor could consent to medical treatment despite parental disapproval, the minor's refusal of such treatment could be disregarded if a parent gave consent.

With regard to *Gillick*, the critical issue to be considered was whether the case gave children rights beyond the statutory rights granted under the Family Law Reform Act 1969 namely the ability to give consent at 16.

> "It clearly did so, as a child who is under 16 may now validly consent to treatment if sufficiently competent. *In Re R* Lord Donaldson had restricted this to a right to *give* consent, not to withhold it, despite Lord Scarman's enunciation that 'the underlying principle' was 'that parental right yields to the child's right to make his own *decisions* (my emphasis) when he reaches a sufficient understanding and intelligence to be capable of making

---

17 (1883) 24 Ch. D 317 which held that parental rights are absolute.

18 [1991] 4 All E.R. 177.

19 *Ibid.*, p.186.

20 Tomkin & Hanafin, *Irish Medical Law* (Round Hall Press, Dublin, 1995), chap.3 "Consent" p.40.

21 [1992] 3 W.L.R. 758.

> up his own mind on the matter requiring decision' ([1986] A.C. 112 at p. 186). Now, in *Re W,* although doubting whether Lord Scarman really intended it, Lord Donaldson was prepared to 'assume . . . so far as the common law is concerned' that Lord Scarman would have decided that parental consent could not be given in the face of the minor's refusal, and that that was of 'considerable persuasive authority' (p. 765). Balcombe L.J., too, was prepared to accept that Lord Scarman had considered that 'the right to refuse treatment was co-existent with the right to consent to treatment' (p. 775). Indeed, he later stated that 'in logic there can be no difference between an ability to consent to treatment and an ability to refuse treatment' (p. 776)."[22]

The Voice of the Child in Ireland

United Nations Convention on the Rights of the Child

Turning to a consideration of Irish law, is there any recognition of the autonomy and self-determination of a minor? How likely is it that the concept of the Gillick competent child would find favour?

The philosophy underlying Gillick competence is enshrined in the United Nations' *Convention on the Rights of the Child* of which Ireland is a ratifying party. Article 12 states as follows:

> 1. States Parties shall assure to the child who is capable of forming his or her own views the right to express those views freely in all matters affecting the child, the views of the child being given due weight in accordance with the age and maturity of the child.
> 2. For this purpose, the child shall in particular be provided the opportunity to be heard in any judicial and administrative proceedings affecting the child, either directly, or through a representative or an appropriate body, in a manner consistent with the procedural rules of national law.

Lack of respect for the voice of the child

In the *Report of the Ombudsman for Children to the UN Committee on the Rights of the Child on the occasion of the examination of Ireland's Second Report to the Committee* the following was noted:

> "[I]t has been the experience of the Office, across all thematic areas, that a high number of complainants reported a lack of respect for the voice of the child. Children themselves reported that when they had made some attempts to complain or suggest changes about a service/facility or about

[22] Eekelaar, "White Coats or Flak Jackets? Doctors, Children and the Courts – Again" (1993) 109 L.Q.R. 182 at 183-184.

a situation that causes them concern, their attempts were disregarded or their views not taken seriously. It was only when their parents or advocate intervened that the issue was dealt with as a complaint. Although not usual, in some circumstances, the child was even disciplined for voicing their opinion. "[23]

Role of Ombudsman for Children

The creation of the function of Ombudsman for Children has undoubtedly created a sense of optimism that children will find greater representation and a clear voice in matters affecting them. Unfortunately, this is something of a false hope.

A legally flawed office?[24]

The Ombudsman for Children Act 2002 is a complex and confusing piece of legislation. In part the Act is a re-statement of the requirements for the office of Ombudsman as outlined in the Ombudsman Act 1980. However, it requires the Ombudsman for Children to act in a general advocacy role or, as was stated in the Explanatory Memorandum, the Act provides the Ombudsman for Children with a promotional role regarding the rights and welfare of children. Such a role compromises the independence and objectivity of an Ombudsman as an impartial investigator seeking redress where appropriate.

Parents' role in children's complaints

Of particular relevance is Chapter 3 section 10(c): "If a complaint is made to the Ombudsman for Children by a child or on behalf of a child by a person other than a parent of the child, the Ombudsman for Children shall, before investigating the complaint, inform a parent of the child of the complaint." It is difficult to make sense of this statutory requirement in that it removes any discretion from the Ombudsman for Children who is **required to inform a parent** of the child, who by definition is a person under 18, **before investigating a complaint**. What if the parent is implicated in the complaint? What if a 17-year old wants to pursue a complaint and the parent does not? Section 10(2)(b)(ii) permits the Ombudsman to discontinue an investigation if the child on whose behalf the complaint is made "has an insufficient interest in the matter." What if the parent of a 17-year old makes a complaint and the child does not want the complaint investigated for reasons unrelated to section 10(2)(b)(ii)? Surely this requirement flies in the face of common sense?

---

[23] April 2006, p.43. Available on the Ombudsman for Children website: www.oco.ie

[24] From Feldman, "Information Law and the Ombudsman" in Byrne R. and Binchy W. eds *Annual Review of Irish Law 2002* (Thomson Round Hall, Dublin) which includes further analysis of the conflicted role of the Ombudsman for Children; for general analysis Shannon, G. *Child Law* (Thomson Round Hall, Dublin), chap. 8. pt. V.

Limited scope

It remains to be seen to what extent the Ombudsman for Children will be able to act independently on behalf of children and to what extent children will have confidence in an office that itself is bound by legislation which has little respect for their autonomy. Further, it is of interest that neither in her report on Child Protection nor on her website does the Ombudsman for Children mention the Protections for Persons reporting Child Abuse Act 1998. This is the only discrete piece of whistleblower legislation in Ireland and affords protection to those who report child abuse to the authorities reasonably and in good faith.[25]

Voice of the child in healthcare

In 2006, the Office of the Minister for Children published two reports into children's experience in healthcare as part of the National Children's Strategy Research Programme. *Giving Children a Voice: Investigation of children's experiences of participation in consultation and decision making in Irish Hospitals*[26] had the aim of examining children's experiences of involvement and consultation in their health care within the hospital setting. Its objectives were:

> "1. To describe children's experiences of consultation in the healthcare setting;
> 2. To identify the factors that enhances children's involvement in care and the decision-making process;
> 3. To identify the factors that hinder children from involvement in care and the decision-making process; and
> 4. To explore strategies that will empower children to participate in their own health care decisions."

The research was carried out by academics in the School of Nursing, Dublin City University.

By contrast, the second piece of research, published in October 2006, was conducted by academics from the Faculty of Law, University College Cork. The principal objective of this second report, *The Child's Right to be heard in the Healthcare Setting: Perspectives of Children, Parents and Health Professionals*[27]

---

[25] For analysis, Byrne R. and Binchy W. eds. *Annual Review of Irish Law 1998*; Feldman, "Whistleblower Protection: Comparative Legal Developments" (1999) 17 I.L.T. (ns) 264 at p.265.

[26] Coyne et al, *Giving Children a Voice: Investigation of children's experiences of participation in consultation and decision making in Irish Hospitals* Office of the Minister for Children September 2006. Available on the Minister for Children's website www.oco.ie

[27] Kilkelly and Donnelly, *The Child's Right to be heard in the Healthcare Setting: Perspectives of Children, Parents and Health Professionals* Office of the Minister for

was to determine the extent to which the voice of the child is heard within the healthcare setting. The research had three core elements:

> "a literature review on the application of the child's right to be heard in the healthcare setting;
> consultation with children and young people (aged between 5-11) parents and family members, health care professionals and voluntary groups active in the area and
> an analysis of the educational and training curricula of the medical professionals who work with children."

Although the two teams of researchers approached the issue of children in healthcare from a different knowledge and experience base, they employed similar methodology and both reports had similar findings.

> "Some children wanted to be involved in the decision-making process, while others were happy for the decisions to be left to parents and health professionals. Leaving decisions to parents/health professionals does not indicate a lack of competence; rather, it demonstrates that children have the ability to choose. Children who may be competent to make their own decisions may, nevertheless, choose to allow parents to make decisions on their behalf. Participation rights do not necessarily confer the right to be the main decider, nor do children want to exclude their parents from the process. It appears that the issue of decision-making should be seen as existing on a continuum rather than an 'all or nothing' approach. The view of 'all or nothing' obscures the fact that there are multiple levels and ways to involve children in decision-making. There are also different types of decisions ranging from minor to major and the decision-making process can change depending on the situational context. …
>
> ….
>
> The findings indicate that decision-making for children is a complex process that evolves over time and that may be shared or contested with parents and health professionals depending on the type of decision. It was evident that parents play an influential role in children's ability to participate, which indicates that an awareness of the family's usual pattern of decision-making can be helpful. It suggests a pragmatic approach, recognising that children need protection while at the same time allowing flexibility for the child's emerging knowledge and self-determination."[28]

Children September 2006 p.3. Available on the Minister for Children's website www.oco.ie

[28] Coyne, *op.cit.* pp.3 and 4.

The interrelationship between the child patient, the parents and the health professionals is obviously complex. Not unexpectedly this was confirmed by the research.

> "Although the duty to listen to children is clearly placed on the shoulders of the health professional, interviews with the professionals themselves confirm that the role of parents in the process is as influential in practice as in theory. Indeed, consistent with other research, interviews with health professionals confirm that the dynamic between them and parents is a hugely significant factor in how they communicate with their child patients."[29]

Moreover, some parents criticised direct communication by the professionals with the child.

> "A commonly expressed view was that parents were better placed than health professionals to determine the level of consultation that was in their child's interests. In this way, some parents are acting as the gate keeper to the child's exercise of his or her right to participate in the consultation process and would seem to be limiting the level of participation that may be achieved."[30]

With regard to the legal implications of the child patient's capacity Kilkelly comments:

> "The particular features of the patient-doctor relationship ... are further complicated by a child's apparent or real immaturity and lack of legal capacity, which mean that the involvement of a third party (the parent or guardian) in the process is nearly always required. The extent of parental involvement and whether it is direct or indirect are important variables here and can distinguish between an essentially paternalistic approach to the child's healthcare — where the adults decide what is best for the child — and a rights-based approach — where the child is listened to and supported to be involved in the process. Moving from the former to the latter requires an acknowledgement that there are complex reasons for the differing views and attitudes of parents and professionals in this area which relate to perceptions of the parental right and need to protect their children, their awareness of the child's rights, the nature of their relationship with their children and what they may perceive as their unique understanding of the child's development, personality and health."[31]

---

29 Kilkelly, *op.cit.*, p.87

30 Kilkelly, *ibid.*, p.49.

31 Kilkelly, *ibid.*, p.11.

Acknowledging the extraordinary complexity of listening to the child in a healthcare situation, from a legal standpoint what is most important is the constitutional position of parents and of children.

Constitutional Position[32]

It is impossible to refer to the relative constitutional position of child and parent without referring to both Article 41 (The Family) and Article 42 (Education) of the Constitution.

Article 41

41.1.1 The State recognises the Family as the natural primary and fundamental unit group of Society, and as a moral institution possessing inalienable and imprescriptible rights, antecedent and superior to all positive law.

41.1.2 The State, therefore, guarantees to protect the Family in its constitution and authority, as the necessary basis of social order and as indispensable to the welfare of the Nation and the State.[33]

Article 42

42.1 The State acknowledges that the primary and natural educator of the child is the Family and guarantees to respect the inalienable right and duty of parents to provide, according to their means, for the religious and moral, intellectual, physical and social education of their children.

42.3.2 The State shall, however, as guardian of the common good, require in view of actual conditions that the children receive a certain minimum education, moral, intellectual and social.

42.5 In exceptional cases, where the parents for physical or moral reasons fail in their duty towards their children, the State as guardian of the common good, by appropriate means shall endeavour to supply

---

[32] The constitutional analysis which follows is derived from the author's lecture notes in Constitutional Law. These notes owe debt to many sources including the four major texts on Irish constitutional law: Casey, *Constitutional law in Ireland,* 3rd ed., (Sweet & Maxwell, London, 2000); Forde, *Constitutional Law of Ireland*, 2nd ed. (FirstLaw, Dublin, 2004); Hogan and Whyte, eds, *J.M. Kelly: The Irish Constitution,* 4th ed., (Butterworths, Dublin, 2003) and Ryan, *Constitutional Law* (Round Hall, Dublin, 2001).

[33] Arts 41.2.1 and 41.2.2 refer to the woman's role in the home.

> the place of the parents, but always with due regard for the natural and imprescriptible rights of the child.[34]

As can be seen, there is a close mutual connection between Articles 41 and 42. Thus, both commentators and case law tend to combine the Articles when commenting on aspects of these provisions.

According to *Kelly* these two Articles are "the most innovatory in the entire Constitution" with advantages as well as disadvantages.

> "Because of the conservative ideology underpinning Articles 41 and 42, aspects of these Articles are arguably under more strain than many other provisions of the Constitution, given the increasing secularisation and liberalisation of Irish society beginning in the 1960s. In particular, the constitutional emphasis on the position of the married family is somewhat at odds with the growing number of non-marital families in the country [births outside marriage rose from 3% in 1937 to 20% in 1996] and arguably precludes the courts from acting wholly in the best interests of the child in custody disputes between a family member and a non-family member. In addition, the reference in Article 41.2 to the role of woman in the home is understandably regarded as sexist and paternalistic in contemporary times, *while concern has also been expressed about the failure of the Constitution adequately to protect the rights of children, though this is arguably due more to judicial interpretation of Articles 41 and 42 than to the actual wording of those provisions*"[35] (emphasis added)

How then have the courts dealt with these two Articles as they might pertain to children?

"Constitutional family" is the family based on marriage

The courts have unequivocally defined the constitutional family as the family based on marriage. In *State (Nicolaou) v. An Bord Uchtála*,[36] the Supreme Court ruled that a father who was not married to the mother of his child could not invoke the provisions of Article 41. This was because the provisions of Articles 41 and 42 were restricted to marital families only. Henchy J. said that "for the State to award equal constitutional protection to the family founded on marriage and the family founded on an extra-marital union would in effect be a disregard of the pledge which the State gives in Article 41.3.1, to guard with special care the institution of marriage."[37]

---

34 Arts 42.2., 42.3.1 and 42.4 refer to education.

35 *Kelly, loc. cit.,* para.7.6.04.

36 [1966] I.R. 567.

37 *Ibid.* at 622. Art.41.3.1° states:"The State pledges itself to guard with special care

Family constitutional rights pertain to social unit not individual member

The rights that are enjoyed by the family are collective rather than individual rights. In other words, the rights of the family are to be enjoyed by the family as a unit. In *Murray v. Ireland*,[38] Costello J. distinguished between the collective rights of the family as an institution, which rights may usually be exercised on behalf of the family by any of its members, and the personal rights of the individual members of the family, acquired by family members by virtue of their membership of that social unit. He said:

> "The rights in Article 41, s.1, sub-s.1, are those which can properly be said to belong to the institution itself as distinct from the personal rights which each individual member might enjoy by virtue of membership of the family. No doubt if the rights of the unit group were threatened or infringed any member of the family could move the court to uphold them, but the cause of action would then be the threat to the rights granted to the unit, and not to those of its individual member."[39]

Some 26 years later, in *L v. L*,[40] Finlay C.J. in the Supreme Court stated: "Neither Article 4.1.1 or 2 purports to create any particular right within the family, or to grant to any individual member of the family rights, whether of property or otherwise, against other members of the family, but rather deals with the protection of the family from external forces."[41]

Family right to autonomy

The family right to autonomy was upheld by Walsh J. in *McGee v. Attorney General*,[42] which recognised the unenumerated right of marital privacy. Similarly, the autonomy of the family unit was a key consideration in *Re Article 26 and the Matrimonial Home Bill 1993*.[43] This was a legislative attempt to provide for joint ownership of matrimonial property regardless of the arrangements that families themselves had made. The Supreme Court, however, held that the Bill usurped the constitutional authority of the family to regulate such matters:

> "Having regard to the extreme importance of the authority of the family as acknowledged in Article 41 of the Constitution and to the acceptance in that Article of the fact that the rights which attach to the family including

the institution of Marriage, on which the Family is founded, and to protect it against attack."

38 [1985] I.R. 532.
39 *Ibid.*, p.537.
40 [1992] 2 I.R. 77.
41 *Ibid.*, p.108.
42 [1974]1 I.R. 284.
43 [1994] 1 I.R. 305.

its right to make decisions within its authority are inalienable and imprescriptible and antecedent and superior to all positive law, the Court is satisfied that such provisions do not constitute reasonably proportionate intervention by the State with the rights of the family and constitute a failure by the State to protect the authority of the family."[44]

Welfare of child rests in family authority

More recently, in *North Western Health Board v. HW*[45] Hardiman J. described the authority of the family as follows:

> "A family, such as the family of which the Respondents are the heads, consist of parents and children. Since a child will not himself or herself be capable of making or of acting upon any decision as to its own welfare, these decisions must necessarily be made by some person or agency on his or her behalf. In practice, this will almost invariably be either the parents or a parent on the one hand or a State or public agency of some sort on the other. The Plaintiff urges us to let a particular decision be taken by an entity of the latter sort because, it says, the decision that such a body will take has been rationally shown to be in the objective best interest of the child. But in the choice of decision maker, the Constitution plainly accords a primacy to the parent and this primacy in my view gives rise to a presumption that the welfare of the child is to be found in the family exercising its authority as such. This reflects the right both of the parents and of the children to have the family protected in its Constitution and authority."[46]

Hardiman J. reiterated this view in the later case of *Lobe v. Minister for Justice Equality and Law Reform:*[47]

> "In *North Western Health Board v. H.W.* [2001] 3 IR 622, which is relied on by the applicants in relation to the rights of the family, the issue centred on whether parents could be compelled to present their child for a particular medical test. This was resisted by the parents, but not on the basis of any view of the test imputed to the child or asserted as the child's by the parents. It was resisted on the basis that the parents, according to our constitutional order, were the appropriate decision makers on a matter plainly within the authority of the family. The fundamental issue in the case concerned who would take the decision to accept or reject the test:

---

44 *Ibid.*, p.326.

45 [2001] 3 I.R. 622, [2001] IESC 90. This case is sometimes referred to as the *PKU* case, below.

46 *Ibid.*, p.323.

47 [2003] 1 I.R. 1.

> a State body or the parents. *It did not occur to either side to suggest that the decision was the child's, and merely articulated by someone else as his agent. It is unrealistic to consider any decision made on the child's behalf as his own. It would not, I think, occur to anyone so to describe a parental decision except under the artificial constraints of a need to support a particular argument.* What is unusual about the present case is that the child has a right, which is not shared by the parents, which he is at present incapable of exercising. Accordingly, he will be bound by whatever decision the parents may lawfully make in his regard. A decision about a child's medical treatment is, *prima facie*, within the authority of his family." (emphasis added)

Family rights not absolute

It is difficult but not impossible to interfere in the workings of a family unit. In *Murray v. Ireland*[48] Costello J. in the High Court commented that notwithstanding the very strong language in Article 41, the rights of the family were not absolute and could be curtailed with a view to upholding the common good. Further, the Supreme Court held in *Matrimonial Home Bill*[49] that the State is entitled lawfully to impose certain rules on the family, provided such intervention is shown to be reasonable and proportionate, that is, no more than is necessary to achieve certain legitimate purposes. For example, the Health Service Executive has statutory responsibilities to promote the welfare of children under the Child Care Act 1991. Ward writes as follows in his annotation of the Act:

> "In performing the primary function of promoting the welfare of children (for example by initiating care or supervision order proceedings) the Health Service Executive can affect the rights of the family as protected under Art.41 and Art.42 of the Constitution".[50]

Rights of unmarried parents and their children

In *State (Nicolaou) v. An Bord Uchtála*[51] the unmarried father of a child was deemed not to enjoy constitutional rights. However, in relation to the unmarried mother, in *G v. An Bord Uchtála*[52] the Supreme Court held that she enjoyed a right to care for and have custody of her child. These rights were derived as part of the personal rights protected by Article 40.3.2:

> "**Article 40.3.1** The State guarantees in its laws to respect, and, as far

48 [1985] I.R. 532.

49 [1994] 1 I.R. 305.

50 Ward, *The Child Care Acts*, 2nd ed., *Annotated and Consolidated* (Thomson Round Hall, Dublin, 2005), p.15.

51 [1966] I.R. 567.

52 [1966] I.R. 32.

> as practicable, by its laws to defend and vindicate the personal rights of the citizen.
>
> **Article 40.3.2** The State shall, in particular, by its laws protect as best it may from unjust attack and, in the case of injustice done, vindicate the life, person, good name, and property rights of every citizen."

With regard to the manner in which the judiciary have interpreted the Constitution by recognising rights of the unmarried natural mother and denying any rights to the unmarried natural father, one legal commentator has noted:

> "This rather patent gender discrimination, the courts have said, is justified by the 'different nature' of the relationship between the mother and the child and the father and the child. While it is inescapably true that the mother, by virtue of her pregnancy, has a closer biological and thus emotional link to her child, it seems unfair in the extreme to say that this means that the unmarried father has no constitutional rights at all in respect of his child. It is especially unfair considering that a married father has full constitutional rights equal to those of the mother in respect of their marital children."[53]

Twenty years ago, Duncan, critically analysing a Supreme Court decision in a custody case,[54] made the following comments:

> "Interpretation of the Constitution involves policy choices, which instead of taking refuge in the natural law, should take more account of prevailing social conditions and values. The Supreme Court should be aware that more than 7% of children born in this country are born outside marriage, that the number of family units comprising a single mother and her child has, with the static adoption rate, increased dramatically over the last 15 years, and that to many the idea that such a family unit is less deserving of constitutional respect and protection is unworthy and un-Christian. This is not to suggest that the non-marital child should become subject to the same strictly protected regime of parental rights which apply to the marital child. What perhaps is needed is a two-fold movement in constitutional doctrine - a movement away from the exaggerated emphasis on married parents' rights combined with a recognition of some constitutional status for the non-marital family."[55]

---

53 Ryan, *loc. cit.* p.198.

54 *In re JH an infant* [1985] I.R. 375.

55 Duncan, W. (1986) D.U.L.J. 76 at 83.

The child's rights[56]

As early as 1946, in *Re M., an infant*[57] Gavan Duffy J., based on a recognition of personal rights under Article 40.3, ruled that a non-marital child enjoyed rights similar to those enjoyed by a marital child under Article 42. These included the right to the care and custody of his mother, and the right to an adequate education and upbringing.

The view, that personal rights of family members, specifically those of the children, are derived from Article 40.3 was classically articulated by O'Higgins C.J. in *G v. An Bord Uchtála:*[58]

> "The child also has natural rights. Normally, these will be safe under the care and protection of its mother. Having been born, *the child has the right to be fed and to live, to be reared and educated, to have the opportunity of working and of realising his or her full personality and dignity as a human being*. These rights of the child (and others which I have not enumerated) must equally be protected and vindicated by the State. In exceptional cases the State, under the provisions of Article 42, s.5 of the Constitution, is given the duty, as guardian of the common good, to provide for a child born into a family where the parents fail in their duty towards that child for physical or moral reasons. In the same way, in special circumstances the State may have an equal obligation in relation to a child born outside the family to protect that child, even against its mother, if her natural rights are used in such a way as to endanger the health or life of the child or to deprive him of his rights. In my view this obligations stems from the provisions of Article 40, s.3, of the Constitution."[59] (emphasis added)

The voiceless child

The full import of the reference to realising the child's full personality and dignity appears to have been ignored in more recent case law. As noted above, Hardiman J. both in *North Western Health Board (NWHB)* and in the subsequent *Lobe* case made it clear that parental authority is well-nigh absolute. The child in *NWHB* was an infant, but this has not been referred to by Hardiman J. in the more recent statement. Is it to be presumed that his *dictum* refers to all minor children irrespective of age? In other words, he appears to make no distinction between the baby and the adolescent in their decision-making ability and their right to autonomy. This is in stark contradiction to the legal philosophy underlying the

---

[56] Children's rights in healthcare is further considered by the author in *The Constitution, the child and health, ignoring the elephant in the room*, in Carolan and Doyle eds, "Essays on Constitutional Law" (Thomson Roundhall, 2008) (forthcoming).

[57] [1946] I.R. 334.

[58] [1980] I.R. 32.

[59] *Ibid.*, p.55.

concept of the Gillick competent child or, indeed, the international view as expressed in the Covenant on the Rights of the Child. While in future proceedings litigants may well seek to have this judgment in *NWHB* distinguished, in its most recent manifestation in *McK v. Information Commissioner*,[60] no account was taken of the fact that the child involved was not an infant but in the early stage of adolescence. It seems as if the constitutional authority of the married parent leaves no space for the voice of the child.

Presumption of parental authority

Thus, in summary, Article 41 can only be pleaded for the benefit of the family as a whole, i.e. the marital family. Individual rights of family members, i.e. the marital family and the unmarried mother and child but not the unmarried father and child, on the other hand, are said to be personal rights protected under Article 40.3 rather than Article 41. There is a presumption that a constitutionally recognised parent,[61] or legal guardian acts at all times in his/her child's best interests. The only way to rebut this presumption is to present evidence that will satisfy Article 42.5. In effect, the parent needs to engage in egregious conduct to fall foul of this provision. In *NWHB* Keane C.J. expressed this in somewhat gentle terms: "The duty of the superior courts to uphold the rights of the child arises, to the extent that it arises at all, because they are not being upheld by the parents and have not been or, cannot be, upheld by the other two organs of the State."[62] A recent example of a breach of Article 42.5 is the case of *Attorney General v. Dowse*[63] discussed below.

Statutory Provisions for Minor's Consent to Medical Treatment

Over 16s may consent to medical treatment

Under section 23 of the Non-Fatal Offences Against the Person Act 1997 a minor over the age of 16 may consent to surgical, medical and dental treatment. It states:

> "(1) The consent of a minor who has attained the age of 16 years to any surgical, medical or dental treatment which, in the absence of consent, would constitute a trespass to his or her person, shall be as effective as it would be if he or she were of full age; and where a minor has by virtue of this *section* given an effective consent to any treatment it shall

---

60 [2006] IESC 2 discussed below.

61 Marital parent, or the biological unmarried mother.

62 [2006] IESC 2 at [122]. The three organs of state are the judiciary, the legislature and the executive.

63 [2006] IEHC 65.

> not be necessary to obtain any consent for it from his or her parent or guardian.
>
> (2) In this *section* "surgical, medical or dental treatment" includes any procedure undertaken for the purposes of diagnosis, and this section applies to any procedure (including, in particular, the administration of an anaesthetic) which is ancillary to any treatment as it applies to that treatment."

Whilst these provisions might seem to confer autonomy on a minor approaching adulthood they must be read in conjunction with section 23 (3) which states:

> "Nothing in this *section* shall be construed as making ineffective any consent which would have been effective if this *section* had not been enacted."

As, absent section 23, the only means of giving consent for a minor is by the parent or legal guardian, by default it would appear that the primacy of parental authority remains unchallenged by the passage of section 23. It remains unclear as to whether a refusal of consent by a minor over 16 must be considered, let alone take precedence, if a parent or legal guardian disagreed and consented to treatment. Moreover, it is unlikely that the purpose of including this provision is to advance the self-determination of children. This legislation provides protection for the health practitioner from suit for battery or negligence.

Taking blood from minors

Similarly, section 39 of the Status of Children Act 1987 refers to consent to, and taking of, blood samples. Section 39 (2) provides for the taking of a blood sample from a person who is not of full age and "where the court considers that he is in the circumstances capable of giving or refusing the necessary consent, any consent given or refused by him shall be as effective as it would be if he were of full age." Section 39 (3) provides for the situation where the court does not consider the minor capable of consenting or refusing consent; in such circumstances the person having charge of the minor may consent. In the situation where more than one person has charge of or control over the minor and they disagree as to whether consent should be given, the minor shall be treated as not having consented.

Again, a superficial analysis of this section might infer that there has been a breakthrough with regard to the autonomy of the minor. However, the Long Title of the Status of Children Act 1987 clarifies that these provisions are for the use of blood tests to assist in the determination of parentage. Nevertheless, the statutory text "where the court considers that he is in the circumstances capable of giving or refusing the necessary consent" appears to approach a *Gillick* type of intervention to assess competence. Unfortunately, the statutory circumstances are so confining it is unlikely that the courts would view with favour an attempt to extend this reasoning to issues of general medical consent.

THE COMPETENCE OF A MINOR CHILD

Criminal Law

Under section 52 of the Children Act 2001 the age of criminal responsibility has been raised from 7 years old to 12 years old. Thus, in criminal law it appears that pre-teens and adolescents are considered competent despite their minority.

Judicial comments on minor child capability

The following are a random selection of cases,[64] and judicial comments on the minors who are the subject of those cases. The purpose is to illustrate that there are occasions on which the judiciary have no difficulty in hearing the voice of the child.

Damages case: 8-year old

In *Mapp, a minor v. Gilhooley*[65] Barr J. in the High Court stated as follows:

> "'The plaintiff, who is now eight years of age, gave evidence at the trial. Although he was not sworn because he had not yet learned the meaning of an oath, I am satisfied that he understood the importance of the occasion and the necessity for telling the truth. He is a remarkably bright and intelligent boy who had no difficulty in giving evidence.'"[66]

On appeal Finlay C.J. (O'Flaherty J. concurring) observed:

> "The learned trial judge did not have, in my view, any jurisdiction to accept the evidence of this young child unsworn even if both parties had expressly agreed to such a course. This is so even if he concluded that the child was a competent witness, in the sense that he understood what he was saying and was able to give a coherent and truthful account of what had occurred.
>
> What should have been done, I am satisfied, on this occasion, having regard to the answers which the young boy gave to the learned trial judge upon inquiry as to his knowledge of an oath, was to have adjourned the commencement of the case for such time as might be necessary to enable this young child properly to be instructed in the meaning and importance

---

64 A selection of results of an opportunistic search of Westlaw.ie.

65 [1991] I.L.R.M. 695.

66 *Ibid.*, p.698.

of an oath and then to have sworn him. The conclusions reached by the learned trial judge as to his intelligence and capacity to understand the nature of the occasion on which he was giving an account of the accident would seem to suggest that had that course been adopted it would not have been a matter of any significant difficulty to have instructed him in the meaning of an oath."[67]

In his judgment McCarthy J. said as follows:

> "At a trial, a child tendered as a witness should be questioned by the trial judge as to understanding the meaning of taking an oath to tell the truth. If the child does not show an acceptable level of understanding, the trial should be adjourned so that the child may be adequately instructed as to the meaning of an oath. If, such instruction having been given, the judge is not satisfied that the child understands the meaning of an oath, then the trial judge should refuse to allow the oath to be administered and must refuse to hear any oral evidence from the witness so tendered."[68]

Guardianship: 6½ year old

Following on *Mapp v. Gilhooley*, in *Southern Health Board v. CH*[69] the Supreme Court suggested that a six and half year old child be reassessed to see if he was competent to give evidence on oath. O'Flaherty J. (Blayney and Barrington JJ. concurring) stated, *inter alia*:

> "S. 3 of the Guardianship of Infants Act 1964 provides:
>
> > where in any proceedings before any court the custody, guardianship or upbringing of an infant … is in question, the court in deciding that question shall regard the welfare of the infant as the first and paramount consideration.
>
> The Act defines welfare as comprising of the 'religious and moral, intellectual, physical and social welfare of the infant.' The 1964 Act, itself a statutory statement of what is inherent in the Constitution, reinforces the common law position that the court is entrusted with the responsibility of the child's welfare. This is of the utmost importance."[70]

He continued:

> "So, the first point to note about this case is that the judge is in essence required to *inquire* as to what is in the best interests of the child. It is

[67] *Ibid*, p.701.

[68] *Ibid.*, p.703.

[69] [1996] 2 I.L.R.M. 142.

[70] *Ibid.*, p.149.

> true, of course, that the rights of the father must be safeguarded, as far as practicable, in a manner consistent with discharging that primary obligation. But when the consequences of any encroachment on the respective rights is considered, it is easy to comprehend that the child's welfare must always be of far graver concern to the court. We must, as judges, always hearken to the constitutional command which mandates, as a prime consideration, the interests of the child in any legal proceedings...
>
> It would seem to be necessary, too, that since the child is now six and a half years old that the district judge should establish anew that she is, indeed, incompetent to give evidence. He will hear such expert evidence as he thinks right and if he receives confirmation that the child is incompetent to give evidence, or, *as a distinct condition*, if he finds that the trauma that she would suffer would make it undesirable that she should come to give evidence, then he will be justified in allowing in the evidence of the video recordings. In this regard, it is well to point out that a courtroom is, in general, an unsuitable environment for a child of such tender years as this child."[71]

Adoption: 17-year old

In *WHB v. An Bord Uchtála*[72] *inter alia*, O'Higgins J. made the following comments about the subject of the adoption:

> "L., who is now seventeen, gave evidence herself. She impressed the court as being an articulate, thoughtful, mature and courageous person. She also impressed the court as being a truthful witness.
>
> For a person aged seventeen, access can be facilitated and encouraged — coercion is not a realistic option
>
> Accordingly, I make an order authorising the Board to make an adoption order in respect of this remarkable and courageous young person."

Child not totally voiceless

One can hardly generalise from these particular incidents presented out of context and brought to light in an opportunistic random fashion. However, they do indicate that in individual cases the courts are prepared to allow, in some instances require, a minor, a child, to express opinions as to their personal circumstances. What is most telling is the acceptance that a 7 year old had reached the age of criminal responsibility until the coming into force of the

---

[71] *Ibid.*, p.150.

[72] Unreported, High Court, O'Higgins J., May 27, 2004.

Children Act 2001. Yet, this age latitude does not extend to the giving or refusing of consent to medical treatment.

Cases Involving Health Issues

Before considering the cases in which the substantive issue relates to health care of a child, it is instructive to consider a recent judgment of the High Court which resoundingly reiterated that the welfare of a child and the proper exercise of his constitutional rights are deemed paramount.

International adoption

Welfare of child

Attorney General v. Dowse,[73] considered the circumstances of Tristan Dowse, an Indonesian boy whose adoption was registered by the Adoption Board in the Register of Foreign Adoptions in September 2001. Consequent on that registration Tristan became an Irish citizen. The Attorney General sought *inter alia* a declaration that the defendants, the adoptive parents, had failed in their duty pursuant to Articles 42.1 and 40.3 of the Constitution to care and provide for their son Tristan and an order directing the defendants to carry out their constitutional duty pursuant to those constitutional articles to care and provide for him. The High Court also considered a request from the adoptive parents to order the cancellation of the registration of foreign adoption.

It is noteworthy that the High Court published its judgment. This was as a result of a second judgment,[74] in which MacMenamin J. had regard to the fact that the position in regard to Tristan Dowse was already very much in the public domain. "His circumstances have already been the subject of extensive public discussion and comment. This renders the position herein quite distinct from the ordinary realm of family law cases which are heard in private and where judgments are issued protecting the anonymity of the parties." The court was also guided by the principle that the welfare of the minor must at all times remain paramount. "In the application of this principle the orders made by the court must have regard to the welfare principle of Tristan both directly – and indirectly."

Parents' breach of constitutional duty

In the substantive case,[75] based on the undisputed facts, MacMenamin J. found that there had been a clear breach of the constitutional duty owed to Tristan by the adoptive parents.

---

[73] [2006] I.E.H.C. 64.

[74] *AG v. Dowse* [2006] IEHC 65.

[75] [2006] IEHC 64.

> "[A]s Tristan is deemed to have been adopted pursuant to an Irish adoption order, he is considered in law to be the child of the applicants, having the same status as if born to them in lawful wedlock and his natural mother, *prima facie*, lost all parental rights and was freed from parental duties in respect of him pursuant to s. 24 of the Adoption Act, 1952 as amended. As he was in law then deemed to be their marital child, the applicants owed and owe constitutional duties to him and he in turn enjoys constitutional rights in respect of them."

MacMenamin J. then considered the Constitutional position:

> "I am satisfied that, pursuant to Article 42.1 of the Constitution of Ireland, 1937 the applicants are obliged 'to provide according to their means for the religious and moral, intellectual, physical and social education' of Tristan. If parents, 'for physical or moral reasons fail in their duty towards their children' the State is obliged to endeavour 'to supply the place of the parents' by appropriate means pursuant to Article 42.5 of the Constitution. In doing so, the State must do so 'always with due regard for the natural and imprescriptible rights of the child'."

Parents' future obligations

Arising from the constitutional position and from the appropriate statutory provisions of the Adoption Acts 1952 and 1991 as amended by the Act of 1998 the High Court made specific orders requiring the adoptive parents to provide maintenance for Tristan, since restored to the custody of his natural mother in Indonesia. The sums of money, both lump sums and continuous, to be lodged in Tristan's behalf were set based on the following:

> "The level of maintenance should not, as a general principle, be set against the background of the standard of living and cost of living in Indonesia. While this may be one factor to be weighed in the balance, against that must be placed the position in which as a matter of certainty Tristan would have been but for the events which have occurred."

Full force of State brought to bear in child's representation

In relation to this case all the organs of the State were united in their desire to represent the child's best interests. The High Court considered evidence from a social worker of the Adoption Board and from members of the diplomatic corps based in the region, all of whom had visited Indonesia and met Tristan and his natural mother. In reading the judgment there can be no doubt that Tristan's best interests were at the core of the State's concern and were the motivating factor for the High Court. This attitude may be compared to the court's position in the following cases.

Only exceptionally can there be intervention in constitutional family

North Western Health Board v. H.W.[76] is a case that causes great concern to health professionals. It is also a case where the judges of the Supreme Court appear to have acknowledged the paramountcy of the marital constitutional family despite their better judgement and in the face of concerns over the infant's interests and welfare.

The Supreme Court (Denham, Murphy, Murray JJ., Keane C.J. dissenting) affirmed the High Court's refusal to grant an order to the plaintiff health board to carry out the standard PKU test on the defendants' infant. The purpose of the PKU test, or "heel-test", is to screen for various medical conditions some of which are life threatening, which are treatable if detected but could lead to serious harm if left undetected.

> "The carrying out of the test involves an invasive procedure for which the consent of parents is required. However, what this procedure involves is, both metaphorically and literally, a pinprick. No evidence was produced and no suggestion made that there is any medical or scientific view which envisages any possible danger to a patient from the PKU test. In my view it is beyond debate that the performance of a PKU test, viewed in medical terms, is unquestionably in the best interests of the infant tested."[77]

The plaintiff health board sought a court order to enable them to carry out the test. The defendants, the infant's parents, refused to consent to blood being taken from their child and offered a urine or hair sample instead in order that the test could be carried out. There was evidence before the Court that such tests were less effective than blood tests.

Brave new world

In the High Court, McCracken J. dismissed the health board's application on the grounds that not even vaccinations were compulsory so that it would be quite wrong to make the PKU test mandatory. Furthermore, there was no evidence that the parents were behaving in such a way as to justify interference with the family authority. He concluded:

> "In my view the decision in the present case by the defendants, who are acknowledged to be caring and conscientious parents, could not be said to constitute an exceptional case, even though the general medical opinion would be quite clear that such a decision was wrong. If the State were entitled to intervene in every case where professional opinion differed from that of parents, or where the State considered the parents

[76] [2001] 3 I.R 622; [2001] IESC 90.

[77] *Ibid.*, p.200 (*per* Murphy J.).

were wrong in a decision, we would be rapidly stepping towards the Brave New World in which the State always knows best. In my view that situation would be totally at variance with both the spirit and the word of the Constitution."[78]

Health board care order

Statutory provisions considered in the case included section 18 of the Child Care Act 1991 which provides that:

> (1) Where, on the application of a health board with respect to a child who resides or is found in its area, the court is satisfied that:
> (a) the child has been or is being assaulted, ill-treated, neglected or sexually abused, or
> (b) the child's health, development or welfare has been or is being avoidably impaired or neglected, or
> (c) the child's health, development or welfare is likely to be avoidably impaired or neglected,
>
> and that the child requires care or protection which he is unlikely to receive unless the court makes an order under this section, the court may make an order (in this Act referred to as a 'care order') in respect of the child.

The care order commits the child to the care of the health board for as long as he remains a child or for a shorter period as ordered by the court. Sub-section (3) requires the health board to give consent for "any necessary medical or psychiatric examination, treatment or assessment with respect to the child".

Balancing responsibilities and rights

In the course of her judgment affirming the High Court decision Denham J. commented:

> "The decision in this case requires the correct constitutional balance between the responsibility of the parents and the health board and the constitutional rights (family and personal) of the child. The fundamental principles by which the community wishes to live are to be found in the Constitution. The Constitution clearly places the family as the fundamental unit of the State. The family is the decision maker for family matters - both for the unit and for the individuals in the family. Responsibility rests fundamentally with the family. The people have chosen to live in a society where parents make decisions concerning the welfare of their children and the State intervenes only in exceptional circumstances. Responsibility for children rests with their parents except in exceptional circumstances.

[78] [2001] 3 I.R. 622 at 635.

> In assessing whether State intervention is necessary the fundamental principle is that the welfare of the child is paramount. However, part of the analysis of the welfare of the child is the wider picture of the place of the child in the family; his or her right to be part of that unit. In such a unit the dynamics of relationships are sensitive and important and should be upheld when possible as it is usually to a child's benefit to be part of the family unit.
>
> In seeking the balance to be achieved between the child's rights within and to his family, and the family (as an institution) rights, and the parents' right to exercise their responsibility for the child, and the child's personal constitutional rights, the threshold will depend on the circumstances of the case. Thus, if the child's life is in immediate danger (e.g. needing an operation) then there is a heavy weight to be put on the child's personal rights superseding family and parental considerations."[79]

Threshold for medical tests

Denham J. continued:

> "In assessing the balance to be achieved in this case it is relevant to consider the threshold which it would set for this and other medical tests and for matters such as inoculations. If the responsibility for making this decision is transferred from the parents to the State then it would herald in a new era where there would be considerably more State intervention and decision making for children than has occurred to date. Every day, all over the State, parents make decisions relating to the welfare, including physical, of their children. Having received information and advice they make a decision. It may not be the decision advised by the doctor (or teacher, or social worker, or psychologist, or priest or other expert) but it is the decision made, usually responsibly, by parents and is abided by as being in the child's best interest. Having been given the information and advice, responsibility remains with parents to make a decision for their child. The parents are responsible and liability rests with them as to the child's welfare.
>
> In exceptional circumstances - such as where a child needs acute medical or surgical care - the expert may be part of an application for a court order to protect the welfare of the child by seeking a judicial decision different from that of the parents. This arises only in exceptional circumstances. Even if some medical experts advise acute medical care and the parents consider that the responsible decision may be to refuse such care it may be within the range of responsible decisions. This may occur where a child is suffering a terminal illness and parents may decide

[79] *Ibid.*, pp. 171-172.

> responsibly that he or she has suffered enough medical intervention and should receive only palliative care."[80]

Danger of overruling caring parents

Concluding his judgment, Murphy J. considered the impact of the court intervening in parents' decisions.

> "If the State had an obligation in the present case to substitute its judgment for that of the parents numerous applications would be made to the Courts to overrule decisions made by caring but misguided parents. Such a jurisprudence and particular decisions made under it would tend to damage the long term interests of the child by eroding the interest and dedication of the parents in the performance of their duties. In my view the subsidiary and supplemental powers of the State in relation to the welfare of children arises only where either the general conduct or circumstances of the parents is such as to constitute a virtual abdication of their responsibilities or alternatively the disastrous consequences of a particular parental decision are so immediate and inevitable as to demand intervention and perhaps call into question either the basic competence or devotion of the parents."[81]

Preferable decision for ward of court

In the course of his judgment Murray J., now C.J., referred to the greater freedom of action the court would have if the child were a ward of court.

> "If this court was exercising a *parens patriae* jurisdiction and stood in *loco parentis* to the child such as would arise if he was a ward of Court then the Court would be free to decide whether the child should be subjected to a PKU. test on the basis of what a prudent and responsible parent would do in the interest of the child. Since the Court does not exercise such a jurisdiction in this case, this approach is not open to it."[82]

Parental primacy superior to authority of State

Further in his judgment, Murray J. recognised the paramountcy of parents even against the State.

> "I think it is well established in our case law that the authority and autonomy explicitly recognised by the Constitution as residing in the family as an institution in our society means that the parents of children

---

80 *Ibid.*, pp. 174-175.

81 *Ibid.*, p.209.

82 *Ibid.*, p.214.

> have primary responsibility for the upbringing and welfare generally of their children. When exercising their authority in that regard they take precedence over the State and its institutions. In this respect I agree with the observation of the Chief Justice that the family is endowed with an authority which the Constitution recognises as being superior even to the authority of the State itself."[83]

State cannot micromanage family

In considering the exceptional circumstances which might warrant intervention, Murray J. expressed concern at possible unwarranted intrusion in the family.

> "If the State had a duty or was entitled to override any decision of parents because it concluded, established or it was generally considered that that decision was not objectively the best decision in the interest of the child it would involve the State, and ultimately the Courts, in a sort of micro-management of the family. Parents with unorthodox or unpopular views or lifestyles with a consequential influence on their children might for that reason *alone* find themselves subject to intervention by the State or by one of the agencies of the State. Similar consequence could flow where a parental decision was simply considered unwise. That would give the State a general power of intervention and would risk introducing a method of social control in which the State or its agencies would be substituted for the family. That would be a infringement of liberties guaranteed to the family. Decisions which are sometimes taken by parents concerning their children may be a source of discomfort or even distress to the rational and objective bystander, but it seems to me that there must be something exceptional arising from a failure of duty, … before the State can intervene in the interest of the individual child."[84]

Extracts from the final judgment, that of Hardiman J. which strongly upholds the authority of the family, have been referred to above in relation to the discussion on constitutional rights. It is his judgment that is the basis for the decision in a later case, described in the following section, to do with a parent's right to his child's medical records.

Separated parents' rights of access to records

NMcK v. Information Commissioner[85] allowed an appeal of a separated parent against a decision of the Information Commissioner that affirmed the refusal of a hospital to grant access to medical records relating to his daughter.

---

[83] *Ibid.*, p.226.

[84] *Ibid.*, p.229.

[85] [2004] 1 I.R. 12; [2006] IESC 2.

Access to minor's records shall be granted

This case involved consideration of the Freedom of Information Act 1997 (section 28 (6)) Regulations 1999,[86] in particular, article 3(1) which states that a request for access to a record which involves the disclosure of personal information shall be granted, *inter alia*, where:

> "(a) the requester is a parent or guardian of the individual to whom the record concerned relates and that individual belongs to one of the following classes of individuals:
> (i) Individuals who, on the date of the request, have not attained full age (within the meaning of the Age of Majority Act, 1985) access to whose records would, in the opinion of the head having regard to all the circumstances and to any guidelines drawn up and published by the Minister, be in their best interests."

Quirke J. held that these terms are *prima facie* "imperative and positive requiring that access to appropriate records *shall* be granted where the requester is a parent or guardian and where the record relates to a minor (as in this case)." The only relevant qualification upon this requirement is that such access:

> "'... would, in the opinion of the head, having regard to all the circumstances and to any guidelines drawn up and published by the Minister, be in [the minor's] best interests....'.
>
> It has been acknowledged that no guidelines of the kind contemplated in the Regulations have been drawn up or published so it follows that the regulation imposes an obligation upon the [Information Commissioner] to form an opinion as to whether access to the records would, having regard to all the circumstances, be in the minor's best interests."

Quirke J. held that the Information Commissioner had misconstrued these provisions by placing an onus on the applicant to prove that granting of access would be a tangible benefit to the child:

> "The respondent is not of the opinion that access by the appellant to the records will accrue to *the detriment* of the minor. The respondent construes the section as requiring that access must invariably be *denied* unless and until *'tangible'* evidence has been furnished demonstrating that the access will result in a benefit to the minor.
>
> I do not believe that this construction is the correct one. It imposes upon an applicant such as the appellant in this case, the obligation to discharge an onus which is not apparent from the terms of the legislation. The Act and the Regulations, when read together, provide that access

[86] S.I. No.47 of 1999.

> *'shall'* be granted where, in the opinion of the deciding officers it is in the best interests of the minor *'having regard to all the circumstances'*."

Strained family relationship irrelevant

The background to the case is that during separation proceedings between the applicant and his wife, an allegation was made that the applicant had sexually abused his daughter. He vigorously denied and still denies this allegation and the Gardaí, having investigated the allegations concluded that there was "no evidence to warrant a prosecution". The applicant was granted supervised access to his children. Subsequently, the wife died and by agreement the two children of the marriage went to live with the late Mrs. McK's brother and his wife, with whom Mr. McK had a strained relationship, and it was agreed, *inter alia* that they and the applicant would be appointed as joint guardian of the two children. In January 2000, the daughter, then aged 12, was admitted to hospital. The applicant had failed in his appeal to the Information Commissioner following the hospital's refusal to grant him access to his daughter's records and he had then appealed on a point of law to the High Court.

With regard to the applicant's history, Quirke J. stated:

> "Although a complaint has in the past been made about the appellant, it remains unsubstantiated and the appellant comes before this Court enjoying the presumption of innocence which is enjoyed by every citizen of the State. The evidence indicates that he is concerned with the welfare of both of his children and avails of his rights of access to them in a conscientious fashion."

The High Court judgment was rooted in the Supreme Court judgment of Hardiman J. in *North Western Health Board v. H.W.*[87] which declared that any legislation vindicating and defending the rights of children must be interpreted in the light of the Constitution particularly Article 41 (The Family) and Article 42 (Education).

Parental primacy

Quirke J. quoted extensively from this judgment and the following points with regard to the role of the family are of particular significance.

> "'... a presumption exists that the welfare of the child is to be found in the family exercising its authority as such. ..... The presumption ... is not, of course, a presumption that the parents are always correct in their decisions according to some objective criterion. It is a presumption that where the constitutional family exists and is discharging its functions as

---

[87] [2001] 3 I.R 622, discussed above.

> such and the parents have not for physical or moral reasons failed in their duty towards their children, their decisions should not be overridden by the State or in particular by the Courts in the absence of a jurisdiction conferred by statute.'"

Having noted that there had been no suggestion of such a failure of duty on the part of the appellant the High Court judgment continued:

> "Accordingly the appellant, as a parent, joint guardian and joint custodian of the child concerned enjoys the parental primacy identified by Hardiman J. in *North Western Health Board v. H. W.* … and the presumption that he has the welfare of his child at heart in the absence of evidence to the contrary.
>
> The presumption is of course rebuttable, but there is no suggestion of rebuttal in this case.
>
> Reluctance by another family member to agree to access does not, in the absence of any supporting evidence, amount to rebuttal sufficient to displace the presumption referred to."

The Information Commissioner appealed the High Court judgment to the Supreme Court.

Parental entitlement to a minor child's medical information

The Supreme Court judgment,[88] which both affirmed and varied the High Court decision, was delivered by the presiding judge, Denham J., McGuinness, Hardiman, Geoghegan, and Fennelly JJ. assenting. The High Court's judgment was affirmed as to the correct test to be used in administering the Regulations, namely a presumption of parental entitlement to a minor child's medical information. However, the Supreme Court remitted the matter to the Information Commissioner for review in accordance with the correct test and in light of all of the circumstances.

Delay when minor child involved

Of most concern to the Supreme Court was the delay from the time the requester had made his initial request to the hospital for the records in January 2000 until the delivery of the judgment in January 2006.

> "The elapse of time has a special relevance where a minor child is involved.
>
> L was born in 1988. The hospital stay in issue was in January, 2000. At that time she was still a minor. Six years later she is in her 18th year,

88 [2006] IESC 2.

> she was born on the 30th May 1988. This alters the circumstances, as her wishes are now most relevant.
>
> The delay is not the fault of the requester, and it is most unfortunate. However, the effects of the delay cannot be ignored in view of the necessity to balance the changed circumstances, including the attitude of L."

Parental family authority affirmed

Noting that the Freedom of Information Act 1997 and the consequent Regulations must be interpreted in accordance with the Constitution, Denham J. agreed that the Commissioner erred in law in requiring tangible evidence of parental interest. This "tangible evidence" test reversed the onus of proof. "The relationship between parent and child has a special status in Ireland. Under the Constitution the family is the primary and fundamental unit group in our society: Article 41.1.1. The State has guaranteed to protect the family in its constitution and authority: Article 41.1.2." Consequently, Denham J. continued, the judicial branch of government has a duty to protect the family and its authority.

Rights of child within family

Denham J. made a clear declaration that each member of the family unit also has rights. "Thus while the parents have duties and rights in relation to a child, and a child has rights to parental care, the child also has personal rights which the State is required to vindicate if the parent fails in his or her duty."

Parent's rights/duties caring for ill child ... a rebuttable presumption

The extent of the Supreme Court's opinion on the parental care of an ill child is as follows:

> "A parent's rights and duties include the care of a child who is ill. As a consequence a parent is entitled to information about the medical care a child is receiving so that he or she may make appropriate decisions for the child, as his or her guardian. The presumption is that a parent is entitled to access such information. That position is not absolute. The circumstances may be such that the presumption may be rebutted. But the primary position is that the presumption exists. Consequently, the approach of the Commissioner was in error when he required 'tangible evidence' that the release of such information would serve the best interests of the minor. The obverse is the correct approach. The presumption is that the release of such medical information would best serve the interests of the minor. However, evidence may be produced that it would not serve her interests, and, in considering the circumstances, her welfare is paramount."

The error of the Commissioner was in not presuming that the parent was entitled to the child's medical records. Based on that presumption the Commissioner should then proceed to consider "any evidence which exists addressing the issue that it would not be in the minor's best interests that the parent should be furnished with such information."

Request remitted to Information Commissioner

Having specified the correct test that the Commissioner must use in deciding whether or not a minor child's medical records should be released to a parent, Denham J. remitted the matter for decision to the Commissioner. This remittal was consequent on three factors: the delay, the circumstances of the case, and "especially the age of the minor [nearly 18 years of age], whose views now are very relevant".

Missed opportunity

The importance of *McK* was signified by the number of judges sitting in judgment, a bench of five rather than three. It was not unreasonable, therefore, to anticipate some significant judicial comments on Articles 41 and 42 of the Constitution which deal with the rights of the family and the right to education. In particular, it had been hoped that the court would comment on the rights of children to preserve confidentiality of information as against the rights of parents as enshrined and inferred in the Constitution and from earlier court judgments. It is to be regretted that there was no expansion on the clear declaration that a child has rights within the family unit. The judgment is a disappointment in these respects; moreover, nothing of great import was said about the Freedom of Information Act itself. Coming hotfoot on the failure of the All-Party Oireachtas Committee on the Constitution[89] to recommend any Constitutional change in the traditional status of the family based in marriage as enshrined in the Constitution, the Supreme Court judgment in *McK* appears to say that neither our elected leaders nor our appointed judges are keeping pace with the changing realities of family life and the growing autonomy of children prior to attaining their legal majority at 18.

Professor Binchy has been critical of the High Court judgment in *McK* as it related to the full emergence of autonomy in children. In the context of balancing the constitutional rights of parents and of children, he commented that the "presumption of parental entitlement to access to joint personal information in relation to children tilts the preference for parental rights too far".[90]Unfortunately, as has been noted above, the Supreme Court judgment failed to address this issue.

---

89 *Tenth Progress Report: The Family,* The All-Party Oireachtas Committee on the Constitution, Dublin, Stationery Office, 2006.

90 In *Family Law* in eds. Byrne and Binchy *Annual Review of Irish Law 2004* (Thomson Roundhall, Dublin 2005), pp.275 *et seq*.

Exceptions to rule of parental autonomy

Doctrine of necessity

Nevertheless, in circumstances that might be categorised as "life or death" the courts will not hesitate to intervene. The High Court issued an interim care order so that that a five-month-old baby girl could receive life-saving open heart surgery at Our Lady's Hospital for Sick Children, Crumlin.[91] The baby, born in the Rotunda Hospital, had immediately been transferred to Crumlin for urgent heart surgery. The mother, a Jehovah's Witness, had signed a consent for the unqualified use of blood and blood products but had subsequently withdrawn the consent following "support" from her Jehovah's Witness community. Abbott J. said he had been satisfied that there was a pressing need for new remedial surgery and he would extend the scope of the orders to encompass such further treatment arising from and consequential to the operation to obviate the necessity of any further application to the court. He also granted the mother her liberty to apply to the court to lift the court wardship for the purpose of bringing the child to England. The child was made a ward of court for the period of time necessary to conduct the life-saving procedure.

Requirement to obtain informed consent from child and parents

In *Quinn v. SEHB*,[92] a medical negligence case, *inter alia* it was alleged that surgical procedures were performed without the full and informed or any consent on the part of the plaintiff or her parents. In November 1994, at the age of 14, the plaintiff underwent an appendectomy as a consequence of which she sustained meralgia parasthetica for which she was incorrectly treated. Rather than conservative treatment the pain was treated aggressively culminating in a neurectomy At the time of the action the plaintiff was aged 22. Ó Caoimh J. held as follows in relation to the consent:

> "With regard to the plaintiff's consent to the neurectomy, I am satisfied that while there was a consent it cannot be considered to have been an informed consent as the plaintiff and her parents were not advised of the risks associated with a failed neurectomy and in particular the possibility that it might not prove successful and might reduce the possibility of other conservative treatment being followed, not to mention other possible side effects from the operation such as anaesthesia dolorosa. It must be emphasised that the plaintiff was not advised appropriately as to the consequences of the neurectomy being an irreversible procedure."

It can be noted that the judgment required that both the child and the parents should have been advised of potential risks.

---

[91] *The Irish Times,* August 6, 2004.

[92] Unreported. High Court, March 22, 2002, Ó Caoimh J.

Children in Hospital Care

Needless to say, the rights of the child patient in relation to consent ought to be at the forefront of medical treatment especially when the child may need to attend hospital either as an in or out-patient. Leading international opinion recommends that a sick child's welfare is best assured when a paediatric hospital is co-located with adult hospital services.[93] Currently there is only one hospital in Ireland that satisfies the co-location requirement and that is the Adelaide and Meath Hospitals, Dublin, incorporating the National Children's Hospital (AMNCH) in Tallaght. This is the hospital with which the author is most familiar[94] and has direct experience of the patient focused approach of the services Indeed, the mission statement of AMNCH, recently reviewed by a large representative group of staff and patients, contains such a declaration. What this means for all patients, be they adults or children, is that there is an obligation on the health professionals to involve them and listen to them in relation to their medical treatment. Nevertheless, the legal position is such that with regard to child patients, if they and their parent or legal guardian do not agree on issues of consent, the parent's view must prevail.

The anomaly of the minor child as parent

The catchment area of the National Children's Hospital, Tallaght shows the highest proportion of teenage births at 6.3% compared to any other area for which the Health Service Executive is responsible. Sadly, therefore, the incidence of female patients who, although minors themselves, are a parent is far from a rarity. Marriage confers majority status. However, the youngest any of these child parents could marry, other than by special exemption,[95] is 18 years old. Thus, being unmarried minors they are unable to give medical consent on their own behalf; yet, in relation to their own child, it is they who have the right to give consent.

Drug addicted neonates

An area of concern to health professionals in both maternity and paediatric settings is the difficult situation where an infant is born with the inherited disease or addiction of its mother. The legal issues associated with this growing problem are extraordinarily complex and they are not the subject matter of this chapter on informed consent for minor children. However, it is hoped that this brief mention of the dilemma facing all concerned might encourage debate.

---

[93] McKinsey Report presented to the Health Service Executive, *Children's Health First International best practice in tertiary paediatric services: implications for the strategic organisation of tertiary paediatric services in Ireland,* February 1, 2006.

[94] Apart from teaching law to paediatric nurses in Tallaght, the author has experience of the adult services as a patient, and is a member of the AMNCH Board.

[95] Under s.33 of the Family Law Act 1995.

Caring for neonates manifesting symptoms of severe illness e.g. HIV or drug addiction is, evidently, not for the faint-hearted as quite often the infants manifest distressing withdrawal symptoms. Of course, as no treatment may be administered to a neonate without parental consent, should that be absent the health professional requires an order making the infant a ward of court. An instance of this extreme measure took place in July 2002 when the President of the High Court dealt with the case of a woman who had refused antenatal treatment to prevent HIV transmission and, further, had refused to attend the Coombe Hospital for the birth. The High Court ordered the woman to accept treatment to reduce the risk of transmission of HIV and directed that, on birth in the Coombe Hospital, the baby be made a ward of court so that the court could direct the neonate's medical treatment.[96]

The chasm that opens before us if the courts should persist in adopting this approach to mothers whose babies may be at this type of risk is that the law will set up an adversarial and combative approach between a mother and her newborn. The preferred option of the health professionals is to engage the putative mother in antenatal programmes whereby, should the newborn require immediate care, the mother has already given her consent to necessary treatment. Thus, even though the newly-delivered mother and her baby may need to be separated so that the neonate can receive appropriate treatment, the mother can be treated in a non-judgmental way as a partner in the process.

Legal Representation of Children

Child subject of litigation uniquely unrepresented in court

In *MF v. Superintendent of Ballymun Garda Station*[97] O'Flaherty J. stated:

> "In a ruling at the commencement of the hearing the court reaffirmed the strictness of the rule against giving a decision on a moot, but recognised that *cases concerning the care and custody of children and the protection of their rights* are in a special and, possibly, unique category. Certainly, they are special because they concern children and *are possibly unique in that the fundamental rights of persons are in issue in litigation in which they are not represented.* The absence of provision for such representation has been the subject of comment in this Court in the past but there is no provision, financial or otherwise, for it."[98] (emphasis added)

While *North Western Health Board v. H.W.*[99] is not about custody, it is most

---

[96] *The Irish Times* July 20, 2002.

[97] [1990] I.L.R.M. 767.

[98] *Ibid.*, p.772.

[99] [2001] 3 I.R 622, discussed above.

definitely about the welfare of a minor child. One might contend that in this case the infant was represented by the health authority. However, it might equally be said that the health authority was motivated by concerns additional to, if not other than, the welfare of the infant; counsel raised the question of future liability if the child were to manifest any of the illnesses avoidable by dint of having the test. Moreover, it is, after all, the health authority that would have to find the resources and bear the cost of a child who had a debilitating illness. It is economically better, therefore, to conduct a blood test of minimal effect on the infant rather than to run the risk of the infant developing an illness so easily detected and prevented. Thus, the health board was not an independent or unbiased party acting on behalf of the minor. Furthermore, it is difficult not to criticise aspects of the judgments which include statements of personal beliefs that the refusal to administer the test is against the child's interest and welfare and, yet, hold that the court must not intervene.

> "I confess that I would be impatient with the attitude of the Defendants/ Respondents. I am alarmed by the real possibility (happily not a probability) that the young boy may be a victim of one of the metabolic conditions which the PKU test could so easily detect and that, because of the absence of detection and treatment, he could suffer appalling consequences. In that event at least the North Western Health Board will have the comfort of knowing that they took every possible step to secure the welfare of the infant. The only solace for myself and those Judges taking a view similar to mine would be that we interpreted the Constitution and the law to the best of our fallible ability."[100]

Again, in *McK v. Information Commissioner* not only was there no independent representation of the minor child, the High Court judgment made no reference to what her wishes might be in relation to her father's request for her medical records. As has been noted, the Supreme Court failed to make any significant comment on the respective rights of child and parent in such an instance. The judgment did give weight to the fact that as the minor was now almost 18, following the remittal of the case for decision based on the correct test, the Information Commissioner should have regard to the child's views. How else can this be read other than that approaching majority the child's views matter but otherwise the parent is paramount?

In the case of the five month-old baby requiring heart surgery, the infant was made a ward of court in order to override, or perhaps facilitate, the mother. In that instance the court could act *in loco parentis*.

Thus, there is a curious legal anomaly with regard to the representation of children. There is a presumption that a constitutionally recognised parent[101]

---

[100] [2001] IESC 90 at 204 (*per* Murphy J.).

[101] Marital parent, or the biological unmarried mother.

or legal guardian acts at all times in his/her child's best interests. As has been indicated previously, the only way to rebut this presumption is to present evidence that will satisfy Article 42.5 which states:

> "In exceptional cases, where the parents for physical or moral reasons fail in their duty towards their children, the State as guardian of the common good, by appropriate means shall endeavour to supply the place of the parents, but always with due regard for the natural and imprescriptible rights of the child."

In effect, the parent needs to engage in egregious conduct to fall foul of this provision. This, of course, was the finding in *Attorney General v. Dowse*, and, as noted, in the circumstances there can be no doubt that the child was, so to speak, most effectively represented by the High Court itself. Thus, the child who may be the subject of a care order or made a ward of court has a far better chance of having his/her true interests represented than the child who remains with loving, caring but irrational or misguided parents. In other words, it might be suggested that a child in care or the child of non-marital parents may be more likely to have true representation in relation to rights than the child of marital parents because of restrictions placed on a child in the constitutional family in relation to expressions of its own autonomy.

Could a third party be given *locus standi* to represent a child of a constitutional family?

Comparing the born child and the unborn is contextual

Arising from Article 40.3.3° of the Constitution, right to life of the unborn, it has been possible for an organisation that is deemed to have a bona fide interest to be granted locus standi to represent the rights of the unborn in court.[102] The rights of the unborn were more recently considered in *Baby O v. Minister for Justice, Equality & Law Reform.*[103] This was a case challenging a deportation order and, *inter alia*, the appellants sought to prevent a mother's deportation on the grounds that she was pregnant; due to the inferior quality of ante and postnatal care in Nigeria it was argued that the unborn child would not have as good a chance of survival as it would if the mother could remain in Ireland. In the Supreme Court, referring to *Attorney General v. X*,[104] Keane C.J. (Denham, Murphy, Murray, McGuinness JJ. concurring) noted that the constitutional provision was intended to prevent the legalisation of abortion either by legislation or judicial decision within the State, except where there was a real and substantial risk to

---

[102] For example *SPUC v. Coogan* [1989] I.R. 734 and *SPUC v. Grogan* [1989] I.R. 753.

[103] [2002] IESC 44.

[104] [1992] 1 I.R. 1.

the life of the mother which could only be avoided by the termination of the pregnancy. He continued:

> "In this case, neither the State nor any of its organs was seeking to terminate the second named applicant's pregnancy and the fact that the standard of ante or postnatal care available to her in Nigeria was less than would be available to her in this country was entirely irrelevant to the legality of her deportation. If the second named applicant had arrived in this country accompanied by a young infant, and both of them had been refused refugee status and ordered to be deported, the life expectation of the infant, and for that matter the second named applicant herself, might have been less. That would plainly not be a ground for interfering with the deportation. If the State's right to deport persons who have been refused refugee status and who have no legal right to remain in this country were thus circumscribed, it would be, in a great range of cases, virtually negated. It is obvious that the rights of the born, in this context, cannot be less than those of the unborn."

Ignoring the somewhat chilling vista that diminished life expectancy of seekers of refuge in Ireland could not be permitted to stand in the way of deportation orders, one has to be struck by the logic of the argument. If it is alright to refuse entry to a living child it must therefore follow that the unborn child in similar circumstances may not be given leave to remain. "It is obvious that the rights of the born, in this context, cannot be less than those of the unborn." This being so is it not logical, therefore, to ask the question: if the rights of the unborn include separate and dedicated legal representation in court actions, surely the rights of the born child must allow for the same procedure? Or, must one rely on the phrase "in this context" and accept that that may only be true in relation to deportation. Does one then ask the question: if the born child is not to be granted the same legal rights as the unborn child, why are born children in this country not granted the same rights as born children who are being excluded from this country?

Who could represent the child?

It might be thought that the role of representing children is within the remit of the Ombudsman for Children. Yet, the Ombudsman is restrained legally from taking on a child's complaint without informing the parents. How then, could the Ombudsman independently represent a child of the constitutional family? Furthermore, to speak of legal representation is to place all decisions regarding children in the courtroom. This is clearly undesirable; moreover, it is neither necessary nor feasible especially if the point at issue is the giving of informed consent to medical treatment. Perhaps what is required is a Child Advocacy Officer within each health authority area and in all paediatric hospitals or hospitals providing services to those under 18. Such a function should resolve any difficulties arising from disagreement between children and parents or legal guardians. It could also act as honest broker for children in care.

Conclusion

Ultimately, if medical treatment is provided, as it should be, with a patient focus rather than a practitioner focus, each child patient should be regarded as an individual and decisions would be made on a case-by-case basis. The ideal solution from the child's point of view would be to enshrine in law that a minor child's ability to consent must be considered based on a reasoned assessment of that child's competence to understand the risks at stake. In a loving, caring family the child will arrive at decisions in consultation with and on the advice of parents, a result that is not in conflict with constitutional requirements. In addition, for the health professionals it is surely more desirable to deal with a patient who has had the opportunity to express a personal viewpoint and who, consequently, becomes a real participant in guiding the actions of the healthcare team.

Chapter 8

Defence Strategies in Medical Negligence Litigation: The New Approaches

John V. Smith II

Introduction

Physicians, hospitals and other health care providers are facing an increasing tide of malpractice litigation and significant awards. The number of medical malpractice claims is increasing. The rising number of malpractice claims and the increase in the malpractice verdicts has a significant impact on physicians, hospitals and other individuals involved in the health care profession. Given this rising wave of litigation that poses an economic threat to physicians and hospitals, the individuals involved in medical malpractice claims should be aware of the new approaches of the courts relating to medical malpractice litigation.

Two factors play a prominent role in the rising tide of lawsuits against physicians and hospitals. First, more physicians are specialists that often handle high-risk patients facing higher probability of death or a traumatic complication. Second, physicians and hospitals are more prone to become the target of a medical malpractice lawsuit because the quality doctor-patient friendly relationship is reduced by the changing economics of medicine. Fewer physicians are allowed to develop a relationship with the patient. Since a long-term relationship with a patient often builds up enough "credit" to overcome the stormy relationship that can develop following a medically related injury or death, the lack of such a relationship increases the likelihood of litigation. For hospitals, the situation is worse. There is little or no sympathy for hospitals in today's medical/legal climate. It is, therefore, not surprising that talented legal counsel in Ireland and the United States of America who represent patients in malpractice litigation earn high yearly incomes generated from lawsuits against physicians and hospitals.

A physician or hospital who is a defendant in a medical malpractice case is often confronted by an attorney representing the plaintiff who is as skilled in the art of advocacy as the medical specialist is skilled in the art of medicine. An insight into the personality and ego of the successful patient's attorney in the United States is seen in the following description by a wealthy plaintiff's attorney from Chicago, Philip H. Corboy, about himself:

> "I have what the jurors want. They want charisma. They want a fight in the courtroom. They don't want placidity. They don't want a one-dimensional lawsuit. They came here for a show! And they want to do what's right."[1]

This description is taken from *The Litigators,*[2] which goes on to note:

> "Corboy earned millions of dollars a year representing clients in personal-injury lawsuits, but instead of shrouding such good fortune he virtually trumpeted it in a profession in which mega verdicts meant mega business. If your injury was bad enough and the defendant big enough, Corboy was yours for a third of the recovery, plus expenses. He'd just earned a twenty-thousand-dollar fee for four hours' work settling a case, and he made no apologies for his hourly rate of five thousand dollars. 'You and I could have the same case,' he boomed, 'and I'm gonna get the client more. And that's why I'm entitled to that contingent fee.'"[3]

This chapter discusses the new approaches of the Courts and of the attorneys who specialise in medical malpractice in the United States. In the United States, defence attorneys, using these tactics, win medical malpractice cases on behalf of defendant physicians and hospitals in more than 80 percent of the trials brought to verdict.

Historical Overview of Medical Malpractice Claims

In the 1970s, the number of medical malpractice cases exploded. Prior to the mid-1970s, there were few medical malpractice actions and even fewer attorneys specialising in medical malpractice. During the past 20 years, however, medical malpractice has become a cottage industry among litigation attorneys in the United States. Certain specialists in the United States are more likely to be sued in a medical malpractice action. A large group of physicians in the United States, the Illinois State Medical Insurance Society, realised that its physicians needed specialised insurance coverage. As a result, the Illinois State Medical Insurance Society formed the Illinois State Medical Inter-Insurance Exchange which remains the largest malpractice insurer in the State of Illinois. Since the insurance company was formed in 1976 and continues to maintain detailed

---

1 Jenkins, *The Litigators – Inside The Powerful World of America's High-Stakes Trial Lawyers* (1989), p.315.

2 *Id.*

3 *Id.*

records, it is interesting to review the table below that lists the frequency of claims against various medical specialists.

Claim Frequency and Exposures by Specialty[4]

Specialists	Number of % of All	Claims from Claims
Obstetricians/Gynaecologists	3,744	11.8%
Internal Medicine	3,044	9.6%
Orthopaedic Surgery	2,989	9.4%
General Surgery	2,889	9.1%
Radiology	2,485	7.8%
Family Practice	1,905	6.0%
General Practice	1,406	4.4%
Anaesthesiology	1,262	4.0%
Neurosurgery	929	2.9%
Paediatrician	916	2.9%

This table represents a 17-year history for approximately 10,000 physicians in the State of Illinois. As these figures demonstrate, the specialists practising in the area of obstetrics and gynaecology run the highest risk of medical malpractice claims. The reason that obstetricians and gynaecologists have the highest number of claims is that these specialists treat two types of patients who can generate very high verdicts: (1) children with brain injuries sustained at birth from oxygen deprivation, and (2) gynaecologic cancer patients. Brain injuries to children generate large verdicts because of the high future medical care costs that are associated with the constant nursing care that may be required for a child who will be unable to feed or cloth himself or herselffor the next 50 to 70 years or more. Cancer patients are often women who die a tragic death leaving a grieving husband and children. The sympathy present in gynaecologic cancer cases has generated high verdicts against physicians.

High verdicts against physicians not only create the risk of a substantial personal financial loss, but also significantly increase the insurance premiums that must be endured on a yearly basis. Listed below are examples of the insurance premiums for those specialists that are the most common targets of malpractice actions. Even though the defendants have continued to win the vast majority of medical malpractice lawsuits, the ever-increasing verdicts cause malpractice premiums to increase. Note the significant increase that is encountered by specialists in one year, between 1994 and 1995.

4 Table from Illinois State Inter-Insurance Exchange regarding claims from July of 1976 through December of 1993.

Yearly Premiums by Specialty - 1994 and 1995 for Coverage of $1,000,000 per Claim and $3,000,000 in the Aggregate

Specialists	1994	1995	2007
Obstetricians/Gynaecologists	$63,452	$69,500	$138,484
Internal Medicine	$20,072	$21,944	$46,688
Orthopaedic Surgery	$67,064	$73,464	$113,284
General Surgery	$39,352	$43,080	$137,048
Radiology	$20,072	$21,944	$59,288
Family Practice	$27,300	$29,872	$50,288
General Practice	$27,300	$29,872	$50,288
Anaesthesiology	$20,672	$22,604	$41,288
Neurosurgery	$91,164	$102,528	$228,484
Paediatricians	$12,840	$14,016	$46,688

Since the medical malpractice verdicts are high and the premiums are climbing ever higher, physicians and attorneys defending physicians are, by necessity, becoming increasingly sophisticated in the defence techniques used to combat medical malpractice lawsuits in the United States.

Recent Developments Relating to Malpractice Payments

Between 1995 and 2001, the average medical malpractice claim payment in the United States rose from less than $200,000 per claim to more than $300,000 per claim.[5] As a result of this significant increase in payments made for medical malpractice claims, there has been a significant amount of political commentary relating to the "medical malpractice crisis" in the United States. The United States Senate rejected legislation in the summer of 2003 to limit awards a patient may win in medical malpractice cases. Nevertheless, the battle between those advocating "malpractice reform" and those claiming that this reform is unnecessary continues to move forward. In addition, state legislatures are posed to fight this issue on a state-by-state basis since state governments are confronted with physicians who leave states with high malpractice premiums in order to practice in other states with lower premiums. In 2000, medical malpractice verdicts totalled $372,000,000 in Pennsylvania and $633,000,000 in New York.[6]

5 Testimony of Lawrence E. Smarr before a Joint Hearing of the United States Senate Judicial Committee of Health, Education and Labor Pension Committee, February 11, 2003.

6 *Health Care News*, January, 2002.

New Approaches to Issues Relating to Expert Testimony

The evolution of expert testimony in medical malpractice litigation

In most medical malpractice lawsuits in the United States, expert testimony is crucial. A jury is often persuaded primarily by the testimony given by experts. The experts will testify as to the standard of care. It is important to note, however, that there is no definition of the standard of care as it applies to any particular medical issue. Instead, the standard of care for a physician is literally whatever opinion is expressed by that expert in court. The Courts have regularly determined that the standard of care is raised where a specialist is involved in the treatment of the patient.

In the United States, a physician is held to the same standard of care as other reasonably well-qualified physicians in similar circumstances. A specialist is held to a higher standard of care. Whereas non-specialists must meet the standards of a reasonably well-qualified *physician*, a specialist must meet the standard of other *specialists* A typical jury instruction setting forth the law applicable to a specialist is found in the Illinois Pattern Jury Instructions.

> "**105.02 Duty of a Specialist Professional-Professional Negligence**
> A physician who holds himself out as a specialist and provides service in his specialty must possess and apply the knowledge and use the skill and care ordinarily used by a reasonably well-qualified *specialist* under circumstances similar to those shown by the evidence. A failure to do so is professional negligence.
>
> The only way in which you may decide whether the defendant possessed and applied the knowledge and used the skill and care which the law requires of him is from expert testimony or evidence of professional standards or conduct presented in the trial. You must not attempt to determine the question from any personal knowledge you have."[7]

This foregoing instruction is an evolution of Illinois common law which originated in the case of *Ritchy v. West.*[8] The court in *Ritchy* reviewed a case involving a physician who was alleged to have improperly immobilised a fractured wrist. The medical malpractice attorney who argued the appeal on behalf of the physician was Abraham Lincoln, later President of the United States. The Illinois Supreme Court declared that, although the physician is not required to possess "the highest order of qualification, to which some men attain, still he must possess and exercise that degree of skill, which is ordinarily possessed by members of the profession."[9]

Note that this standard jury instruction emphasises that the jury must not

---

7 Illinois Pattern Instruction, 105.02 (November 1990) (emphasis supplied).

8 23 Ill. 329 (Ill. Sup. Ct. 1860).

9 *Ibid.,* p.330.

decide the case based on any personal knowledge. Yet, it is rare that a jury member will not attempt to apply his or her own logic to the medical situation in order to determine whether the medical physician's care was appropriate. Therefore, the best preparation of a physician or hospital usually involves the heavy use of visual evidence that allows a judge or jury to reach a conclusion that is sympathetic to the defendant physician or hospital.

The court's role of gatekeeper for expert witnesses

One of the newest and most important approaches by the court relating to medical malpractice litigation involves the standard for determining the admissibility of expert testimony. In the Federal Courts, the test has been changed from the *Freye*[10] standard to the *Daubert* standard. The *Freye* standard requires that the expert testimony has gained "general acceptance" within the specific scientific community. In *Daubert*, the United States Supreme Court changed the standard for expert witnesses by requiring the trial judge to undertake "preliminary assessment" of whether the reasoning or methodology for the expert testimony is "scientifically valid."

Expert testimony is extremely important in cases involving medical malpractice. Not only is expert testimony required to establish the standard of care applicable to a physician, hospital or other health care provider, but expert testimony is also required to prove that a proximate cause existed between the alleged medical negligence and the plaintiff's claimed injury. In addition to challenging an expert's credentials during trial, a trial court is now often confronted with challenges to an expert's credentials made prior to the commencement of trial. The *Daubert* standard applies in Federal courts and in those State courts in the United States following the *Daubert* standard. It is important to note that in states that follow the *Freye* standard, the court will also carefully review the expert's credentials.

Where an expert is offered by a plaintiff to establish the applicable standard of care and a breach by the defendant, there is usually a two prong test that is used by the court in its role as the "gatekeeper." The first test is that the expert must be *licensed* in the same "school of medicine" to which a defendant physician belongs.[11] The second prong of this test is whether the expert is qualified to give opinions relating to the specialised medical field. A good example of the new direction that the courts are moving in medical malpractice litigation is contained in the decision rendered by the court in *Northern Trust Company v. The Upjohn Company, et al.*[12] In this decision, the court reviewed the qualifications of the plaintiff's expert witness, Dr. James Mathews, a board-certified emergency room physician. Even though Dr Mathews had significant experience in the

---

10 *Freye v. United States* 293 F. 1013 (D. C. Cir. 1923) and *Daubert v. Merrell Dow Pharm., Inc.* 509 U.S. 579 (1993).

11 *Dolan v. Galluzzo* 77 Ill.2d 279, 396 N.E.2d 13, 32 Ill.Dec. 900 (1979).

12 213 Ill.App.3d, 390, 572 N.E.2d 1030, 157 Ill.Dec. 566 (First Dist. 1991).

treatment and management of patients who had suffered a cardiac arrest, the court ruled that Dr Mathews was not qualified to establish the standard of care against the defendant physician who was an obstetrician. The court reasoned that the defendant physician, who was an obstetrician, might have reacted to vital signs and symptoms of the patient in a distinctly different manner than an emergency room physician. The court emphasised that Dr Mathews was "not qualified" to give an opinion on the standard of care applicable to an obstetrician because Dr Mathews could not know what was "custom and practice" for an obstetrician.[13]

Therefore, the new approaches of both the Federal and state courts in the United States indicate that, as medicine becomes more specialised, the expert witnesses who testify as to the standard of care and causation issues must also be aware of the "custom and practice" of the defendant physician's specialty.

The Courts' New Approaches to the Increased Risk of Future Injuries

Although there is pressure on legislatures and courts to limit medical malpractice awards, there is a significant number of cases that have expanded liability theories against physicians, hospitals and other health care providers. One significant area of expansion is related to future damages. The majority view in the United States is that, where a plaintiff can prove that there exists a "more likely than not" chance that his injury is permanent or that future injury will result, he may receive full compensation for that injury.

An example of this issue is discussed in the Illinois Supreme Court case of *Dillon v. Evanston Hospital*,[14] where the court allowed a new category of damages to be awarded to the plaintiff. In *Dillon,* the court reviewed a verdict against a physician and hospital where a fragment from a catheter remained in the plaintiff's body following a procedure. The fragment was discovered on x-ray. The defendant physician recommended that no attempt be made to remove the catheter because of the risks associated with the removal. The court allowed an award for potential future injury because of the increased risk of an infection potentially caused by the catheter fragment. Although the Illinois Supreme Court has historically rejected assessing damages for potential future injuries, the Court set forth its approach by allowing an award for a potential future injury, which had *not* occurred and might *never* occur. The court held that the plaintiff must be permitted to recover for the risk of potential future injuries.

The court in *Dillon* represents the majority rule in the United States.[15] In determining whether to award damage for "potential future injuries," a court will impose the "reasonably certain" standard. To meet this standard, the plaintiff is generally required to prove that it is "more likely true than not true" (described

---

13 *Ibid.*, p.407.

14 199 Ill.2nd 483, 771 N.E.2d 357, 264 Ill. Dec. 653 (2002).

15 *Dillon* 199 Ill.2nd at 499.

as a greater than 50% likelihood) that the potential future injury will occur. If the court decides that a potential future injury is "more likely than not" to occur (again, a greater than 50% chance of occurring) then the court will award full compensation for the injury.[16]

An opposite result was reached by the Supreme Court of Connecticut in *Petrillo v. Kalman:*[17]

> "In essence, if a plaintiff can prove that there exists a 51 percent chance that his injury is permanent or that future injury will result, he may receive full compensation for that injury as if it were a certainty. If, however, the plaintiff establishes only a 49 percent chance of such a consequence, he may recover nothing for the risk to which he is presently exposed. Although this all or nothing view has been adopted by a majority of courts faced with the issue, the concept has been severely criticised by numerous commentators. By denying any compensation unless a plaintiff proves that a future consequence is more likely to occur than not, courts have created a system in which a significant number of persons receive compensation for future consequences that never occur and, conversely, a significant number of persons receive no compensation at all for consequences that later ensue from risks not rising to the level of probability. This system is inconsistent with the goal of compensating tort victims fairly for all the consequences of the injuries they have sustained, while avoiding, so far as possible, windfall awards for consequences that never happen."

As courts continue to analyse whether or not to assess damages for a *potential future injury,* the court will be confronted with whether or not to accept expert testimony on the likelihood of future damages.

Recent Developments Involving Hospitals in Medical Malpractice Actions

A hospital, acting through its agents, must also comply with the accepted standard of care. In the case of *Zajac v. St. Mary of Nazareth Hospital Center*,[18] the court ruled that a hospital is under a duty to conform to the legal standard of reasonable conduct. In most malpractice actions, however, it is the physician who acts as the "Captain of the Ship" and directs the action. Therefore, a common defence

---

[16] *Wilson v. Johns-Manville Sales Corp.* 684 F.2d, 111, 119 (D.C. Cir. 1982). *Accord 2 D. Dobbs, Remedies* § 8.1(7), at 4507 (2d ed. 1993); King, "Causation, Valuation, and Chance in Personal Injury Torts Involving Preexisting Conditions and Future Consequences" 90 Yale L.J. 1353, 1370-72 (1981); "Note Damages Consistent Upon Chance" 18 Rutgers L.Rev. 875, 876 (1964). Cited in *Dillon*, 199 Ill.2d at 499.

[17] 215 Conn. 377, 576 At. 2d 484 (1990).

[18] 212 Ill. App. 3d 779, 571, N.E.2d 840, 156 Ill. Dec. 860 (1st Dist. 1991).

tactic for hospitals is to separate the hospital's actions from the actions of the physician who is considered an independent contractor.

A developing trend in the United States is to impose liability on hospitals in cases where physicians are found to be "apparent agents" of the hospital even though these physicians are not employees or agents of the hospital and are acting as independent contractors. In *Gilbert v. Sycamore Municipal Hospital*,[19] the Illinois Supreme Court determined that a hospital assumes responsibility for the emergency room physician who is an independent contractor. It is important to note that the emergency room physician in the *Gilbert* case was not employed by the hospital, but was employed, instead, by a separate medical corporation. The emergency room physician had discharged a patient from the emergency room who died later that evening from a myocardial infarction. The Supreme Court held that the hospital could be found liable under the doctrine of apparent agency for the negligent acts of the physician. The Illinois Supreme Court reasoned that patients who seek care through the emergency room of a modern hospital are usually unaware of the employment status of the emergency room physicians. These patients have relied on the reputation of the hospital, rather than the emergency room physician. In addition, the patients have often been led to believe that the emergency room physicians are employees of the hospital based on the signs in and around the emergency room and the hospital coats supplied to the emergency room physicians. The Illinois Supreme Court held that, therefore, the hospital must assume responsibility for the actions of the emergency room physician since the hospital created the impression that the emergency room physician was the hospital's "apparent agent."

Successful Trial Tactics for Medical Specialists

Simplify the medical issues for the judge or jury

There is an important principle that significantly increases the likelihood that a judge or jury will return a verdict in favour of a physician who is a defendant in a medical malpractice action. A successful defence attorney will keep in mind that the trier of fact is neither a physician nor a lawyer, but is a lay person who is attempting to determine whether a physician correctly treated the patient. Medical malpractice actions are becoming more complex. The defence of a medical physician is usually a mixture of overwhelming facts of a complexity not normally faced by a layman. Successful attorneys have a way of simplifying the most complex issues in a fair and logical manner that best illustrates the physician's practice and explains the complex logic involved in making important medical decisions.

---

[19] 156 Ill. 2d 511, 266 N.E.2d 788, 190 Ill. Dec. 758 (1993).

Preparing the defendant physician

The defendant physician is the cornerstone of the defence. In order to successfully defend a physician, the legal counsel must master the objective historical facts of treatment so that those facts are crystal clear at the time of trial. Only after the physician is able to master the historical facts of the case can the physician then approach all of the nuances of the complicated medical issues.

The physician who hopes to be successful at a medical malpractice trial must be so prepared that he believes that he or she can handle any question posed by the plaintiff's attorney at trial. A common tactic when preparing the defendant physician for trial in the United States is to use several videotaped practice sessions. The purpose for the physician's review of his attorney's critique of the videotape is not to repackage or recreate the physician's personality. Instead, the videotape is used to demonstrate to the physician that he can more effectively communicate to the judge or jury by improving his testifying ability. In addition, a physician's anxiety relating to a lawsuit is often reduced when he enters the courtroom and finds that he is facing the same questions and issues that have already been presented to him under tough mock cross-examination conditions.

Locating the best defence expert witnesses

There are two issues related to expert testimony on behalf of physicians. First, the defendant must obtain the best expert possible. A defence attorney has a definite advantage that should not be relinquished. That is, the defence attorney usually has developed contacts and created good will in the medical community based on his representation of a number of physicians. These physicians can certainly provide a source of experts or, at the very least, provide insights for the defence attorney as to potential experts with their individual strengths and weaknesses. It is not uncommon for a defence attorney to look for more than one expert on a specific subject, and then select the best expert from the group. This can become expensive for the insurance carrier since many experts charge in excess of \$500 per hour for their time with an agreement that trial testimony will cost more than \$2,000 per day. When combined with trial preparation including a pre-trial deposition, the defence expert will often charge in excess of \$10,000 to review and defend a lawsuit.

The second issue relating to expert witnesses involves the availability of the particular expert. If the defendant's expert is not available to testify in person at trial, a significant portion of the expert's ability to communicate directly to the judge or jury is lost.

Tools of persuasion

> "The principal nemesis of any trial lawyer is not so much adversary as boredom on the part of the fact finder."[20]

The medical physician's case will not be presented to the jury until the plaintiff has rested. By the time the defence attorney presents evidence on behalf of the physician, the jury will have heard many issues on numerous occasions. Therefore, it is extremely important for the defence attorney to keep the case interesting. Modern visual demonstrative evidence is a marvellous way to keep the evidence interesting.[21]

Anatomical drawings

A jury must understand the precise anatomy involved in the medical malpractice action. The best way to present this anatomy to the jury is to obtain anatomical drawings that are specifically tailored for the lawsuit. In that manner, the rough drawings can be given a trial run and reviewed by a lay person who is not involved in the case. This allows a polishing of the anatomical drawing in order to best portray the issues that are important in the lawsuit. These anatomical drawings must, of course, fairly and accurately depict the medical issues involved in the lawsuit. If mistakes are made, the opposing counsel will be happy to point out the mistakes when the exhibit is before the jury.

Computer animation

Computer animation is usually presented in a videotape format and can show the anatomy in motion, such as how the heart valves open and close to move oxygenated blood. The case for computer animation is significant. Whereas a standard anatomical drawing will typically cost between $500 and $2,000, the computer animation will usually cost $10,000 to $20,000. The computer animation can be placed on a video disk and can be indexed so that a witness or lawyer can immediately jump to any portion of the computer animation.

Video testimony

Although a defence attorney may be able to obtain experts throughout the country or world who specialise in a specific area of medicine, insuring that the physician travels to the trial is impossible. Therefore, the defence attorney must often rely on a videotaped evidence deposition that will be shown to the judge or jury at the time of trial.

---

20 Joseph, *Modern Visual Evidence* (1987), pp.1-3.

21 Belli, "Demonstrative Evidence: Seeing Is Believing," *Trial Magazine*, July 1980; reprinted in *Best of Trial*, 1990.

Enlargements of actual medical records

Many medical records are difficult to decipher. A common defence tactic is to enlarge the exhibit with a highlighted portion translated on the side of the exhibit. In that way, the jury is drawn to the clearly typed portion of the translation, rather than to an illegible entry in the medical chart.

Chronology

It is very important that the jury understand the important chronology of the plaintiff's treatment. The chronology can be presented on enlargements. The defence attorney should teach the "history" to the jury with the use of a chronological outline so that the jury can understand the historical framework for the treatment. Important dates or times within the treatment should be highlighted so that the jury's attention is drawn to the dates and times that the physician and his or her attorney consider important.

The co-defendant

If two or more physicians or hospitals are involved in the lawsuit, it is usually a significant handicap for the defendant physician for strong disagreements to develop among the defence witnesses at trial. Therefore, a tactic among defendants is to make sure that the defence attorneys present a consistent description of the treatment in a manner that does not cause fireworks to occur during the trial.

Jury selection

In the United States, medical malpractice actions are typically decided by a jury.

> "There is no one phase of any jury trial which is more important than the *voir dire* examination. It is the engine that starts the vehicle. It is the act, if you will, that gets the show off the ground. It is the first, and best opportunity for the lawyer to perform and sell himself and his product.[22]

There are numerous books and articles written on the theories applicable to jury selection. One process in the selection of a jury in a case involving a physician may be mentioned here. Since many of the malpractice cases that involve physicians also involve circumstances relating to serious injury or death, the defence attorney may sometimes request that the court present to potential jurors the most sympathetic aspects of the plaintiff's case, in order to

---

22 *The Trial Masters: A Handbook of Strategies and Tactics that Win Cases* (Warshaw, ed., 1984), p.93.

determine whether the potential jurors can actually render a fair verdict after being exposed to powerful sympathetic evidence. For example, a *Day in the Life* film is often used to portray the difficulties that an injured plaintiff faces on a daily basis. The video contains footage showing the difficulty involved in eating, dressing or with other daily chores. If the court allows the defence attorney to show the potential jurors a *Day in the Life* film or other similar sympathetic evidence to potential jurors, the defence attorney can then seek to exclude those individuals who admit that the very sympathetic evidence would prevent them from rendering a verdict in favour of the physician. The rationale is that this weeding out process allows a physician to obtain a jury that will be able to render a verdict after considering the liability issues, rather than being overcome by the sympathy.

Opening statement

When defending a specialist, it is especially important to remember that trials involving specialists are typically longer and more complex than lawsuits involving non-specialists. Since the defendant physician's portion of the lawsuit will not proceed until the plaintiff rests, the jury must have a clear understanding of the defendant physician's position from the outset of the trial. An attorney representing a defendant will often present a significant majority of the visual evidence to a jury during the opening statement so that the jury has some idea as to the response of the defendant to the mountain of evidence that will be transported through the courtroom during the plaintiff's case.

Therefore, a common tactic employed by defence attorneys who represent specialists is to have several practice sessions involving the opening statement with the physician present as an additional critic of the defence attorney's performance. The physician's presence is useful for two reasons. First, the physician can provide insights into how the opening statement can be improved. Second, the physician is better able to understand the theory of his case presented by the defence attorney if the specialist is allowed to see, or at least discuss in detail, the relevant portions of the opening statement.

Attacking the plaintiff's expert

The expert on behalf of the plaintiff often has less impressive credentials and more "baggage" related to a high volume of prior service as a highly paid plaintiff's expert. There is usually a much smaller number of plaintiff's experts who are willing to testify, especially in cases where the liability issues are in favour of the defendant physician.

Attorneys who defend physicians in the United States have formed the Defence Research Institute.[23] The plaintiff's attorneys have organised a similar

---

23 The Defense Research Institute is located at 750 North Lake Shore Drive, Suite 500, Chicago, Illinois 60611.

organisation that also provides material for use in medical malpractice cases.[24] The Defence Research Institute provides deposition transcripts and the names of defence attorneys who have contacted the Defence Research Institute with inquiries regarding specific plaintiffs' experts. In this manner, the defence attorney can obtain transcripts of effective cross-examinations that have occurred in other lawsuits. In addition, the defence attorney can obtain information concerning the wide-ranging testimony habits of certain plaintiff's experts who travel to various states on a regular basis.

One common tactic to be used against an expert who testifies in various areas of the country is to display a map with the localities of the various trials pinpointed on a map so that a lay jury or judge can visually appreciate the frequent travel that is encountered by this specific expert. This tactic allows a judge or jury immediately to see that a plaintiff's expert is being flown around the country for one specific purpose. That purpose is to provide testimony to plaintiffs' attorneys and their clients for a high fee.

Organising the mountain of documents and facts

Trials involving physicians move at a quick pace. Attorneys representing physicians must be able quickly to retrieve specific parts of medical records, medical literature or deposition transcripts that apply to an unexpected twist in the lawsuit. Defence attorneys are making better use of computer technology. An index can be prepared relating to various witnesses and their testimony so that there can be a "key word" search for specific testimony or particular medical records. Computer technology is used to access the information for quick retrieval.

Portraying the defendant physician

Judges and juries will usually enjoy the specific colourful detail of a specialist's practice. An attorney representing a physician should show the jury actual relevant equipment, or at the least photographs of the equipment, that is used by the physician. This allows the physician to explain medical equipment that is familiar to him or her and will usually create good will.

Conclusion

The defendant physician has dedicated a good part of his or her life to the medical techniques that are growing more and more complex. As the complexity of medicine increases, the number of lawsuits against physicians will continue to increase. So too must the defence counsel have available those techniques that can be put to good use defending physicians.

---

[24] The American Association for Justice, formerly the American Trial Lawyers' Association, consists primarily of attorneys representing plaintiffs.

CHAPTER 9

Some Statutory Responses to the American Medical Malpractice Crisis

JOHN H. SCHEID

INTRODUCTION

An article in *The Irish Times* over a decade ago began with this sentence: "Ireland has become the 'USA of Europe' in suing doctors and dentists." Since history, as the adage goes, tends to repeat itself, the health care profession in Ireland could possibly profit from observing the direction that American medical malpractice law has taken. And healthcare professionals in Ireland, hopefully, may also profit by observing how the American healthcare profession has defended itself from some of the more egregious excesses found in the American legal system.

The law of medical malpractice in the United States has progressed along very similar lines in the 50 separate States. There are significant differences in the admissibility of evidence among the several States. But for the most part there is a common current among all States on the fundamental requirements for establishing a *prima facie* case. To establish a *prima facie* case of medical malpractice in 2007 in the United States, all that is necessary is to state a series of facts, supported by a physician's affidavit, that the defendant physician failed to meet the standard of care. In some States,[1] the plaintiff's expert witness "who in good faith prepares a report used in conjunction with an affidavit required by this section shall have civil immunity from liability which otherwise might result from the preparation of such report." Thus, the plaintiff's expert should fear no reprisals from his/her fellow physicians, nor from any medical liability insurer by way of increased premiums.[2] It is relatively easy therefore to plead a cause of action that will withstand a motion to dismiss.

Almost none of the basic American law governing medical malpractice has emanated from the state legislatures. The courts have been virtually the sole source of professional negligence tort law, and the courts have tended to favour the plaintiff patient. The medical, dental, and other health care professions

---

1 See, e.g., in Illinois 735 ILCS 5/2-622 (f).

2 See 735 ILC5 5/2-622 (a)(1).

therefore have been forced to look to the legislatures of their various States for relief from some of what the healing arts professions envision as the more egregious problems created through successive, and allegedly "progressive", court decisions. What follows herewith are some legislative responses to eight distinct areas where the scales of justice appeared to have been out of balance.[3]

I. Bad Press—*Ad damnum*—Unknown and Possibly Large Verdict and Judgment

The first major problem facing the medical profession during the past twenty years has been the bad press that physicians receive upon the commencement of a lawsuit. It may surprise the reader but, in the United States, plaintiffs' attorneys were once allowed to simply pick an arbitrary number to insert in their prayers for relief. The "prayer for relief" is generally referred to as the "*ad damnum*" clause in a plaintiff's complaint. Every complaint, prior to remedial legislation, required the plaintiff to demand of the defendant the maximum amount of money which the plaintiff would seek from the jury. Therefore, the last paragraph of a plaintiff's complaint would read something like the following:

> "Wherefore, plaintiff demands judgment against the defendant in the amount of $[insert dollar amount]."

A plaintiff's attorney would, prior to receiving any detailed medical diagnosis and/or prognosis, simply choose a figure he believed reflected the plaintiff's injuries. In defence of this practice, the plaintiff's attorney frequently did not know the extent of the injury when he filed suit. Perhaps the statute of limitations was close to expiring and it was necessary to file suit in order for the plaintiff's attorney to avoid being charged with legal malpractice. Nevertheless, the plaintiff's attorney had it within his power to pick a dollar figure that was utterly out of line with the to-be-determined injuries.

However, the press was all too happy to report that Dr Smith had just been sued for three million dollars. Almost never would the press follow up on Dr Smith's case to report that this case had been dismissed because it was worthless, or that it had been settled for a nominal sum.

Therefore, until some time had passed and discovery was finally concluded, no one ever knew how serious the plaintiff's injuries actually were. Although it was theoretically possible to increase the *ad damnum* prior to trial, it was hardly ever done because the initial demand had originally been so high. Also, in a

---

3 An earlier version of much of what follows appeared originally in the *Medico-Legal Journal of Ireland*, (1998) Vol.4, No.1, which I authored in 1998, and is used here with the kind permission of that journal. The reader is referred to that article for additional case citations and statutes.

closing argument a plaintiff's attorney was never permitted to ask the jury for more money than he had originally demanded in his *ad damnum*, the "prayer for relief." Accordingly, when the case settled for perhaps a pittance, the physician's name had already been besmirched. The press never reported the settlement. The appellate and supreme courts in the various States, in turn, did absolutely nothing to rectify this problem.

Some States like California then enacted statutes that require a plaintiff to give a defendant health provider an advance 90 days notice before filing suit.[4] This is mandatory, and precludes the plaintiff from filing suit and thereby going public with his allegations for at least 90 days. The legislature's hope was that the parties might negotiate and, possibly through binding arbitration, resolve the matter without the plaintiff having to file suit.

> "The purpose of the 90-day waiting period of section 364 … is to decrease the number of medical malpractice actions filed by establishing a procedure that encourages the parties to negotiate outside the structure and atmosphere of the formal litigation process."[5]

Read in conjunction with California's one year discovery rule for the running of the statute of limitations,[6] the practical result is that the window during which suit may be filed is cut back to nine months.

In a case where the defendant physician was alleged to have negligently inserted a shunt into the plaintiff's brain without properly affixing it in the abdomen, the California appellate court held that the 90 day notice provision, having been given once, could not be given again in order to extend the limitation period. The court held this even though the plaintiff did not know that his first lawyer had given the 90 day notice early on in the one year period. In the United States, an attorney's knowledge is imputed to his client. Therefore when plaintiff retained his second lawyer, someone who specialised in medical malpractice, and this second lawyer gave the 90 day notice to the defendant within three months of the running of the statute of limitations, this second notice could not be used to extend the statute of limitations, even though the injuries complained of in the second notice were different than those complained of in the first notice. The bottom line is that, in California, the plaintiff must address himself to a possible medical malpractice claim as quickly as possible, but he cannot go public for at least 90 days. Many States, such as Illinois, have now enacted statutes which forbid the plaintiff from demanding in his complaint the precise amount of money he will eventually seek from the jury. The only thing the plaintiff may now plead in his complaint resembles the following:

---

4 West's Ann. Cal. Code of Civil Procedure (C.C.C.P.) § 364(a) and (d).

5 *Bennett v. Shahhal*, M.D., 75 Cal. App. 4th 384, 389 (4th Dist. 1999) citing *Woods v. Young*, 53 Cal. 3d 315, 320 (1991).

6 *West's Ann.* C.C.C.P. § 340.5.

> "Wherefore, plaintiff demands judgment in an amount sufficient to satisfy the jurisdictional requirements of the court."

This statute therefore makes it impossible for a reporter to discover how much a patient/plaintiff is seeking from a particular doctor/defendant.

However, this statutory relief could possibly become a two-edged sword because the defendant-physician does not know his exposure.[7] In short, the defendant will never know the extent of his exposure. Prior to trial, the defendant's attorney may inquire what amount of money the plaintiff will seek from the jury. The plaintiff frequently responds in general terms. But, until the plaintiff's closing argument, the defendant does not know precisely how much the plaintiff's attorney will ask the jury to return in its verdict.

Frequently, four years have elapsed between the time suit is filed and the time the case comes to trial. It now takes an average of 3.75 years for a civil case to reach trial in Cook County, Illinois, which is deemed an improvement over previous years. During this intervening period, the defendant's attorney attempts, as best as he can, to determine the gravity of the plaintiff's injuries. But one is hard pressed to estimate the true worth of the injuries and the amount of any potential verdict for the plaintiff until actually observing the plaintiff in the courtroom. Thus, the defendant physician confronts an unknown in terms of damages. Much of a plaintiff's recovery is for pain and suffering; this cannot be calculated until the plaintiff is observed on the witness stand. Also, one never actually knows the true extent and nature of the plaintiff's injuries until the plaintiff's medical expert has testified. Nor does one know what future care will be needed, nor its cost, until the plaintiff's economics expert has testified.

A personal friend of the author's, an obstetrician, was sued for alleged failure to diagnose breast cancer, which alleged failure arguably resulted in the patient's death. During discovery, it was the considered judgment of the defence counsel and the defendant's insurance company that the plaintiff's decedent was not a particularly appealing or winsome person because of her behaviour while under the doctor's care. She had basically refused to follow the doctor's orders. The evidence was that after her cancer became manifest, she lied to obtain medical coverage, thus attempting to defraud the health insurance company. There were other unsavoury facts about her. Much of this, however, was not admissible at trial.

Nevertheless, the plaintiff's argument was that the doctor failed to warn, in effect frighten her enough into returning for subsequent diagnostic tests. When she finally did return, the cancer had metastasised throughout her body. The defendant-physician carried one million dollars of malpractice coverage. This was, at the time, the maximum coverage that any physician could purchase. During closing arguments the plaintiff's attorney requested that the jury return a "fair verdict somewhere between three and four million dollars." In the United

---

7 75 I.L.C.S. 5/2-604 (2007).

States, about 70% of all medical malpractice cases are found in favour of the defendant. But in those cases where the jury finds in favour of the plaintiff, the jury returns rather substantial verdicts.

Had the jury in the author's friend's suit returned a verdict, for example, of three million dollars, the insurance company would have paid the first million and the defendant-physician would have been personally responsible for the remaining two million. Of course, this verdict would bankrupt any individual practitioner. Thus, one case could end a doctor's professional life.

Frequently, the plaintiff's attorney on the eve of trial will demand that the defendant pay the entire amount of insurance coverage then in force, for example, one million dollars. The defendant physician's personal lawyer, who often believes his client is guilty of no malpractice, is thereafter placed in the illogical and somewhat uncomfortable position of demanding that the defendant's insurance company pay the policy limit to settle the lawsuit. The defendant through his personal counsel is begrudgingly forced to threaten his own liability insurance company that if the plaintiff seeks to collect any excess verdict from the defendant personally, the defendant himself will look to the company to pay the excess. Hence the doctor and his own liability insurance company become adversaries.

In the case of the author's friend, there was ample evidence that the claim was not a meritorious one. Neither the defendant physician, his lawyer, nor his outside experts believed the plaintiff had a meritorious cause, nor did the malpractice insurance company. Nevertheless, to defend the obstetrician against the possibility of an excess judgment being collected from him personally, the author was forced to demand that the insurance company settle the case and pay the entire one million dollar policy limit. Otherwise, the physician would risk personal liability for any excess over his policy limits. In sum, the defendant is frequently between a rock and a hard place when he is unsure of the amount the plaintiff's attorney intends to seek from the jury.

The defendant physician does not know until the jury's verdict whether his liability insurance will cover the loss.

However, as discussed below in section II, State legislatures have found a way to avoid this inequitable situation through the enactment of caps on the amounts plaintiffs can obtain for non-economic losses in medical malpractice cases. These caps limit the defendant's liability to the amount established by the legislature.

In conclusion, by virtue of this statutory enactment precluding the plaintiff from demanding a specific amount of money in his written complaint, the press cannot discover the amount for which a physician is being sued. But, neither can the physician determine his exposure with any degree of accuracy until the eve of trial. For those cases that settle, the physician enjoys a desirable protection. For the doctor who goes to trial, it is a "mixed blessing."

II. Large Awards—Caps on Non Economic Damages—Constitutionality of Caps

The second crisis facing the medical profession is extremely large jury awards. A review of cases reported from January 2006 to September 2007 in Cook County Illinois indicates that in those cases that went to verdict, the plaintiff prevailed in approximately 34% of the cases. See Appendix A. Thus, the physician prevailed in two-thirds of the cases. But in a review of the most recent data covering the period from September 2006 through September 2007 for the Chicago metropolitan area, in those cases where the plaintiff won, the average verdict was $3,139,191. The lowest verdict was $136,131 and the highest verdict was $31,351,107. As can readily be seen, there were numerous defendant physicians whose malpractice liability insurance coverage of one or two million dollars was woefully inadequate. As noted elsewhere, unless there are other defendants from whom the judgment could be collected, such a defendant physician may face personal bankruptcy.

Some preliminary studies have been done on the effect that caps versus no caps have on doctor placement. A study in the journal Health Affairs published in May 2005 concluded that doctors tend to set up their practices in those States where there are caps on non-economic losses. For example, between the years 1975 and 2000, the number of obstetricians increased 40% in States that had caps during the 80s, as opposed to only an 8% increase in those States without caps, to detriment of the residents of the latter States.

In addition to the size of the awards, plaintiffs' attorneys are very inventive in creating novel theories of liability. In a July 2001 case, an Indiana appellate court held that a physician, who performed a sterilization procedure in an allegedly negligent way so that the woman remained fertile, could be liable to the mother for the cost of raising an unwanted, though perfectly normal and healthy, child to majority. The court held that although she was not morally opposed to abortion, the woman need not terminate her pregnancy. Nor must the woman, to mitigate her damages, surrender the newborn infant for adoption.[8]

However, the case was reversed by the Indiana Supreme Court.[9] Indiana decided to follow the majority of States and permit recovery, in the case of a previously unwanted although healthy child, for all economic damages resulting from the unwanted pregnancy and consequent birth. But the defendant physician's liability stops as the plaintiff, with newborn babe in arms, exits the hospital.

The major response to large jury awards has come from the various State legislatures in establishing limits or caps on the amounts recoverable for "non-economic" losses such as pain and suffering, psychic distress, and disability and disfigurement. Caps like this, specifically for medical malpractice, have

---

8 *Chaffee M.D. v. Seslar*, 751 N.E.2d 773 (Ind. Ct. App. 2001).

9 786 N.E. 2d 705 (Ind. 2003).

passed in many States. Surprisingly, one State, Indiana, also limits recovery even for economic damages. This statute seems to the author to be violative of public policy, because "economic losses" are true out-of-pocket expenses that the plaintiff has and/or will incur in the future.

Although the caps on non-economic damages are supposedly public knowledge because they are mandated by statute, most jurors are unaware of the cap and the court does not inform the jurors of the cap. The jury is simply instructed to award itemised amounts for economic and non-economic losses. The judge then reduces the judgment, if the verdict exceeds the limit, after the jury has returned its verdict. Consequently, in a State with a $500,000 cap for non-economic damages, if the jury were to return a verdict of $1.2 million, consisting of $200,000 for economic damages and $1,000,000 for non-economic damages, the judge would thereafter enter a judgment for $700,000.

As a result of the "tort reform movement," a number of factual studies have been conducted by American Association for Justice, formerly the American Trial Lawyers' Association (ATLA), a largely plaintiffs' attorneys organisation, depicting certain injuries that have been incurred, the verdicts attributable thereto, and the number of verdicts exceeding the cap. Plaintiff lawyer associations have already made a concerted attack on caps. Even before the legislation passed, the Illinois Trial Lawyer's Association vowed to attack its constitutionality. Immediately prior to the signing of the legislation, lawyers "filed an avalanche of personal-injury complaints" in order to avoid the caps and limitations of this new legislation. Minutes after the Bill was signed into law, a challenge was filed in a Cook County Circuit Court.

However, due to the Republican Party's landslide victories in State legislatures throughout the United States in 1994, many such tort reform packages capping non-economic damages were passed throughout the United States. Hard on the heels of tort reform have come the empirical studies attempting to depict the legislation as disproportionate and unfair. These studies have resulted, in the last few years, in a debate over the propriety of all tort reforms. In the meantime, and during all this ebb and flow, some States have partially provided the medical profession with its long-desired protection.

In Illinois, in all tort cases for personal injury, property damage or wrongful death, the cap on non-economic damages was found unconstitutional in *Best v. Taylor Machine Works.*[10] The court ruled that the caps violated the Illinois Constitution's Separation of Powers section, and such caps also violated the prohibition against special legislation. Recently, caps in medical malpractice cases only were enacted. These caps were immediately attacked in the case of *LeBron v. Gottlieb Memorial Hospital.*[11] As of this writing, a motion to find this new legislation unconstitutional is pending before Judge Diane J. Larsen in the Circuit Court of Cook County.

---

[10] 689 N.E. 2d 1057 (Ill. 1997).

[11] No.2006 L 12109.

Statutes mandating caps only for physicians have generally been found to be unconstitutional as special class legislation. Some courts have held that the legislation violates due process; other courts have relied upon the Equal Protection Clause of the Fourteenth Amendment. The Equal Protection Clause prevents States from enacting legislation which favours a particular class. Thus, if a cap exists only for physicians, and not for manufacturers or premises owners, the cap may very well be considered to be class legislation. As Justice Starcher in his dissent in *Verba v. Ghaphery*,[12] stated: "Why should hospitals get more protection for their carelessness than I do as a driver or homeowner?" As a result, legislation which grants quasi-immunity to only one discrete group tends to be violative of the Equal Protection Clause. The present argument in the United States, when considering the enactment of caps on non-economic damages, is currently based on this ground, viz: we must have caps in medical malpractice cases or otherwise physicians and dentists will leave the state. The argument in favour of caps is not so much grounded on the protection of the doctors as it is on the safeguarding of the public and the preservation of a balance between the number of health care providers and the public they serve.

To determine whether legislation violates the Equal Protection Clause, the courts apply two different tests. If a "fundamental right or suspect class" is involved, strict scrutiny is applied. If the legislation deals with social or economic considerations, the "mere rationality" test is applied. Under a "mere rationality" test, there is a presumption that the statute was meant to remedy a perceived problem affecting citizens generally and therefore it would not violate the Equal Protection Clause.

Generally, the caps that have been passed throughout the several States limit damages for all defendant groups. Those State courts that have addressed the issue of the constitutionality of non-economic loss caps for all defendant groups have frequently found the caps to be constitutional.

However, in a 1999 Ohio Supreme Court opinion *State ex rel. Ohio Academy of Trial Lawyers v. Sheward,*[13] the court held that a cap on non-economic damages, recoverable in any tort action, as the greater of $250,000 or three times the economic loss to a maximum of $500,000 (except for certain kinds of permanent injuries), was unconstitutional because such a statute "is unreasonable and arbitrary, irrespective of whether it bears a real and substantial relation to public health or welfare," [14] The Ohio Supreme Court, in a 4 to 3 opinion that ran over 70 pages, simply rejected the legislature's findings of fact. The court disregarded the usual presumption of statutory validity that courts normally accord to a legislative enactment.

Although caps on "non-economic damages" will undoubtedly curb excessive jury awards, the caps may also unduly penalise plaintiffs deserving more than the

[12] 543 S.E.2d 347, at 363 (W. Va. 2000) .

[13] 715 N.E.2d 1062 (Ohio 1999).

[14] *Id.* at 1095.

cap permits. In order to remedy this disparity, the author recommends the creation of a compensation fund to compensate for serious injuries, the seriousness of which exceeds the cap. In this way, proportionality and a certain semblance of fairness would be accorded individual plaintiffs. The implicit assumption is that all plaintiffs are not exactly the same. In Ireland, the bench and bar are possibly more conservative, thus precluding exorbitant judgments against negligent doctors so that their careers do not founder. But good news travels fast. Once it becomes public knowledge that, for example, a comatose child's case has resulted in a million euro verdict against the doctor, it would seem to this author that the court has established a precedent. Although there may be alternative solutions to runaway awards, it is important for Ireland's health care professions to address this issue before it takes on an identity of its own.

Generally, by statute punitive damages are not allowed against physicians in the United States. These statutes have been extremely helpful in protecting doctors, dentists, nurses and, for that matter, lawyers. Statutes prohibiting punitive damages seem sensible. Wilful and wanton misconduct, a *sine qua non* for punitive damages, is almost impossible to prove in a medical malpractice suit. As a New York court stated, an award of punitive damages would require that the defendant's actions be "morally culpable or actuated by evil motives." In the author's opinion, it would be virtually impossible to prove wilful and wanton misconduct against a physician who is essentially a fiduciary and has the health of his patient primarily in mind.

The Supreme Court of West Virginia found a $1,000,000 cap for non-economic loss constitutional in *Verba v. Ghapery*[15]. The court held that the courts must defer to the legislature, and if there were a semblance of a rational basis for making a distinction between tort victims of medical negligence and victims of other tortious behaviour, the court must yield to the presumed legislative wisdom of capping awards. We "must exercise due restraint, in recognition of the principle of the separation of powers in government among the judicial, legislative and executive branches."[16] The court also stated that: "The general powers of the legislature … are almost plenary."[17]

In the *Verba* case, the defendant performed anti-reflux surgery on a 68 year old female. Within 10 hours of her discharge, four days post-op, she died due, according to an autopsy, to a surgical nick in the stomach causing her to contract peritonitis. The jury returned a verdict of $2,500,000 for the survivor's "non-economic loss," which was reduced to $1,000,000 per the legislative cap.

The court applied as a test for constitutionality "whether the classification is a rational one based on social, economic, historic or geographic factors, whether it bears a reasonable relationship to a proper governmental purpose,

---

15 543 S.E.2d 347 (W. V. 2000).

16 *Id.*, at 349.

17 *Id.*

and whether all persons within the class are treated equally."[18] The plaintiff's argument that inflation over the years had reduced the value of the $1,000,000 cap, initially enacted in 1986, to approximately $650,000 and therefore the cap was unconstitutional in its application was unavailing. The court held that it was up to the legislature to adjust the numbers. Lastly the plaintiff's argument that caps on non-economic damages does not reduce malpractice premiums and/or make medical care more readily and widely available was countered by empirical evidence that limiting damages does reduce malpractice insurance. The court also pointed out that legislatures impose limits on lawsuits by enacting statutes of limitation and repose, creating presumptions, and abolishing some causes of action. As of August 2003, a majority of State supreme courts throughout the United States has validated their legislatures' attempts to cap non-economic damages.

The main counter argument to the constitutionality of caps on non-economic damages is that there is a lack of equal protection. Plaintiffs' advocates argue that it is illogical that someone who suffers a moderate injury can receive up to, for example, a cap of $500,000, whereas someone who has been rendered quadriplegic through a physician's negligence is limited to that self same $500,000. There appears to be, they argue, no proportionality. One size does not fit all. [19] They argue that the more severely injured are penalised. Using this point as her main rationale, Justice Mary Ann McMorrow in *Best v. Taylor Mach Works*,[20] found the entire Illinois Tort Reform Act unconstitutional. Or viewed from a defendant's perspective, the worst offenders receive the most protection. Plaintiffs then rhetorically ask: "Is this socially desirable?"

In 2002, Congress considered a comprehensive bill (107 H.R. 4600) entitled the Help, Efficient, Accessible, Low-Cost, Timely Health Care (HEALTH) Act. It was passed on September 26 of the same year, while the Senate's companion bill, 107 S. 2793, had five cosponsors at the time of adjournment. Both H.R. 4600 and S. 2793 sought to cap malpractice damages, specifically non-economic damages, to $250,000. The bill also shortened to one year the time within which the patient could "discover" his injury, and it would have shortened to three years the time within which any suit could be brought. The bill was not passed in the Senate, despite much urgency from American physicians to put an end to "runaway verdicts."

II. Meritless Suits—Lack of an Expert

The third crisis facing physicians is the filing of meritless suits by a plaintiff simply to harass a physician in the hope of forcing a settlement. A related problem includes the practice of filing suit against all physicians, some of whom

---

18 *Id.*, at 350.

19 See *Verba*, 543 S.E.2d at 361.

20 689 N.E.2d 1057 (Ill. 1997).

were only remotely connected to the occurrence. The plaintiff is unsure of the physician's liability, but the plaintiff does not want to miss his opportunity to be compensated for the injury.

The common law briefly gave the doctor a remedy, namely to sue the plaintiff's lawyer for malpractice, malicious prosecution, or abuse of process. Besides these common law responses, the Federal Rules of Civil Procedure and most state rules of civil procedure provide sanctions for filing frivolous lawsuits. But to the doctor's chagrin, counterclaims based on lawyer malpractice, malicious prosecution and abuse of process have been generally unsuccessful because the countersuing physician cannot plead, let alone prove, the classical elements of these torts.

As to a malpractice action against the patient's lawyer, the doctor is not the lawyer's client. The courts generally hold that only a client has a right to bring a malpractice action against the lawyer. Consequently, a doctor cannot maintain a legal malpractice action against the patient's lawyer.

To prove a malicious prosecution action against a lawyer, a plaintiff physician has to show that:

(1) The suit was instituted by the defendant attorney;
(2) the suit was terminated in favour of the plaintiff physician;
(3) there was an absence of probable cause by the attorney to file the suit;
(4) the defendant attorney was motivated by malice in filing the suit; and
(5) the plaintiff doctor suffered a special injury, that is, an injury beyond general damage to his reputation.

Of course, the lawyer invariably maintains that he harboured no personal malice against the doctor when filing the suit. He was simply trying to represent a client who ostensibly had a viable medical malpractice case. Consequently, malicious prosecution suits by doctors against lawyers fall on deaf ears in United States' courts.

Finally, to prove the tort of abuse of process, the plaintiff physician must plead and prove the existence of an ulterior purpose or motive and an act of harassment. This is also difficult to do. The lawyer invariably responds by stating that, in hindsight, perhaps the physician is correct and no lawsuit should have been filed. However, the existence of an ulterior purpose must always be viewed with foresight and the lawyer may justifiably say that at the time of filing, there existed no ulterior purpose. Indeed, at the time of filing it appeared that the patient had a very good chance of recovering against the physician, especially since the plaintiff's medical expert has sworn under oath in an affidavit attached to the complaint that he believes the plaintiff's complaint is "meritorious."

Whereas a physician has found it impossible to sue the patient's lawyer for legal malpractice and may find it difficult to successfully sue for malicious prosecution or abuse of process, many state supreme courts have made it decidedly easier for patients to prove malpractice against the physician. Although, in all 50 States, the plaintiff in a medical malpractice case is required to produce an expert at trial to testify against the defendant, this expert need no longer come from the same community that the defendant practices in. Originally in the United States the plaintiff's expert had to practice in the same locality in order to be qualified as an expert. This was known as "the locality rule".

However, today the plaintiff's expert need only be familiar with the standard of care in either the defendant's particular locality or in similar localities under similar circumstances. This is known as the "modified locality rule" Thus the plaintiff's expert could practice in either the defendant's community or in a similar community hundreds of miles from the community where the defendant practiced. In the recent case *of Robinson v. LeCorps*, [21] a case where the defendant physician allegedly misdiagnosed the plaintiff's ankle sprain with the result that the plaintiff developed post-traumatic arthritis and had to have his ankle fused, the plaintiff's expert testified as to the national standard of care, but failed to establish the local, or similar locality standard of care. Since Tennessee uses a local standard, the plaintiff's expert's testimony was ruled inadmissible. However if the state utilises a "national standard" – frequently employed for the more sophisticated medical procedures – then the plaintiff's expert may come from anywhere.

As to the type of expert, formerly, if the plaintiff sued a specialist, e.g. an orthopaedic surgeon, the plaintiff was required to produce an orthopaedic surgeon to testify against the defendant. A podiatrist would not suffice as an expert witness against an orthopaedic surgeon because of the differing schools of medicine. Currently, courts are beginning to allow any person who is an MD to testify against any other MD, even someone who is not board certified in the defendant physician's specialty. In *Groudin v. Curi,*[22] the defendant allegedly failed to diagnose lung cancer in an 11 year old child until the cancer reached stage three. The court held that plaintiff's expert need not be board certified to testify against the defendant-physician, but that the proposed expert had to have been teaching or practicing in this area of medicine within five years prior to the incident. The credibility of that particular expert is, of course, subject to the scrutiny of the fact-finder. Therefore, even if the plaintiff's expert is not board certified in the defendant's specialty, the expert will be allowed to testify if he can convince the court that he is sufficiently familiar with the general procedures and practices of that specialty.

Thus, a plaintiff's expert who was board certified in internal medicine and infectious diseases was allowed to testify against a plastic surgeon, an orthopaedic surgeon and a general surgeon. The Illinois Supreme Court stated in *Jones v. O'Young*,[23] that there are two foundational requirements that must

---

[21] 83 S.W. 3d 718 (Tenn. 2002).

[22] 817 A.2d 61 (Conn. 2003).

[23] 607 N.E.2d 224 (Ill. 1992).

be satisfied to determine whether a physician is competent to testify as to the defendant's standard of care and his alleged departure therefrom:

> "First, the physician must be a licensed member of the school of medicine about which the expert proposes to testify [namely, an MD to testify against another MD], and second the expert must show that he is familiar with the methods, procedures and treatments ordinarily observed by other physicians in either the defendant physician's community or a similar community."

If the trial court, in its discretion, determines that the plaintiff's expert has met those two threshold foundational requirements, then the expert is permitted to testify. Thus, whether the expert is qualified to testify depends upon whether the defendant's alleged negligence concerns matters within the expert's knowledge and observation. As the court said in *Jones v. O'Young*:

> "Restricting the qualification of experts to those physicians who are members of the same specialty or sub-specialty as the defendant would only upset the balance necessary for an adversarial system without any compensating benefit."[24]

Thus, courts in the United States have liberalised the requirements for expert testimony. It is not overly difficult to find some doctor from somewhere who, although not board certified in the defendant's specialty, can establish to the court's satisfaction that he is familiar with the applicable standard, be it a "modified locality" or a "national standard", and that the defendant has violated that standard. Of course, defence counsel has the opportunity to cross-examine the expert as to his competency and/or any alleged deficiencies in his qualifications. However, the case will go to the jury since the plaintiff has produced some expert testimony, no matter how weak, that the defendant physician was guilty of malpractice. The only exception to the requirement of an expert's testimony is if the case satisfies the classic elements of *res ipsa loquitur* – "the thing speaks for itself" – then an expert's certificate to the effect that the claim is meritorious and his testimony at trial are not necessary. But the facts of the case, e.g. operating on the wrong patient, or leaving a surgical sponge inside the patient must be within the ordinary knowledge of the jurors so that they could reasonably draw the inference of malpractice without the need of expert testimony.[25]

In order to avoid surprise at trial, and also to force the parties to more realistically negotiate a settlement, the Illinois Supreme Court enacted Rule 213. This rule provides that, upon written interrogatories being submitted by

---

24 *Id.*, at 226.

25 *Anderson v. Assimos*, 572 S.E. 2d 101 (N.C. 2001).

one party to the other regarding the 2nd party's expert witness, the second party must disclose:

1. The subject matter about which the opinion witness expects to testify.
2. The conclusions of the witness, and the basis for those conclusions.
3. The qualifications of the opinion witness.
4. All reports of the opinion witness.

Seef v. Ingalls Memorial Hospital,[26] was a case of a stillborn birth, allegedly due to a nurse's failure to deliver a fetal monitoring strip to the attending obstetrician. By virtue of defence counsel submitting precise and pointed interrogatories to the plaintiff's counsel, the defence counsel came to trial prepared to challenge the plaintiff's proposed expert witness, namely an RN. The plaintiff's expert nurse was held to be an improper witness.

Although there is a movement towards a national standard of care, generally a plaintiff must prove that the defendant physician violated a standard of care of the locality or similar localities under similar circumstances. Unless an egregious occurrence, that is, one within the "common knowledge" of laymen, is involved, the majority standard is a "modified locality" standard. A doctor who practices in a small rural community will not be held to the same standard of care as a physician who practices in New York or Chicago. However, a physician who is on the staff of an urban hospital will be held to the standard of similarly situated doctors in other urban areas.

To further curb frivolous suits, legislation in some States now requires the plaintiff's lawyer to sign an affidavit stating that the plaintiff's case is facially valid. Illinois enacted a statute that required the plaintiff, or the plaintiff's attorney himself, to swear under oath as to the validity of the claim. If a malpractice suit were finally determined to be frivolous, the lawyer himself could be assessed costs and fees. As noted above, in Illinois, the plaintiff's attorney must also attach a report from an expert who has analysed the medical records and believes "there is a reasonable and meritorious cause for the filing of such action." The written report from the reviewing physician must also be attached to the complaint.

Similarly, in Florida, an attorney must execute a certificate that he has "a good faith belief that grounds exist for an action against the defendant." If the court determines that the attorney was not "in good faith and that no justiciable issue was presented" against the defendant physician, not only does the court award attorney's fees and costs against the plaintiff's attorney, but the plaintiff's attorney may be brought before the Bar Disciplinary Board for sanctions. A plaintiff's attorney in Florida would be lax indeed if he accepted a malpractice case without some real ammunition against the defendant for trial. The threat of

---

[26] 724 N.E. 2d 115 (Ill. App. Ct. 1999).

disbarment might initially seem rather draconian, but it appears to this author that the threat properly encourages thorough investigation prior to filing suit.

In addition to non-meritorious claims, physicians in the United States have objected to being named defendants in a suit when they were perhaps only peripherally involved. A recent Illinois statute now allows a physician to be named merely as a "Respondent in Discovery." This statute, 735 ILCS 5/2-402 (2007) provides that:

> "The plaintiff in any civil action may designate as respondents in discovery in his or her pleadings those individuals or other entities, other than the named defendants, believed by the plaintiff to have information essential to the determination of who should properly be named as additional defendants in the action."

This prevents a blunderbuss approach when filing suit, whereby a doctor who happened to be in the emergency room at the time of the occurrence is dragged into the lawsuit. Instead, if the plaintiff's attorney does not know at the outset who, if anyone, could have been responsible for the patient's injury, the plaintiff's attorney may name doctors X and Y "respondents in discovery." These doctors, although not named as party defendants, will have to turn over copies of their records to the plaintiff. The hope is that, once it has been determined by an independent medical expert that doctors X and Y were not involved in the occurrence, these doctors will never be joined as defendants.

The defence bar in Ireland would do well to enact similar legislation to the effect that no malpractice suit could be filed without the plaintiff's attorney having first reasonably documented the existence of a viable claim. Preliminary boards of review composed of doctor-lawyer experts could be established that could winnow out frivolous claims. At a minimum, the plaintiff's attorney should be required to have available an expert, certified in the defendant's specialty, who is willing to testify and establish a prima facie case. Cases of malpractice require more knowledge by the fact-finder than that normally possessed by the man on the Clapham omnibus, and fairness to the judicial system itself mandates specialised preparation.

IV. The Medical Standard of Care

If a defendant had been operating an automobile and he believed that he could successfully navigate through an intersection without striking a pedestrian, but he indeed did strike a pedestrian, the driver would be foolish to testify in court that he simply committed a "mere error of judgment." In fact, the verdict would probably be larger than it otherwise would have been if the defendant admitted to making "an error in judgment." However, throughout the United States, professionals such as physicians, dentists, attorneys, and accountants are not generally considered liable for what are denominated "mere errors of judgment."

This means, for example, that if there happened to be three different medical positions as to the proper course of treatment for a particular ailment, and the defendant physician followed one of these schools, although it was followed by only a few doctors, then the defendant cannot be found liable. The defendant may not have utilised the most common treatment, but if the defendant followed one of the recognised methods of treatment, albeit a minority one, the defendant cannot be guilty of malpractice.

The Illinois Pattern Jury Instruction on "professional negligence," which also includes medical malpractice, is typical of instructions given throughout the United States. This instruction states that:

> "Professional negligence" by a ______is the failure to do something that a reasonably careful ______ [practicing in the same or similar localities] would do, or the doing of something that a reasonably careful ______ would not do, under circumstances similar to those shown by the evidence.
>
> The phrase ["violation of the standard of care"] ["deviation from the standard of practice"] means the same thing as 'professional negligence.'
>
> [To determine what the standard [of care] [of practice] required in this case, you must rely upon (opinion testimony from qualified witnesses) (evidence of professional standards) (evidence of by-laws/rules regulations/policies/procedures) (evidence of community practice) (and other sources). You must not attempt to determine this question from any personal knowledge you have.] The law does not say how a reasonably careful ______ would act under these circumstances. That is for you to decide."

Thus, in a medical malpractice case, the plaintiff's attorney generally must have an expert testify against the defendant physician, and the expert must testify that the defendant did not use the skill or care ordinarily used by reasonably well-qualified physicians practicing in this or similar localities under similar circumstances. In establishing a plaintiff's expert doctor's competency to testify to the standard of care that the defendant physician should be held to, the expert must demonstrate: that he is a licensed member of the school of medicine about which he is to testify; that the defendant is a member of that same school of medicine; and that the expert is familiar with the methods, procedures and treatments ordinarily followed in either the defendant physician's community or in a similar community.[27]

---

[27] See *Kotvan v. Kirk*, 747 N.E. 2d 1045 (Ill. 2001) where the plaintiff lost sight in her eye following what initially appeared to be a successful cataract surgery. However, the 5th

All States recognise a theory of physician liability called *res ipsa loquitur*, "the thing speaks for itself". This theory would be utilised in those situations where the ordinary layman would be reasonable in saying: "that doctor was a careless doctor". The trial judge makes the threshold decision whether *res ipsa loquitur* is applicable in the particular fact situation. In *Ybarra v. Spangard*, [28] a patient was operated on for an appendectomy, but suffered a paralysed shoulder. This was held to be *res ipsa loquitur* Or, in cases where the wrong eye is enucleated, the wrong patient is operated on, no expert is needed to establish the standard of care. But in *Brannon v. Wood*, [29] the patient was operated for the excision of a mediastinal tumour. Because of bleeding and the doctor's subsequent attempts to stop the bleeding the patient suffered paraplegia. Do we need an expert to testify, or is this *res ipsa loquitur*? The court held that the plaintiff had to produce an expert.

Does such a case, where an expert must testify to the applicable standard of care, preclude the use of *res ipsa loquitur* as an alternative theory of liability? The Missouri Court of Appeals in *Spears v. Capital Region Medical Care Center, Inc.*,[30] held that if the facts of the case as testified to at trial do not allow a *res ipsa loquitur* theory, and therefore an expert must be used to establish the applicable standard of care via an expert, then the plaintiff cannot use *res ipsa loquitur* as a fall-back position. In short, Missouri holds that the plaintiff must pick his theory, either specific negligence, for which he must establish the standard of care, or *res ipsa loquitur* The majority of States, however, allow the plaintiff to argue in the alternative and plead specific negligence in one count, and then argue in the alternative, if the facts are strong enough, *res ipsa loquitur*. Finally, if, on cross-examination, the plaintiff's expert admits that the defendant physician followed one of the generally recognised schools of medicine, although the expert himself would not have followed it, the plaintiff's expert has failed to prove a prima facie case against the defendant.

It is insufficient for the plaintiff to simply establish that the procedure ended in tragedy. An accident, mishap, or tragedy in the operating room does not, by itself, constitute evidence of malpractice. For example, if a newborn child falls into a coma because of lack of oxygen during the birth process, the coma is not sufficient evidence to prove malpractice. The plaintiff must produce an expert who will testify that the defendant anaesthesiologist failed to exercise the standard of care ordinarily used by reasonably well-qualified anaesthesiologists under similar circumstances. Otherwise, the trial judge will "direct a verdict"

District Illinois Appellate Court recently held, in a case where an infant suffered bacterial meningitis due to an alleged failure to diagnose an alleged delay in starting the infant on antibiotics, that the defendant's negligence could be proved by circumstantial evidence without the need of an expert witness. *Koehler v. Neighbors M.D.*, 751 N.E. 2d 149 (Ill. App. Ct. 2001). This is the functional equivalent of a case based on *res ipsa loquitur*.

[28] 154 P. 2d 687 (Ca. 1944).

[29] 444 P. 2d 558 (Or. 1968).

[30] 86 S.W. 3d 58 (Ct. App. Mo. 2002).

and enter judgment for the defendant. Once, however, a jury receives a case with terrible injuries and begins its deliberations, the doctor runs a serious risk of a substantial verdict.

V. Statutes of Limitations and Repose

The fifth crisis is the possibility that a physician may be exposed to malpractice liability for a long period of time after an alleged act of malpractice occurs. The reason physicians are subject to liability for a protracted period of time is that in the United States, as is apparently the case in Ireland, courts have adopted the "Discovery Rule." In theory, the statute of limitations begins to run on the date that the plaintiff is injured. Basically, the "Discovery Rule" holds that the statute of limitations does not begin to run until the plaintiff knows, or should have known, of the injury that the physician allegedly caused the plaintiff.

In the United States, medical malpractice insurance is currently sold on a "claims made" basis. This means that a liability insurance policy will cover the insured only if the policy is actually in force at the time the claim is made, not when the alleged malpractice occurred. Therefore, since the "Discovery Rule" extends the period within which a plaintiff is permitted to sue, a physician, even after he has retired, should carry malpractice insurance until the statute of repose (really) has completely expired. This is called "tail coverage", with the tail being the length of an unknowable statute of limitations.

Also, a statute of limitations usually does not run against minors. Therefore, for example, an obstetrician who is alleged to have negligently injured a child during delivery is subject to suit until two years after that minor reaches majority, generally 18 years of age. Currently in the United States attorneys and financial planners are recommending that clients avoid the cost of probate by creating revocable trusts and putting all their property into that trust before they die. However, one benefit of the probate process, and one defence against delayed suits after a physician has died, is to probate the deceased physician's estate and lay potential claims to rest. This should preclude potential suits brought by an adult or even a minor. In short, estate planners and malpractice defence attorneys can have radically different views about the wisdom of probate.

An example of what could happen if there were no outer time-limit to a malpractice claim can be found in the 2003 case of *Broek v. Park Nicollet Health Services*.[31] In *Broek,* the defendant physician treated the plaintiff seven years before the plaintiff suffered a fatal heart attack. The plaintiff's allegation was that because the defendant failed to advise the deceased to limit any vigorous activity, his congenital heart condition led to his death. The three year statute of limitations for wrongful death began, of course, only when the deceased died. Without a statute of repose, a Minnesota physician could be liable for

[31] 660 N.W. 2d 439 (Ct. App. Minn. 2003).

an indeterminate amount of time for a later death. Although causality gets progressively more difficult to prove, the suit may still be filed.[32]

To address the problem of an extended statute of limitations, many States have enacted a combination statute of limitations and statute of repose. Under a statute of repose, even allowing for the "Discovery Rule," in no event will a cause of action be maintainable after a certain number of years has elapsed. The Illinois statute of repose bars minors' claims once eight years have elapsed. Therefore, if a child were to allege that he was injured at birth, that child's cause of action would be barred once that child reaches his eighth birthday. This statute was found to be constitutional as protecting an important public policy of laying stale claims to rest.

Therefore, although a patient might be unaware, for example, that a sponge had been carelessly left inside him during a surgical procedure, once a certain number of years has elapsed, the statute of repose bars the cause of action. Whether it is desirable for a minor's cause of action to be barred after eight years is debatable. Some parents may not be diligent in protecting the rights of their own children. Similarly, children have always enjoyed a special place and heightened protection under United States tort laws. Nevertheless, an Illinois Appellate Court found that, on balance, precluding stale claims outweighed any potential injustice to minor plaintiffs.[33]

In *Aicher v. Wisconsin Patients Compensation Fund,* [34] the Wisconsin Supreme Court held that, even for minors, statutes of repose requiring that medical malpractice actions be commenced within 5 years after the act or omission, or by the time the minor reaches age 10, whichever is later, is constitutional. In that case the attending physician, during the plaintiff's newborn examination, misdiagnosed a condition in the infant's right eye, known as "poor red reflex." As a result, the plaintiff had an untreatable cataract in her right eye that caused permanent blindness. The misdiagnosis occurred in December 1982. She, really her parents, discovered the condition in September 1993. Suit was filed in 1996, when the girl was 13 years old.

Although the "discovery rule" provided that suit had to be filed within 1 year of discovery, the 10 year statute of repose obviously ran out long before the malady was discovered. Apparently the little girl adapted to the blindness in her right eye, which malady was only discovered on a routine school eye exam. The plaintiff's argument that the 10 year statute of repose was unconstitutional, because it violated Wisconsin's constitutional provision of a "right to a remedy", was unavailing. Through a bit of tortuous logic the Wisconsin Supreme Court held that the 10 year statute of repose had already run out before the little girl's cause of action accrued.

In the United States a cause of action "accrues" when all the elements of

---

32 See also *Campo v. Correa,* 828 So. 2d 502 (La. 2002).

33 *Partin v. St. Francis Hospital,* 694 N.E. 2d 574 (Ill. Ct. App. 1998).

34 613 N.W.2d 849 (Wis. 2000).

the tort occur. The classic elements of a negligence action, of which medical malpractice is a sub species, are "duty," "breach of duty," "proximate cause" and "damages". The little girl was damaged when she went blind at approximately age 2. But the court said she did not suffer damage until her parents actually discovered the blindness, i.e., at age 11. By this time the 10 year statute of repose had already run out, and therefore the court reasoned she never had a viable cause of action. By this same argument, the court denied plaintiff's "due process" argument stating that no property right was taken from the little girl, because she never acquired a right to sue in the first place. It is analogous to arguing that someone was killed before she was conceived.

As to the plaintiff's equal protection argument, the Wisconsin Supreme Court held that because it is necessary to keep medical insurance premiums down and not deter physicians from providing medical care to the indigent, the legislature was within its prerogatives when it set up a separate classification for medical malpractice claims by minors. The court found a rational basis for the classification, pointing out that 23 other States and three federal circuits have found that such a classification is reasonable, given the desire of controlling medical malpractice insurance costs. The court lastly pointed out that the statute of repose for minors can run for 10 years—as it did in this case—whereas the statute only runs five years for adults. In Wisconsin the minor's claim is barred at age 10, whereas in other States the minor's claim is barred at ages such as 8, 6, and 4. Thus, the court reasoned, this minor in Wisconsin had no standing to complain.

In conclusion, a statute of limitations starts the period of time within which a suit may be filed. The "Discovery Rule" extends this time depending on the plaintiff's actual or constructive knowledge. The problem with applying a "Discovery Rule" to a physician's alleged malpractice is that the time within which a plaintiff could sue could theoretically run forever. Different States, adopting different forms of the "Discovery Rule", have enacted different statutes of limitations. If the plaintiff does not "discover" his injury, and the alleged fact that Doctor X caused this injury, until 25 years later, no physician could ever rest easy.

A statute of repose establishes an outside time limit from the date of the occurrence within which the cause of action may be brought, regardless of the "discoverability" of the injury. Thirty-four States have established different outer limits. For example, in Missouri, the outside limit for adults is two years, in California three years, in Florida and Illinois four years, in Wisconsin five years, and in Nebraska ten years. Consequently, in the United States this particular potential medical crisis of unlimited exposure is being effectively solved by the adoption of statutes of repose.

VI. Liability for the Acts of Another—Vicarious Liability

The sixth crisis that physicians in the United States are occasionally faced with is that of vicarious liability. If A is a physician in one office and A's partner, B, is a physician in a second office, and A thereafter commits malpractice, A's liability is imputed to his partner, B, through the doctrine of vicarious liability.

An argument, it seems to the author, could be made in both the United States (the argument to date has been unavailing) and likewise in Ireland that the entire doctrine of vicarious liability is antiquated and no longer necessary. The legal maxim "*cessante ratione legis, cessat et ipsa lex*" (the reason for the law ceasing, the law itself must cease) seems eminently applicable in cases alleging medical malpractice among partners. The fundamental reason for vicarious liability was to find a "deep pocket" from which the plaintiff's judgment might be paid. But with the almost universal presence of malpractice insurance, there is no longer a need to besmirch the name of Doctor B for the negligent acts of Doctor A. Nevertheless, vicarious liability is very much with us in the United States.

Prior to the Illinois Tort Reform Act, the most recent appellate decision assisting the defendant physician in Illinois, albeit inadvertently, was *Gilbert v. Sycamore Municipal Hospital.*[35] In *Gilbert*, the hospital was held vicariously liable for an emergency room physician's negligence under the doctrine of "apparent agency." Generally, the negligence of an independent contractor such as a staff doctor is not attributable to the hospital.

The vast majority of physicians who enjoy privileges in a hospital are independent contractors, and consequently the negligence of the surgeon, the internist, etc., would not technically be attributable to the hospital.

However, in *Gilbert*, the court held that a hospital may be held liable for a physician's negligence if that physician appeared to be an employee of the hospital. This vicarious liability indirectly benefits the physician because plaintiffs will invariably seek the deep pockets of the hospital after having been awarded a favourable judgment. Therefore, any judgment against both the doctor and the hospital will likely be collected from the hospital.

The physician may not escape unscathed, however, because of "implied indemnity," whereby the party who is passively negligent (in this case the hospital) may seek to recover from the negligent physician any money it pays to the plaintiff. The likelihood of this is probably minimal, but it is theoretically possible. Under American tort law, if the party who pays the judgment was only vicariously liable, that party is entitled to indemnification from the party who was actively negligent. Indemnification is meant to prevent unjust enrichment by allowing the vicariously liable party to recover from the wrongdoer, the actively negligent doctor.

The *Gilbert* case was sharply curtailed in 1995 by the Illinois Tort Reform Act making it more difficult for plaintiffs to prove apparent agency. Under that Act, in order to find a hospital vicariously liable for a doctor's negligence, the plaintiff must plead and prove that:

---

[35] 622 N.E. 2d 788 (Ill.1993).

(1) The hospital affirmatively represented to the patient that the doctor was employed by the hospital;
(2) the patient reasonably relied upon the hospital's representation that the doctor was the hospital's employee; and
(3) a reasonable patient would not have sought medical services from the doctor if he had known the doctor was not employed by the hospital.

However, since this Act was found unconstitutional, *Gilbert* has once again returned as the law in Illinois.

A further help for the plaintiff occurred in Illinois when the jury instruction on apparent agency was modified by deleting the word "reasonable", insofar as the nature of the plaintiff's reliance. Thus, since 1993 a plaintiff may recover against the hospital for the physician's negligence if the plaintiff proves that he simply "relied" on the apparent agency of the doctor. His reliance need not be "reasonable". Illinois Pattern Jury Instructions 105.10.

In *McCorry v. Evangelical Hospitals Corp.*,[36] a hospital referred in its marketing literature to the staff doctors as "our physicians" As a result of this advertisement the appellate court held that a hospital could be liable for the negligence of one of its "staff physicians". It was simply a question of fact as to whether the plaintiff relied on the hospital, rather than on the particular physician, in seeking treatment. The court stated:

> "If a plaintiff shows that he relied in part on the hospital when he accepted treatment from an allegedly negligent doctor, he has met the reliance element of proof . . . under . . . apparent agency."

I have already referred briefly to the famous seminal tort case in the United States, *Ybarra v. Spangard.* There were four doctors involved in the patient's care in Ybarra. Doctor Tilley was the internist, Doctor Reser was the anaesthetist, Doctor Swift was the owner of the hospital, and Doctor Spangard was the surgeon. Mr. Ybarra came to the hospital where Dr Tilley diagnosed his ailment as appendicitis. He was later cared for by the anaesthetist and surgeon, who was assisted by a nurse under the control of Dr Swift. After the appendectomy was performed, the patient experienced paralysis and atrophy of the muscles around his right shoulder. Although each of the individual physicians was actually an independent contractor, there being no express partnership involved, the court looked upon all of them as partners. As a result, all the doctors were held jointly and severally liable for the acts of one physician, or perhaps nurse, who committed the negligent act. Thus vicarious liability was enforced notwithstanding the fact that these four physicians were not, nor had they ever been, partners. This case has been universally followed by other courts throughout the United States.

[36] N.E. 2d 1067 (Ill. App. Ct. 2002).

Thus, in *Dias v. Brigham Medical Associates Inc.*,[37] a doctor's group was held vicariously liable for the negligent acts of only one of its doctors, a negligent act that resulted in a stillbirth.

As noted above, where two or three individuals are actual partners, the negligence of one is legally attributable to the others. Therefore, it is theoretically possible for B, while on vacation, to be liable for the negligent acts of A practicing back home. This result is now being alleviated throughout the United States by the enactment of a statute called "Registered Limited Liability Partnerships." The gist of the new statute is that a physician may be held liable for his own negligence or for the negligence of someone under his direct supervision. However, a physician who has followed the legal formalities and registered under this statute may not be held liable for the negligence of his partners. Lawyers in Illinois were allowed in April 2003 to form these partnerships. Therefore, lawyers and physicians have achieved a modest degree of protection from vicarious liability. If Ireland still utilises the doctrine of vicarious liability, perhaps similar legislation could be enacted to protect the innocent medical partner.

VII. The "Good Samaritan" Statutes

The next crisis a health care provider has faced in the United States is the risk of exposure to liability if he follows his conscience and medical ethics by stopping and aiding a stricken victim in an emergency. The author has a physician friend who accompanied him to an American football game. At the game, someone, apparently inebriated, fell down and struck his head. The physician ministered to the individual and accompanied him to the hospital, but was unable to leave the patient because no other physician was initially willing to assume the patient's primary care, that is, assume the role of attending physician. The law in the United States is, in effect, that once you put your hand to the task you may not look back. The author's friend felt compelled, indeed he was legally duty bound, to continue his care of the individual patient for two days at a hospital located four miles south of the stadium, even though he practiced ten miles north of the stadium, until another physician finally took over. If this doctor had left the patient without properly delivering him into the welcoming care of another physician, it would have constituted the tort of abandonment.

The bottom line is that many physicians in the United States were formerly reluctant to stop and volunteer aid because of the potential charge of abandonment and because of the common law rule requiring that reasonable care be rendered once someone begins to furnish assistance. However, physicians in the United States have acquired statutory protection, namely "Good Samaritan" statutes. All fifty States plus the District of Columbia afford the physician protection for voluntarily aiding a stricken victim. Good Samaritan statutes afford protection to the health care provider who renders emergency care to a patient without a

---

37 780 N.E. 2d 447 (Mass. 2002).

fee. Such a provider can only be liable if he is found guilty of wilful and wanton misconduct. The likelihood of a patient, having received free care, proving that the physician was guilty of wilful and wanton misconduct is virtually nil. The various jurisdictions in the United States have construed the statute very broadly to protect the kindly physician. For example, in *McCain v. Batson*,[38] a "Good Samaritan" doctor sutured a hiker's wound, not at the scene of the accident, but long afterwards in the quiet of the plaintiff's condominium. The court held that the plaintiff, in a malpractice action against her benefactor, was required to prove wilful and wanton misconduct, an almost impossible task. However, in order to avoid the strictures of the Restatement (Second) of Torts, namely the legal inability to abandon a patient, the doctor rendering such free care nevertheless may not leave the patient until another physician assumes responsibility. The "Good Samaritan" protection has been extended by statute to nurses, dentists, and a qualified immunity has been granted "if good faith is exercised" even to an in-hospital emergency resuscitation team that is paid to perform emergency CPR.[39]

In the author's opinion, a plaintiff's lawyer would be foolish to prosecute a case against a physician who, protected by the "Good Samaritan" statute, stopped and without fee ministered to the helpless plaintiff. To prevail, the plaintiff would have to prove that his saviour was guilty of wilful and wanton misconduct, a truly Herculean task. The plaintiff's attorney must always remember that unsubstantiated and frivolous pleadings can result in fees, costs and also sanctions against both the attorney and his client. Further, as noted supra, in some States lawyers have to sign personal affidavits stating their belief that the plaintiff has a meritorious claim. If the facts at trial do not cry out for relief against the physician "Samaritan," the plaintiff's lawyer will lose all credibility before bench and bar. As a matter of fact, the author has been unable to find any reported case successfully brought against a physician where the patient proved that the physician was guilty of wilful and wanton misconduct. If physicians in Ireland begin to experience mounting judgments against them, the medical fraternity might consider protective legislation insulating them from liability in emergency situations, except for egregious conduct. The Law Reform Commission has already opened debate on the subject.

VIII. Double Recovery of Certain Expenses—Collateral Source Rule—Attorney's Fees

The final crisis that the medical profession, along with other defendants, has faced in the United States is what is called the "collateral source rule." This rule States that any judgment rendered against a defendant may not be reduced by monies the plaintiff has received from "collateral sources," such as insurance

---

[38] 760 P.2d 275 (Mont. 1988).

[39] See Calif. Health and Safety Code, s.1317.

companies, wage continuation plans and social security. Courts usually justify the collateral source rule by stating that the defendant should not be allowed to receive the advantage of any monies the plaintiff was prudent enough to provide for himself in the event of an accident. Therefore, if a plaintiff has been wise enough to obtain disability insurance and health insurance which cover lost wages and medical bills, the courts hold that the defendant should not be the beneficiary of the plaintiff's prudence.

In reality, however, most of the insurance benefits that accident victims receive are not due to their own foresight, but are due to company plans provided by their employers. Of course, the counter argument is that if there were no employer benefit plans, the individual's wages would be higher, and therefore, in effect, the employee is paying for his own insurance.

This argument becomes weaker as medical insurance becomes a universal employee perquisite and the cost of coverage is spread among the entire populace. Finally, defendants argue that the entire reason for the collateral source rule evaporates when the plaintiff receives government reimbursement following an accident.

Approximately 34 States have modified the collateral source rule through legislation ranging from mandatory reduction of compensatory damages to various discretionary reductions. In *Reid v. Williams*,[40] the plaintiff sued Dr Williams for a sense of fullness in his ear. Dr Williams diagnosed a "perilymphatic fistula" and performed surgery, dislocating a small bone in the plaintiff's inner ear. Plaintiff prevailed against the surgeon at trial but his recovery of $25,000 was reduced by $6,000, the amount that plaintiff's medical insurer paid on his behalf. This reduction took place because of an Alaska statute that abrogated the "collateral source rule" in a medical malpractice case. The plaintiff attacked the statute on both due process and equal protection grounds. But the Alaska Supreme Court held that the statute was reasonably related to the legislature's stated purpose of reducing medical malpractice insurance premiums and increasing the delivery of medical services throughout the state. The court noted that as of the date of its opinion, October 1998, 23 States had enacted statutes abolishing the collateral source rule in medical malpractice cases. And in California, Pennsylvania, Rhode Island and Maryland the right of subrogation by a third party payer is eliminated when a plaintiff's damages are reduced by the sum of benefits paid by a collateral source, such as a medical insurer.[41]

Further, and ironically, certain statutes provide that the plaintiff attorney's compensation, which is frequently agreed upon as a one-third contingency fee, is to be based not on the jury verdict, but on the verdict only after being reduced by collateral source payments. In effect, the plaintiff lawyer's fee becomes based upon the net recovery and not the gross verdict. Consequently, the hope is that plaintiffs' attorneys will be less willing to take cases where their ultimate fee

---

[40] 964 P.2d 453 (Alaska 1998).

[41] See *Narayen v. Bailey*, 130 Md. App. 458 (2000).

will be proportionately reduced by any monies that the plaintiff will receive from collateral sources.

Plaintiffs have consistently argued that the "American Rule," relative to attorneys' fees, especially in light of statutory caps on damages, should be disregarded. The "American Rule" States that, except in cases where the losing party has acted in an egregious or fraudulent way, each party to a suit pays his own respective attorney's fees. Plaintiffs argue that when damages are artificially capped, the plaintiff attorney's one-third contingent fee so depletes the plaintiff's recovery that the plaintiff is denied a full recovery. Professor Jeffrey O'Connell, a pro plaintiff advocate, long ago stated: "[p]ayment for pain and suffering has, for years, served substantially to pay claimants' lawyers."[42] In *Estate of Verba v. Ghaphery*,[43] a dissenting opinion urged that an exception to the American rule be adopted in medical negligence cases. But as of this writing, a large majority of courts, Alaska being a notable exception[44], has refused to follow the suggestion. The implicit and succinct reason for such refusal is that sometimes injured plaintiffs do not recover against the defendant physician, and if the prevailing defendant had the right to recover his attorneys' fees from the losing, and still suffering, plaintiff, this would deter many injured patients from ever filing suit.

Conclusion

The foregoing are the major areas where United States physicians have sought statutory relief from the evolving court made common law. If history indeed does repeat itself and Irish healthcare providers face some of these self-same crises, perhaps the more egregious consequences can be forestalled and/or remedied by appropriate statutory measures.

---

42 Jeffrey O'Connell, "A Proposal To Abolish Defendants' Payment for Pain and Suffering in Return for Payment of Claimant's Attorneys Fees" (1981) U.ILL.L.REV. 333, 351 (1981).

43 543 S.E.2d 347 (W. Va. 2000).

44 Alaska Civil, rule 82.

INDEX